THE
FRESH-WATER
FISHERMAN'S
BIBLE

REVISED EDITION

Vlad Evanoff

THE FRESH-WATER FISHERMAN'S BIBLE

REVISED EDITION

Illustrated by the author

DOUBLEDAY & COMPANY, INC. / GARDEN CITY, NEW YORK

Library of Congress Cataloging in Publication Data

Evanoff, Vlad.
  The fresh-water fisherman's bible.

  1. Fishing.   2. Fishing—North America.
I. Title.
SH441.E856   1980   799.1'1'097
ISBN: 0-385-14405-9
Library of Congress Catalog Card Number 79–7684

CONTENTS

Chapter 1

BASIC FRESH-WATER FISHING OUTFITS

I started fishing in fresh water in the traditional country-boy manner. When I needed a fishing "pole" I would look for the nearest long, straight tree sapling. Then I would take out my pocket knife, cut the sapling down, and trim off the branches. Next, I would get a length of string and attach a bent pin to the end for the hook. With this makeshift gear, I caught sunfish and chubs in a small brook. Later I graduated to genuine fishhooks and long cane poles with which I caught panfish and trout. Still later I got a steel bait-casting rod and reel with black braided line, with which I could cast lures for bass and pickerel.

The bamboo cane pole is still a popular fishing tool with millions of fresh-water anglers. Such bamboo poles run anywhere from eight to twenty feet in length and come in one piece or in sections (the latter can be broken down into three or four pieces for easy carrying and storing). You can buy these poles in most fishing-tackle, sporting-goods, or country-hardware stores.

If you want a stronger, longer-lasting pole you can get one of the telescopic glass poles that can be extended from a short three-to-five-foot length to anywhere from ten to twenty feet. They generally have from two to five sections, which slide into each other.

These cane and glass poles are mostly used for still fishing with live baits, especially for such panfish as sunfish, yellow perch, crappies, white bass, and bullheads. But they can also be used to work artificial lures or baits such as spoons, spinners, jigs, pork chunk, pork rind, plastic baits for the same panfish, and for occasional catches of bass, trout, pickerel, and other so-called game fish. Cane and glass poles, however, are limited to fishing short distances from shore, piers, docks, and boats. When buying poles, get the shorter, lighter ones for children and the longer ones for adults.

Because of the many limitations of a cane or glass pole, most fresh-water anglers turn to a more versatile outfit such as a rod-and-reel combination. These enable the fisherman to cast farther and fish deeper; they also work lures better and offer more sport. Since World War II the spinning rods and reels have become very popular with fresh-water anglers. The spinning reels work on a "fixed spool" principle and enable almost any angler to cast a light lure a good distance with only a little practice. There are no "backlashes" or "birdnests" to plague an angler, as in the days when only bait-casting, revolving-spool reels were used.

The many different spinning outfits available today enable an angler to handle almost any kind of fresh-water fishing. To simplify matters we can divide fresh-water spinning outfits into four groups: ultralight, light, medium, and heavy. The ultralight rod ranges from about four to six feet in length. With this light rod you use one of the small ultralight spinning reels filled with monofilament line testing from two to four pounds. The whole outfit—rod, reel, and line—will weigh only a few ounces, and is a pleasure to use.

The ultralight spinning outfit is best for small fish, small waters, and very light lures weighing from $5/16$ to $1/4$ ounce. It is often a deadly outfit when used for wary game fish such as trout and

A Wright & McGill open-faced spinning reel, typical of the many models, in a wide variety of sizes, used for most fresh-water angling.

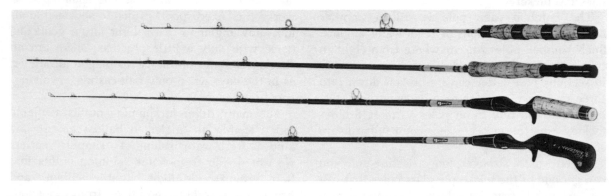

From top to bottom: A Garcia spinning rod, fly rod, spin-casting rod, and bait-casting rod. All of these are used for fresh-water fishing.

small bass in low, clear, heavily fished waters. And you can't find a better outfit for seeking the smaller panfish. However, for the fresh-water angler who can afford only one spinning outfit, the ultralight is not the best one to get. It limits your fishing to small fish in open waters and to casting very small, light lures.

The light fresh-water spinning rod and reel are more practical for fresh-water fishing in streams, rivers, and lakes. These rods, which range from 5½ to 7 feet in length, will best cast lures weighing from ⅛ to ⅜ ounce. You can use this rod with most of the fresh-water spinning reels made, but the smaller, lighter models will balance the rod better and add less weight to the outfit. Monofilament lines testing from 4 to 6 pounds are usually used with the light spinning outfit.

The medium fresh-water spinning rod will also run from 5½ to 7 feet in length. But it will be stiffer in action, especially at the butt end, and have the backbone to cast heavier lures and handle bigger fish. Lures from ⅜ to 1 ounce can be cast with this outfit. This includes most of the spinning lures made and most of the bait-casting lures that are too heavy to use with the lighter spinning rods. This rod can accommodate most spinning reels filled with lines testing 6 or 8 pounds. The medium-weight spinning rod is the nearest thing to an "all around" rod for fresh water such as big trout, bass, walleyes, pickerel, small pike, steelhead, small catfish, and carp. Yet it is still light enough to be used when you are fishing for panfish. If you can afford only one rod for fresh-water fishing, the medium spinning rod is the one to get.

Heavy fresh-water spinning rods can range from about 6 to 9 feet in length. The shorter rods in this class may be cast with one hand, but the longer ones, with longer butts or handles, are cast with two hands. Some of these rods are made especially for big fresh-water fish, but other rods in this class are really salt-water models. These heavy spinning rods can be used with the larger fresh- and salt-water spinning reels with lines testing anywhere from 8 to 25 pounds. They will handle lures and sinkers weighing from about ½ ounce to 2 ounces, depending on the strength of the line and the power or action of the particular rod being used. Rods in this heavy class can be used for big black bass and for steelhead, salmon, lake trout, pike, muskellunge, big carp, sturgeon, gar, and big catfish.

The heavy spinning rods are most suited for big fish, big waters, strong currents, deep rivers, and for fishing in areas where there are many obstructions such as weeds, logs, sunken trees, and rocks. They can also be used to cast heavy lures long distances and for fishing on the bottom with bait and heavy sinkers. They also make good trolling rods for coho and chinook salmon, lake trout, and muskellunge.

The "spin casting" and "push button" type reels are very popular, especially with kids, beginners, and those who do not fish too often or

A Zebco closed-face spin-casting reel.

haven't acquired the skills to use other outfits. These reels are similar to the open-faced spinning reels in that their spools are stationary (but covered rather than exposed). Like bait-casting reels, spin-casting reels are mounted above the rod. In order to cast with them you simply push a button, then release it to send the lure out to the target. They are almost foolproof, quite accurate, fast, and very easy to use. They also preclude the loose coils of line that plague open-faced spinning reels, which is one of the reasons many expert anglers like to use spin-casting reels for night fishing.

The push-button-type reels are now made in various sizes for use with lines testing anywhere from 4 to 20 pounds. The average reel of this type will hold from 80 to 150 yards of line, depending on the test used, which is enough for most kinds of fresh-water fishing.

The rods used with the push-button-type reels are called "spin casting" rods. They are similar to bait-casting rods except that they may have somewhat larger guides and may be a bit longer. Actually, you can use a spin-casting reel with most bait-casting rods, and a bait-casting reel with most spin-casting rods. Most rod manufacturers make the spin-casting rods in three or four different actions, ranging from extralight to light, medium, and heavy. The lighter, more limber rods of this type are used with lines testing 4 or 6 pounds and can cast lighter lures weighing ⅛ and ¼ ounce. The light and medium rods are used with 6-to-10-pound-test lines and can cast lures weighing anywhere from ¼ to ⅝ ounce. The heavy spin-casting rods are used with the larger spin-casting reels that hold lines testing from 10 to 20 pounds. These rods can cast lures weighing from ⅝ ounce to 1½ ounces. Most spin-casting rods range from 6 to 7 feet in length.

If you are buying your first casting rod and reel for fresh-water fishing, you can't go wrong by getting one of the spin-casting rods and push-button reels. For all-around use get a medium-weight rod and reel holding 8- or 10-pound-test line. This can be used for most fresh-water fish. With such an outfit you can go out on a pond, lake, river, or stream and in a short time learn how to cast a lure or sinker or even a bait a good distance. With regular practice you will be able to cast accurately too.

Our next alternative is the bait-casting rods and reels used for many kinds of fresh-water fishing. These rods can be divided into three classes: light, medium, and heavy. The light bait-casting rod will run from 5 to 6½ feet and has a limber action for casting light lures from ¼ to ½ ounce. It is used with the revolving-spool bait-casting reel. (For the light rod, the smaller, lighter, narrow-spool bait-casting reel is best.) This can be filled with braided line or monofilament line testing from 8 to 10 pounds. The light bait-casting outfit is used for small or medium-sized fish such as big trout, bass, pickerel, and panfish. It is also used mostly in open waters with no snags, vegetation, or obstructions.

The medium bait-casting rod can run from 5 to 6 feet and can cast lures weighing from ½ to 1 ounce. Since most bait-casting lures weigh around ⅝ ounce, the medium bait-casting rod is perfect for handling such lures. The bait-casting reel used with this rod is filled with line testing from 10 to 18 pounds. This rod makes a good all-around fresh-water tool for catching bass, walleyes, big trout, and the smaller pike and muskies.

The heavy bait-casting rod ranges from 5 to 6½ feet and is stiff and powerful enough to cast the heavier lures. Many of these rods will handle lures ranging from ⅝ ounce to 1½ ounces in weight. The larger-sized bait-casting reel used with this rod can be filled with lines testing from 15 to 25 pounds. This rod is best for fishing the larger game fish such as big black bass, pike, muskies, steelhead, salmon, and lake trout. It can also be used for bottom fishing with sinkers, usually for big catfish, carp, and the like.

In addition to being a good trolling rod for many fresh-water fish, the heavy bait-casting rod is also most practical for fishing in strong currents, lakes, or rivers filled with weeds, logs, rocks, sunken trees, and other obstructions.

Many fishing-tackle companies also make a stiff, heavy bait-casting rod called a "worm" rod, which is used for fishing with plastic worms. Usually available in 5½- or 6-foot lengths, these rods are made to set a hook buried inside a plastic worm that is being fished deep near the bottom. They can also be used for working the heavier lures in thick cover for big bass.

There is also the "popping" type rod made especially for salt-water fishing but that can be used for heavy fresh-water fishing. This rod, ranging from 6 to 8 feet in length, has a long handle, suitable for casting with two hands when using heavier sinkers, lures, or baits. Popping rods can also be used for still fishing on the bottom with bait for the larger fish. This is the rod many anglers prefer to use for coho or chinook salmon, lake trout, big pike, muskies, striped bass, and big catfish. If you cast heavy lures or suckers for muskies this is the rod to use.

There are many companies making bait-casting reels today. The best ones, though rather expensive, have such features as a light spool, free spool, star drag, high-speed retrieve ratio,

This Garcia "Ambassadeur" bait-casting reel can be used with bait-casting rods for casting or trolling.

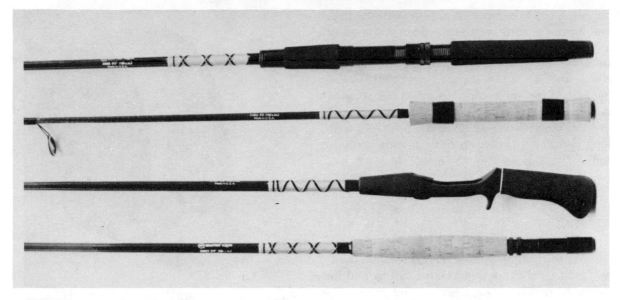

Graphite rods, such as these by Graftex, are now made for all kinds of fresh-water fishing.

and antibacklash control. The antibacklash control makes it easier to cast with these reels with fewer backlashes. However, it still requires more skill and practice to cast far and accurately with a bait-casting reel than with one of the spin-casting or spinning reels, a fact you should bear in mind when buying your first outfit. Later on, if you feel you need a bait-casting outfit, you can get one.

Many fresh-water anglers feel that for the most sport and thrills you can't beat a fly-fishing outfit. If you plan to do any trout fishing or Atlantic salmon fishing, a fly rod is needed. It is also being used more and more for the black-bass fishing with bass bugs and flies. And to get the maximum sport from the smaller panfish, go after them with a light fly rod.

Fly rods are made in various weights, lengths, and actions, depending on the waters you are going to fish, the fish sought, the size of the flies or bass bugs used, and other conditions. Generally, the smaller the fish and the smaller the waters, the shorter and lighter the rod. For the bigger fish and big waters, the longer and heavier the rod. Also, for casting the heavier, bigger, and bulkier lures long distances, the heavier and longer rods are more practical.

Not too long ago, most fly rods were made from split-bamboo or Fiberglas, but in recent years graphite rods have become popular and are being used by more and more fly fishermen.

Although still expensive when compared to Fiberglas, graphite rods have many features that make them superior to rods of any other material. A graphite rod is stiffer and lighter than a glass or bamboo rod of the same length and diameter. Yet it has more power, less rod vibration, and is also more sensitive, all of which means that you can make longer and more accurate casts with less effort. Being thinner in diameter, a graphite rod also offers less resistance during the cast. In addition, the rod tip is extremely sensitive and responsive to the bite or strike of a fish or to the action of a lure. However, if you are buying your first fly-fishing outfit, you can do very well with a good-quality Fiberglas fly rod. Later on, as you become more skilled and experienced, you may want to buy a graphite rod.

The lightest fly rods will range from 6 to 8 feet. The shorter, lighter ones may weigh only 1 ounce, while the longer ones may run up to 3 ounces. They are used with No. 4, No. 5, or No. 6 weight fly lines, and with the smallest, lightest fly reels to fish the smaller, heavier wooded streams where trout are not too big and casts are short. They are also fine for panfish and small bass. The light fly rods are excellent for fishing with dry flies where fine leaders and tiny flies are needed to fool wary trout.

Fly rods in the medium range will run from 8 to 9 feet in length and weigh from 2½ to 4 ounces. They take No. 6, No. 7, or No. 8 fly lines and are used with regular-sized single-action or automatic fly reels. The rods in this class are suitable for general trout fishing in streams, rivers, and lakes, but are also good for bass and panfish. Many anglers also use them for Atlantic salmon, landlocked salmon, coho and chinook salmon, steelhead, and pike. An 8- or 8½-foot-long fly rod is the nearest thing to an all-around rod for dry-fly, wet-fly, nymph, streamer, and bass-bug fishing.

Heavy fly rods will range from 8 to 14 feet in length and weigh from 4 to 10 ounces. They take No. 8, No. 9, No. 10, and No. 11 weight fly lines. The longest and heaviest of these fly rods, used for Atlantic salmon, may have extension butts and long handles for two-handed casting and for fighting big fish in heavy waters and strong currents. With the advent of graphite as a rod material, however, you can now make long rods in this class that weigh less than shorter rods made from bamboo or Fiberglas.

Heavy fly rods are best for fishing big fish in big waters as well as for making long casts. They are also the most efficient tools for casting the larger, bulkier lures such as big streamers, bucktails, and big bass bugs. This is the rod that is often used for Atlantic salmon, steelhead, coho and chinook salmon, pike, big bass, and striped bass in fresh water. The heavy fly rod calls for the largest single-action fly reels capable of holding the fly line and backing line. Anywhere from 100 to 200 yards of backing line is put on

Automatic fly reels, like this model by the Martin Reel Company, make retrieving a fly line much quicker and easier.

the reel to take care of long runs made by such fish as salmon and steelhead. Many good-quality large fly reels are now made for use with a heavy fly rod in fresh and salt water.

The fly line you use with fly rods will depend on the type of fishing you will do. For casting dry flies, a double-tapered floating fly line is best. For casting wet flies, nymphs and streamers that are worked anywhere from just below the surface to very deep, you need sink-tip, slow-sinking, fast-sinking or extra-fast-sink-

Single-action fly reels, such as these by Orvis, come in different sizes to match the different fly rods available today.

ing fly lines, depending on the depth you want to reach. For casting bass bugs and streamers, as well as for making long casts, a weight-forward or bug-taper fly line is used. The size or weight of the fly line should match the fly rod you are using. This information can best be obtained from the rod manufacturers, who usually list the correct size line for a particular rod either in their catalogs or on the rod itself. Some knowledgeable tackle dealers will also be able to recommend the correct weight line to use with a particular rod.

Fresh-water anglers sometimes use salt-water rods and reels for various kinds of fishing or in specific areas and waters. Anglers seeking coho or chinook salmon or lake trout will often use salt-water boat or trolling rods and salt-water reels to handle heavy-wire lines and weights and big lures (not to mention the big fish that may be hooked). If you plan to use wire lines for deep trolling, get a rod with roller guides or at least a roller tip, as well as a reel with a metal spool.

Other anglers going after big carp, buffalo, catfish, sturgeon, and fresh-water striped bass may resort to salt-water spinning rods and reels or to boat and surf rods and reels. The longer rods of this type are used to make long casts from shore. Shorter and somewhat lighter salt-water rods can be used from boats. Lines for these rods may test from 15 to 80 pounds if you are after the bigger fish.

Before you buy any of the above tackle you should decide where you plan to fish most of the time and what kind of fish you expect to catch—essential information that should determine your choice of tackle. Often you can obtain advice from an expert fishing friend as to the best fishing outfit for your area. Most fishing-tackle dealers will also recommend a suitable outfit, if you tell them where you plan to fish.

Fresh-water anglers also need various accessories such as boots or waders, vests or jackets, hat, fly, tackle boxes, landing net or gaff, fish stringer, creel, bait bucket, knife, pliers, oil, reel grease, sunglasses, and insect repellent. And, of course, there are the various kinds of fishing lures, baits, hooks, and rigs, which will be covered in the following chapters as they pertain to a particular species of fish.

Chapter 2

LARGEMOUTH BASS

The largemouth bass is one of the most widely sought of the fresh-water game fish in the United States. It is especially popular with expert and dedicated anglers who seek a challenging fish that is not too easily fooled. Largemouth bass, smart and unpredictable, meet these requirements. They learn quickly from experience and tend to avoid ordinary lures, baits, methods, and techniques. This is especially true of big, old bass, who are more wary and feed less often than younger, inexperienced bass.

Fortunately, however, most largemouth bass are also almost always hungry, curious, and pugnacious. If they don't strike a lure or bait because they are hungry, they may strike it because they are curious or angry. Time and again, anglers have seen bass that seemed indifferent to all the lures cast to them. But by continuous casting and reeling past the noses of the fish, they finally succeeded in teasing the bass into grabbing the lure. Spawning bass will also guard their homes and nests against all intruders, even if that means chasing and grabbing a bait or lure.

At one time largemouth bass had a limited range: from southern Canada and Maine, through the Mississippi Valley to northern Mexico, the Gulf states, and Florida, and up along the East Coast. But extensive introductions have been made through the years and now you'll find largemouth bass in almost every state. Together with the bluegill and the bullhead or catfish, it has become one of the most commonly stocked fishes in farm ponds or man-made lakes or reservoirs. One of the factors in its favor is that the largemouth is more adaptable to various waters and water temperatures than the smallmouth bass.

The largemouth bass is also called the bigmouth bass, green bass, green trout, lake bass, mossback, and linesides. Although there are several species of bass recognized by scientists, in this book we'll deal only with largemouth black bass and smallmouth black bass. The latter will be covered in the following chapter.

Fishing for largemouth bass has grown tremendously in popularity in recent years, as is evidenced by the proliferation of bass tourna-

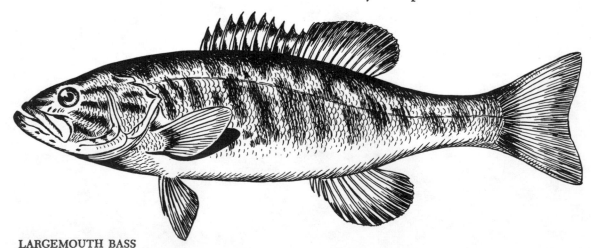

LARGEMOUTH BASS

Today most serious bass fishermen invest in a special "bass" boat, a big outboard motor, an electric motor, and electronic gear to aid them in locating and catching fish. (Evinrude Motors Photo)

ments, bass-fishing clubs, and even the bass seminars or classes conducted all over the country. There have been many new developments and improvements in the design of big, fast bass boats, and motors, electronic depth finders or fish finders, fishing rods, reels, lines, and lures. New methods and techniques have been discovered and developed, and a great deal more has been learned about the behavior of the largemouth bass. So while the present-day bass angler is better equipped, more knowledgeable, and more highly skilled than his predecessors, he also faces more competition for fewer bass in many heavily fished waters. With more fishing pressure you have to fish longer and harder to make a decent catch of largemouth bass.

You can catch largemouth bass with cane or glass poles, spin-casting or spinning tackle, bait-casting tackle, or fly-fishing tackle, all of which were discussed in the previous chapter. Your choice will depend on the waters you are fishing, the methods and lures used, and your own personal preference. Later in this chapter, we will mention suitable tackle for particular methods, techniques, and waters, and for the lures or baits being used.

The time of year, water temperature, water level, light, weather, and the availability of food all play a big part in largemouth-bass fishing. The fishing will vary according to the seasons. One of the best times to catch bass is in the early spring, when the water first starts to warm up and before the fish are ready to spawn. At this time, they are hungry and will feed near the surface not far from shore.

Largemouth bass spawn as early as January, February, and March in Florida and the other southern states and from April to June in more northern climes. If the fishing season is open during these months, you can have excellent action on the spawning beds near shore. This is the best time to catch the big "hawg" bass in the trophy class. Largemouth bass are aggressive at this time and are prone to strike at lures moving near them.

As the water warms and the sun gets bright and strong, largemouth bass tend to drop back into deeper water. The depth will vary accord-

Many women enjoy catching largemouth bass, as is evidenced by the growing number of women's bass-fishing clubs and tournaments all over the country. (Georgia Department of Industry and Trade Photo)

ing to the type of water being fished as well as to other factors such as the preferred water temperature, oxygen content, structure, and presence of food. The bass may return to feed in shallow water at dusk, during the night, and around daybreak. But during the daylight hours, deep fishing will be the rule, especially during the hot summer months.

Then in the fall, as the water and weather cool again, the largemouth bass will return to shallow water near shore. September and October can be two delightful and productive fishing months.

Not many anglers fish for largemouth bass during the winter months in the North. But in our southern states you can still catch bass in December, January, February, and March, if you fish in deep water where the bass are holed up. Of course, in Florida you can catch bass year round, and winter fishing can be very good.

The biggest problem confronting the largemouth-bass angler is locating the fish in the lake, reservoir, pond, or river he plans to fish. This is especially true if you are fishing a strange lake and are not familiar with the bottom structure, the depths, contours, and hot spots that have produced in the past. The best way to get this information in a hurry and enjoy good fishing is to go out with an angler who knows the waters or hire a fishing guide for a day or two.

If you are on your own, try to find out from the local marina operator, fishing-camp owner, tackle shop, or a local angler which part of the lake is producing. Get a topographic map or hydrographic map of the lake or reservoir you plan to fish, and study the contour and depths, points, coves, and dropoffs shown on it. Your boat should also be equipped with a good electronic depth finder or fish finder to enable you to know the bottom and the depth you are fishing.

Largemouth bass are easiest to locate when they are in shallow water in the spring or fall, around daybreak, dusk, and during the night. In such shallow water largemouth bass like to be under or near some kind of cover. They like shady spots under lily pads, hyacinths, weeds, brush, overhanging trees, or else they lurk under or near driftwood, rocks, boulders, piers, docks, and rafts. Any kind of "stick-ups" such as sawgrass, cattails, reeds, branches, and cypress trees, stumps, or knees also attract them.

When fishing warm, sluggish rivers, look for largemouth in the quieter portions such as the backwaters, coves, eddies, pools, and shorelines, especially those with mud bottoms covered with weeds, reeds, sunken trees, logs, and stumps.

Points of land sloping into deeper water and elevations, ridges, or ledges in shallow water (but close to deep water) are prime fishing spots. If these areas contain brush, tree branches, rocks, or boulders, so much the better. A creek or stream entering a shallow cove is another hot spot. The running water brings food into the lake and attracts minnows and small fish, which in turn bring the bass.

Locating largemouth bass in deeper water is more difficult; in this case you should use your depth finder to read the bottom and determine the location of schools or groups of fish. Try to pinpoint the underwater structure such as channels, creekbeds and riverbeds, old roads and depressions, elevations, submerged islands, and dropoffs leading to deeper water or adjacent to it. Bass will often gather along a sharp dropoff. Look for rock walls or other steep structure in fifteen to twenty feet of water, especially if they are next to a deeper channel. Along channels and riverbeds the most productive spots are the bends or curves, culverts, bridges, and dropoffs.

Individual bass and small schools of bass may be scattered throughout the lake, at different levels or depths. Bass also move around or migrate from their feeding areas to their holding or resting areas depending on the time of day and water and weather conditions. The bass anglers who catch the most fish are those who know several potentially good spots in a lake or reservoir and fish them all, eventually focusing on those that contain fish. Successful anglers usually don't spend too much time in one spot. They make a few casts and try different lures, but if they get no hits they move on to the next spot. Experienced fishermen, however, do spend many hours on a lake, reservoir, or river and make hundreds of casts during the day.

The bass pros also try to establish a pattern for the day: They try to find out the type of structure or cover the fish prefer, the best depth or depths to fish, the best lure to use, and the action that best produces hits. But they are also alert to conditions that will change the established pattern, such as time of day, moving fronts, wind shifts, waves, changes in temperature, fishing activity by other anglers, heavy

Largemouth bass like cover such as these standing cypress trees. Try to cast your lure as close to the trunks as you can. (Texas Parks & Wildlife Department Photo)

boat traffic, and other factors that can affect the fishing.

The important point to remember in bass fishing, whether in shallow water or deep water, is that bass, large ones in particular, are smart and wary, especially when they are found in calm, clear, shallow water. A sloppy or noisy approach or a big splash or commotion will scare them away or at least alert them. Expert anglers usually cut their motors when nearing a fishing spot and row or drift quietly to the fishing area. (Another alternative is to use a quieter electric motor to reach the area.) They try not to approach too close to where the fish can see the boat or angler. Once in a good location, these anglers make long casts from a sitting position, and, of course, they don't bang metal boxes, oars, paddles, or other objects against the boat.

After you have located the bass your biggest problem will be to find out which lure they want and how it should be presented and manipulated to bring a strike. In the spring and fall and at daybreak and toward dusk during the summer months you can use a surface plug in shallow water. Such surface plugs as poppers, chuggers, crippled minnows, darters, gurglers, and torpedo or cigar shapes that kick up a fuss or create a commotion on top are the ones to use. They are especially effective when the lake or river is calm. Most of these plugs are supposed to imitate a crippled or injured minnow or a frog, so an action that duplicates the struggles of such food is best. Good examples of these surface plugs are the Jitterbug, Hula-Popper, Devil's Horse, Zara Spook, Plunker, and Spin-I-Diddie.

For best results cast most surface plugs right

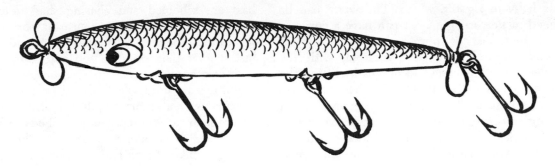

Top-water plug for largemouth bass.

next to or into cover. Let it rest for a minute or so; twitch it, let it rest, then jerk and twitch it again. Keep doing this for several feet, then reel in and cast to the same spot again or a bit to one side. Some surface plugs such as the Jitterbug can be reeled in steadily but slowly, so that it rolls, wobbles, and crawls along the surface.

Other surface plugs such as the torpedo shapes and the crippled-minnow propeller types can be reeled faster or "walked" on top of the water in a zigzag fashion. They can be fished along shorelines or out in deeper water when bass are schooled up and chasing shad minnows or other small fish on the surface. Surface plugs are also very good to use at night near shore.

Shallow-running underwater plugs can be used in shallow water near shore or in somewhat deeper water up to several feet. The Rapala, Rebel, Red-Fin, and Creek Chub Pikies are examples of these plugs. Some of these plugs run only a few inches to a couple of feet under the surface, while others may go down a bit deeper. Slow reeling will keep them closer to the surface, while faster reeling will make them dive deeper. Most of these plugs have a built-in action such as a wriggle, dart, or wobble, but you can also give them some added action by varying the speed of the retrieve at intervals and jerking the rod tip occasionally. Use them throughout the day and also at night. They are often better than surface plugs when the water is choppy, rough, or a bit discolored.

Deep-running, diving, and sinking plugs are used in deeper water, usually from eight to twenty-five feet deep. The sinking types go down slowly to even deeper water but must be reeled slowly to stay there. Some have no built-in action but must be jerked or twitched to provoke strikes. The "crankbaits" are plugs of the deep-running type that come in different

sizes, shapes, designs, and colors. The bodies are usually round, deep, and short. They have big plastic lips that make them dive deep and wriggle in a lively manner at a certain depth when reeled at a fast speed. They are usually labeled as shallow runner, medium shallow runner, medium runner, deep diving, or extra-deep diving.

The deep-diving and deep-running underwater plugs are most effective during the daytime when bass are lying in sunken weedbeds, among trees and logs, on submerged islands, river channels, rock piles, off rocky points and bars, along dropoffs, in holes, and in other structure. Here you anchor or drift not too far from the chosen spot and cast beyond it, then reel fast to get your plug down to the structure or cover. Since fast reeling usually brings the most strikes, most anglers use fast-retrieve reels. But if you are using a floating-type plug, try reeling fast to get it down deep, then pause and let the plug rise a short distance. Reel fast again, pause, and let it rise and so on during most of the retrieve. Bass will often hit the plug as it starts to rise.

The lure that has really revolutionized largemouth-bass fishing in recent years is the very popular plastic worm, which now comes in sizes ranging from three inches to the twelve-inch-long jumbo "snakes" used for the big "hawg" bass. Some of these plastic worms have wavy or curly tails, split tails, or even tails like skirts. The bodies can be smooth, segmented, or ringed. Plastic worms come in colors such as white, yellow, natural, blue, green, purple, and black. Most of them are covered with some kind of oil or scent to attract the fish.

Plastic worms can be rigged in various ways. For fishing in shallow water or water that is not too deep, they can be hooked with a single hook whose point and barb can be either exposed or buried inside the worm. Or you can use a weedless hook to rig the worm. The worm can be rigged to ride straight or it can have a curve in the body to make it spin or revolve slowly. Most worms, however, are used straight, with the angler imparting some rod action by lifting the rod and then letting it drop so that the worm rises and sinks. The weedless-type unweighted worms can be cast into heavy weeds or cover or close to it; after it sinks a few inches you can reel the worm back slowly. Or you can reel it faster over lily pads or in open pockets so that it slithers like a small snake on top of the water.

To fish the plastic worm deeper you can add a clincher sinker or Rubbercore sinker a foot or so above the worm. But the most popular rig for deep fishing is the Texas rig, in which a cone-shaped sinker slides against the worm and rests at its head. The hook point and barb are buried inside the worm to make it weedless. The weighted plastic worm (from six to eight inches long) rigged in this manner should be cast out and allowed to sink to the bottom. Give the rod tip a short jerk, reel in the slack line, let the worm settle once more, reel in the slack again, and let it settle, etc. Try to keep the worm bumping bottom at all times so you will know you are deep enough. Watch where your line enters the water to detect a strike. If you get a pickup, lower your rod, reel in the slack, and set the hook fast and hard. A stiff rod such as the special "worm" bait-casting rod is best for such deep fishing with plastic worms.

Another highly effective and versatile lure for largemouth bass is the jig, which has become very popular in recent years. Formerly used mostly in salt water, jigs have now become a standard lure for bass and other fresh-water fish. Jigs have a weighted head, usually of lead, in front and are dressed with skirts of hair, feathers, nylon, rubber, and other materials. You can also add a strip of pork rind or even a plastic worm to the hook. The jig heads with short plastic grubs, tails, or curly tails are very good. Jigs come in various colors, with white, yellow, black, brown, and red or combinations of these colors being the most popular. The best jig sizes or weights for bass are the ⅛-, ¼-, ⅜-, and ½-ounce models.

When using jigs you have to determine the depths you want to fish and the speed of the retrieve. Jigs can be reeled fairly fast, steadily, or with short jerks, just below the surface when bass are schooled and chasing shad minnows. When used with a plastic worm or pork chunk jigs can also be used in shallow water and reeled fast so that they skim on top and through lily pads or other weeds.

But jigs are most effective in deeper water, especially over and through heavy structure and cover such as submerged weedbeds, islands, points, or bars along dropoffs, ledges, and through sunken brush and branches. When such conditions are present, you should cast out and let the jig sink until it hits bottom, then raise and lower your rod tip so that the jig bounces on the logs, through the branches, and along ledges and dropoffs. If you are right over the structure you can just lower the jig to the bottom or into the cover and then "jig" it up and down. Here you have to keep a sharp eye on your line because bass usually hit the jig as it is sinking.

Spoons are old-time largemouth lures, but they are still very effective in many waters and on many occasions. Around lily pads and other weeds use a silver, gold, copper, or black spoon with a weedless hook and a strip of pork rind, plastic worm, or a rubber skirt on it. Cast right into the pads or weeds and pull it along on top of the pads until the spoon comes to an open pocket of water. Then let it sink a few inches, reel, and jerk it until it comes up on the pads again. You can also cast the spoon in shallow open water near shore and let it sink, then retrieve it in a darting, stop-and-go fashion with erratic action of the rod tip. When you see bass schooled up and chasing minnows or other small fish you can cast the spoon right into them and retrieve it fairly fast below the surface.

The heavier-type spoons can be used for vertical jigging in much the same manner as described above for jigs. This is especially effective during the hot summer months when bass are very deep in the daytime and also during the cold winter months when they are schooled and holed up in deep water.

Spinners are also old-time lures that are still effective for bass. In recent years weighted

Weedless spoon with pork frog.

Weedless spoon and plastic worm.

spinners with skirts of hair or feathers around a treble hook have become popular. The Mepps is a good example. Spinners come in different sizes, weights, and colors, such as silver, gold, brass, black, or with painted blades. Most of the time a bass will take a spinner that is reeled steadily, but at times a stop-and-go or erratic retrieve with some rod action is better. Spinners are good to use in roily or murky water because they give off vibrations.

Spinner baits have also become popular in the past few years too, as they are very deadly for largemouth bass. These lures consist of two wire arms with single or double blades on the top arm and a leadhead hook dressed with a plastic or rubber skirt on the bottom arm. When bass are in shallow water you can fish the spinner bait by "buzzing" it on top of the water so that the blades churn the surface of the water and leave a wake. This is done around lily pads, weeds, grass, reeds, logs, rock piles, stumps, and brush. At other times you can reel the spinner bait so that it travels just below the surface. In deep water you can cast the spinner bait out and simply let it sink or drop, or else you can jig it up and down as it sinks. Bass will often hit it on the way down. And finally you can let the spinner bait sink all the way to the bottom, then raise and lower your rod tip, reeling in very slowly so that the spinner bait bumps the bottom.

More and more anglers are discovering that catching largemouth bass on a fly rod can be exciting and a lot of fun. For bass, you should use one of the heavier and longer fly rods capable of handling a heavy-bug-taper fly line. Bass bugs are great lures to use when the bass are in the shallows near shore. The various cork, plastic, and deer-hair poppers, frogs, bugs, and minnow types are all good at different times, especially around weedbeds, lily pads, stumps, logs, and rocks along shore. Most of the bugs should be worked very, very slowly, with long rests,

In recent years spinner baits such as this one have caught many largemouth bass. They can be buzzed on top or reeled below the surface. (Oklahoma Department of Wildlife Conservation Photo)

pauses, short jerks, or twitches to imitate a bug, moth, dragonfly, or other insect or a small frog. The bullet-shaped minnow-type bugs (as well as big streamers and bucktails) can be retrieved more steadily and faster to simulate a frantic minnow trying to escape.

When casting doesn't produce or when you want to locate bass in a strange lake, trolling is often effective. Underwater plugs, spoons, spinners, jigs, and plastic lures can be trolled at various depths and speeds until you find the fish.

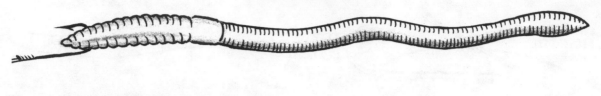

Two ways of hooking nightcrawlers for largemouth bass.

In the morning and evening, troll close to shore along the edges of lily pads, over weedbeds, around rocky points, and over sandbars or rockbars. During the middle of the day trolling should be done in deeper water over structure with lures that travel near the bottom or even bump it. One of the best lures for this is the Spoonplug, designed by that great bass master Buck Perry.

A lot of bass are still caught on natural bait; if it swims, crawls, creeps, or flies, it will be eaten by the largemouth bass. Worms, either a big single nightcrawler on a hook or several smaller garden worms on a hook, make good baits, as do frogs of small to medium size. Minnows of various kinds, from 2½ to 4 inches for small bass and up to 5 or 6 inches for big bass are also effective. In fact, in Florida, anglers use shiners and small fish up to 8 or 10 inches for the big bass. Suckers, small bullheads, gizzard shad, chubs, yellow perch, and killifish can all be used where legal. Largemouth bass have also been caught on hellgrammites, salamanders, leeches, crayfish, snakes, mice, crickets, grasshoppers, locusts, grubs, and caterpillars.

Largemouth bass put up an exciting fight, often standing on their tails and shaking their heads violently to throw the lure or bait. They should be played carefully until they give up before an attempt is made to boat or land them. This can be done with a landing net by leading the bass head-first into it. Some anglers also grab the bass by the lower lip, but this can be dangerous if plugs or other lures with treble hooks are used.

In most of our northern lakes, largemouth bass will run from a pound to three or four pounds. A five- or six-pound bass is a big one in these waters. Farther south, especially in Florida, fish grow much bigger, and lunkers are more numerous. Florida bass have also been introduced into California waters, and big ones are now being caught there too. The world record on rod and reel is a twenty-two-pound, four-ounce largemouth bass taken by George Perry in Montgomery Lake, Georgia, on June 2, 1932.

Largemouth bass are found in so many waters all over the country that it would require a book to list them all. In fact, there is a book that lists the top bass waters state by state. It is *The Bass Fisherman's Bible*, written by Erwin A. Bauer and published by Doubleday & Company.

Chapter 3

SMALLMOUTH BASS

Most anglers like to fish for both the largemouth bass and the smallmouth bass, but those who have caught both species agree that, when it comes to fighting, the smallmouth has a slight edge. This is especially true when you compare the smallmouth bass of the fast, cold rivers to the largemouth bass of the warm, muddy lakes. But even when both are found in the same waters, the smallmouth has that extra dash, speed, and stamina that make him the superior battler. And most anglers who have caught both species also agree that the smallmouth bass is harder to fool, more wary, fussy, and temperamental! In other words, these fish offer a real challenge even to the expert angler when it comes to locating them and making them hit.

Unfortunately, not every angler gets an opportunity to fish for smallmouth bass, since their distribution is somewhat limited. These fish cannot stand very warm waters, nor do they thrive as well as the largemouth bass in small, still waters. Smallmouth bass like cool, clean, swift rivers and deep, cool, clear, rocky lakes. Such waters are not as numerous as the warm,

muddy, weedy lakes and ponds that the largemouth prefer. So, while smallmouth bass have been introduced into many of our states, there are still vast areas in the South and West where smallmouth bass are scarce or nonexistent.

Originally the smallmouth bass was found from southern Canada south to Alabama, Georgia, northern Mississippi, and Arkansas. But it has been introduced throughout New England, along most of the East Coast, and on the West Coast from California to British Columbia.

The smallmouth bass goes by a variety of names, inluding black perch, brown bass, tiger bass, swago bass, gold bass, redeye, bronze bass, and bronzeback. The smallmouth vary in color from a pale yellow to a dark brown, depending on where it lives. Usually it is a dull olive-gold with a luster of bronze. The belly varies from a creamy white to a gray. The sides usually have dark bars, bands, and patches. The eye of a smallmouth bass is bright red. The maxillary or upper jaw reaches only to the middle of the eye and not beyond it, as in the largemouth bass.

You can use the same fishing tackle for small-

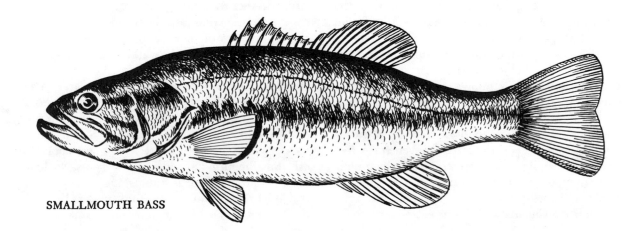

SMALLMOUTH BASS

mouth bass as for largemouth bass. The same bait-casting, spinning, spin-casting, and fly tackle covered in the previous chapter are equally effective for smallmouth-bass fishing. However, in most waters you can use somewhat lighter rods and lines to fool the smallmouth in the clear lakes and rivers and open waters where they are found.

The same is true of the lures such as surface and underwater plugs, spoons, spinners, jigs, plastic worms and grubs, bass bugs, streamers, flies, and pork rind. All these lures will catch the smallmouth bass, but as a general rule you'll find that the smaller and lighter lures are better for the smallmouth than the larger, heavier lures used for the largemouth bass.

The smallmouth bass will also take many of the natural baits that appeal to the largemouth bass. The favorites are worms, minnows, hellgrammites, crayfish, lamprey eels, salamanders, frogs, crickets, and grasshoppers.

The seasons for catching smallmouth bass will, of course, depend a great deal on regional laws affecting fishing for this popular species. They are protected in some states during the spawning season, but where fishing is allowed at this time, it can be out of this world. In southern waters, smallmouth bass may be caught during the winter, but fishing usually doesn't begin there until March or April. Farther north, fishing doesn't start until May or June, when the bass in many areas are in shallow water on their spawning beds. June especially is considered a top month. Fishing in Canada and in some of our northern states may be fair to good during July and August. September and October are usually excellent months for smallmouth-bass fishing in many areas.

Early in the spring and fall and during the spawning season, smallmouth bass will be found in waters ranging from two to fifteen feet in depth. Even during the hot summer months they'll come in close to shore or into shallow water to feed (on minnows, crayfish, frogs, and various bugs and flies) at daybreak, dusk, and during the night. But in the middle of a summer day, smallmouth bass will be found in waters ranging from fifteen to thirty or even forty feet in depth, usually over deep structure, along cliffs and sharp dropoffs, over humps, underwater islands, and rock piles, and in the pools and holes of rivers. In Canada and in our extreme northern states, smallmouth bass will stay and feed in shallow water more often and for longer periods during the summer, even in the daytime, than in our southern states, where the water is warmer. When the water is low, clear, and warm in a river, wait for a shower or rainstorm, which raises the level of the water, lowers the temperature, and makes the water slightly brown. In these circumstances, bass will often go on a feeding spree and you'll have fast action.

In rivers look for smallmouth bass in the shallow water near shore in the spring and fall and during the spawning season. They'll be in spots flooded by rising water such as coves, grass, gravel, sandbanks, sandbars, and around logs or fallen trees. Rocky stretches, especially where there is fairly deep water with plenty of big rocks and boulders scattered throughout, are good hiding and feeding spots for bass. They'll be found lying behind and beneath these boulders, in the pockets between the rocks, and under ledges. When actually feeding, smallmouth bass will often come into fast rapids, riffles, slicks, and runs, and into the shallow tails and head of pools. At other times, particularly during the summer months, they will be lurking in the deeper pools and eddies, deep runs, and in the shade of a rock, log, ledge, or overhanging limb of a tree. Eddies bordering fast water and dropoffs into deeper water from the shallows are all good spots.

In the bend or curve of a river smallmouth bass will often be lying at the deeper side under rock ledges, behind rocky outcroppings, and under the banks. In the rivers and tailwaters below dams such as those found in Tennessee and Alabama, smallmouth bass will often be found in the main channels where the current is strong, rather than along the shoreline.

In lakes, smallmouth bass prefer the rocky shores, bottoms of rock, sand, or gravel, offshore bars and reefs, and underwater islands. Look for shorelines where there are big rocks or boulders above and below the surface of the water. Also look for rocky points sloping out into the lake. Here the deeper sides and the sharp dropoff out on the end are most productive. Sharp ledge rocks formed like steps are also good spots to fish. Smallmouth bass like shady spots, so look for them around brush, stumps, logs, sunken tree trunks, bridge abutments, and under bridges, docks, and piers. But in some lakes smallmouth

By the bend of that rod you can tell that this angler has a fight on his hands. The smallmouth bass gives a good account of itself when caught from a lake or a river. (Ontario Ministry of Industry & Tourism Photo)

bass will also be found feeding over sunken weedbeds growing on the bottom or along weedy and reedy shores. Here they will often find crayfish, minnows, and frogs to feed on. Inlets, streams, or rivers entering a lake are also hot spots.

When fishing narrow or small streams and rivers, smallmouth bass should be approached carefully and quietly. These waters are often shallow, clear, and confined—smallmouth bass are very spooky here and will take off for deeper water or hide under a rock, log, or bank at the slightest disturbance. So try to avoid wading if possible, keep low or hidden, and make your casts from shore. If you do have to wade, do it slowly without creating too much of a disturbance, and watch where your shadow falls. The same is true when fishing shallow water near the shores of big rivers or lakes, from a boat. Move into the spot with oars, paddle, or an electric motor, stop a good distance away, and make long casts. When the water is clear and calm, light tackle with light lines and small lures or baits are best for such shallow-water fishing.

Plugs aren't used as often for smallmouth bass as for largemouth bass, but they can be effective on many occasions. In shallow water and when bass are feeding on minnows, frogs, or hatching mayflies, a small surface plug such as a popper or darter can be deadly. The small, slim plugs with a single or double propeller are among the best to use. They should be cast out near shore or where fish are breaking and twitched with short jerks and pauses in an erratic manner to imitate a crippled minnow or frog. For smallmouth bass do not work a surface plug too violently or with too loud a splash, pop, or other commotion. Gentle twitches and jerks are best.

Small underwater plugs are often effective in lakes and rivers. Here the slim minnow-type plugs that float and dive, such as the Rapala or Rebel, are excellent. In shallow water they can be worked on top slowly in a snaky, swimming action. Or you can reel them faster so that they dive and wriggle below the surface from a few inches down to a foot or two. They have a good built-in action, but sometimes added rod action and a change in the speed of retrieve will bring more strikes.

For deeper waters, the deep-diving or sinking plugs are better. Crankbaits in the smaller sizes are often productive, especially the dark-colored ones (in black, brown, or dirty green) that imitate crayfish. They can be worked at various depths in water from five to twenty feet deep. Cranking them fast so that they travel close to the bottom is often deadly. In fact, you can even let the plug dig into the bottom to stir up some mud or sand or to bump the rocks.

The smaller spoons also account for many smallmouth bass, especially in rivers. Here you can cast upstream and across and let the lure sink to various depths. Then raise the rod, reel in fast, and stop; lower the rod, let the spoon sink once more, then raise the rod again, speeding up your reeling as you do so. This gives the spoon a tumbling, sinking, rising, crazy action that often brings strikes.

Spinners are old-time favorites for smallmouth bass and they are still very good, especially the weighted types, such as the Mepps, with hair skirts around the treble hook. These can be used in rivers and lakes at various depths. Reel them in straight or give them action with the rod tip so that they rise and fall in an attractive manner.

The small tail-spinner baits such as the Little George and the Pedigo Spinrite are highly effective when smallmouth bass are down deep. A good way to use them is to cast out and keep a tight line while the lure is sinking so that you can set the hook if a fish hits it on the way down.

In recent years jigs have become smallmouth-bass killers in rivers and lakes. Jigs used for smallmouth bass should be small and short, with the feather or hair not much longer than 2 or 3 inches, and should weigh $\frac{1}{16}$, $\frac{1}{8}$, $\frac{1}{4}$, or $\frac{3}{8}$ ounce. The best jigs are those with black, brown, or gray bucktail hair or marabou feathers. You can add a short strip of pork rind, a pork eel, or a plastic worm to the hook to make the jig even more deadly.

In streams and rivers cast the jig upstream and let the current swing it around and down deep where the bass are lying. Then retrieve it with short, gentle twitches of the rod tip. In the quiet pools of rivers or in lakes, let the jig sink to the bottom, then reel it in steadily so that it crawls along the bottom like a crayfish. If a steady retrieve doesn't produce, let the jig hit bottom, slowly move the rod up and to the side, and then let it settle back to the bottom. You can also try shaking the rod as you lift the jig so that it quivers and pulsates and looks alive.

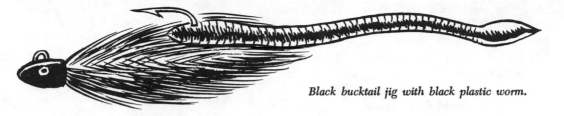

Black bucktail jig with black plastic worm.

Plastic worms will catch smallmouth bass at times but not as often as they do largemouth bass. They are more effective when used with jigs or weights than they are plain. And, most important, worms should be short—not much longer than five or six inches. In fact, the short plastic grubs and curly tail lures only about two or three inches long are usually better than the longer plastic worms.

Fly-rod anglers will find the various bass bugs, popping bugs, streamers, bucktails, wet flies, big nymphs, and, at times, dry flies very effective for smallmouth bass. These usually work best near the shores of lakes and in rivers in the early morning, late afternoon, and evening when flies are hatching and bugs are flying. But bass bugs of the minnow type, streamers, and bucktails are also good when smallmouth bass are feeding on minnows in the shallows or tails of pools. These should be cast and retrieved by stripping in line in short spurts and in an erratic manner to simulate a frightened or frantic minnow. When you see smallmouth bass rising for insects such as mayflies and making rings on the surface, cast to the disturbance with your bug or fly. Then twitch it several times so that it acts like a bug or fly on top of the water. When smallmouth bass are down deep you can still catch them on streamers, bucktails, wet flies, and big nymphs by using a fast-sinking fly line. Buoyant flies are best because you can let the line touch bottom while the fly will float higher and is less likely to foul in rocks, weeds, or logs.

Trolling is often effective when smallmouth bass are in water from 6 to 20 feet deep. You can use an outboard motor or electric motor, trying slow, medium, and fast speeds as you go. Trolling can be done with fly rods equipped with a sinking or lead-core fly line and leader, with a streamer such as the Muddler, Gray Ghost, Black Ghost, Black-nosed Dace, Mickey Finn or one of the marabous on the end. In rivers you can troll very slowly against the current. In lakes you can troll not too far from shore over structure. You can also use spinning and bait-casting tackle and troll with underwater plugs, spinners, spoons, and jigs with the lines anywhere from 30 to 150 feet out, depending on the depth you are trying to reach and the weight of the lure being used. For best results the lures should travel close to the bottom. It will require some experimentation to find out which lures are best, the right speed to use, and how much line to let out. In deeper water you may also have to add a trolling weight about three or four feet in front of the lure to get it down near the bottom.

Smallmouth bass are not always easy to catch with artificial lures, and there are times when natural baits are much more effective. Worms, both the big nightcrawlers and the smaller garden worms, can be used for smallmouth bass. Put a single nightcrawler on the hook by running the hook through the worm's head. Or hook three or four of the smaller worms through the middle so that their ends wriggle.

Hellgrammites are a deadly bait for smallmouth bass, especially in streams and rivers where they are naturally found. Hook this bait by running the hook under the collar. Both worms and hellgrammites can be used in streams and rivers by casting them across and upstream and then letting them drift freely into pools, holes, deep pockets, eddies, and glides, around rocks and boulders, and alongside ledges, crevices, and under cut banks. Most of the time you can fish without a sinker or weight, but there are occasions (particularly if you are fishing in fast currents) when you may have to add some split-shot or clincher sinkers above the hook. Or you can fish in the deeper pools with a bottom rig and sinker to let the worms or hellgrammite lie on the bottom.

In lakes and in the quiet pools of big rivers you can also cast worms into shallow water near shore from a boat. Shady spots and cover such as rocks, boulders, roots, and logs, and under overhanging branches of trees are especially productive. Let the bail of your reel remain open so that the bait sinks with plenty of slack line.

When smallmouth bass are down deep in a lake you can drift or slow troll a single night-crawler on a slip-sinker rig such as the "Lindy" type. Here you should feel the sinker hit bottom and slide along on it. Keep the bail on your spinning reel open (or on free spool with a bait-casting reel) so that when a bass picks up the worm you can let line out. A live minnow or leech can be fished the same way for smallmouth bass.

In the tailwaters of rivers in Alabama and Tennessee anglers use minnows to catch big smallmouth bass from a boat anchored above a good spot. Then they hook a shad minnow through both lips with a No. 1 or No. 2 hook and let it out in the fast current. If the current is too fast they add a couple of split-shot sinkers about eighteen inches above the hook. Here again, the reel should be on free spool or with the bail open to allow the bass to take line when he picks up the minnow.

In lakes and deep pools, a similar minnow rig with a couple of split-shot sinkers can be cast out and allowed to sink to the bottom. You then bring it back slowly along the bottom, and when you feel a pickup give the bass some slack line so that it can swallow the minnow before you set the hook.

One of the best baits for smallmouth bass is a live crayfish. The soft-shelled variety is preferred, but it is hard to keep on a hook. You have to attach it to the hook with thread, rubber bands, or plastic tie, as indicated in the accompanying drawing. A hard-shelled crayfish can also be used, but the two big claws must be removed. You then simply hook the crayfish through the tail.

In a lake or deep pool one of the best ways to use a crayfish is to add a couple of split-shot sinkers a couple of feet above the hook. Then let the bait out from a drifting boat so that it moves slowly and bumps bottom. Or you can cast out the crayfish and let it sink deep to where the fish lie, then reel it back slowly with occasional twitches. During the summer months use the crayfish in water from ten to thirty feet deep along underwater points, reefs, bars, ledges and submerged islands.

In streams and rivers cast your crayfish across and upstream and let it drift into pools, holes,

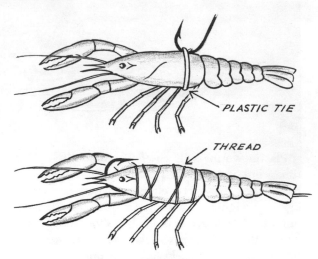

How to hook soft-shelled crayfish.

deep pockets, eddies, and around rocks and boulders. Here you usually don't need a sinker or weight because if you cast well upstream of the spot to be fished, the crayfish is heavy enough to sink even in a current.

Small frogs also make a good bait for smallmouth bass. Here you can hook the frog through both lips with a No. 1/0 or No. 2/0 hook and cast it near shore around logs, weeds, and rocks, and under overhanging bushes and trees. Let it swim around until a bass grabs it. In deeper water in lakes or deep pools in rivers you can add a clincher sinker on the leader or line about three feet above the hook to take the frog down into the depths. Here again, best results are obtained when fishing over structure such as submerged weedbeds and islands, along dropoffs of bars and points, and in holes between big rocks and boulders. Salamanders, small lizards, and newts can also be used as bait in the same way for the smallmouth bass.

Other effective smallmouth-bass baits at times are live grasshoppers, crickets, and locusts. They should be hooked lightly through the neck and cast out on top of the water where they can kick around. If that fails, let them sink slowly to various depths and even way down to the bottom.

A smallmouth bass on the end of a line in a fast river will put up a fight that will remind you of a big trout. The smallmouth bass will often make a long, fast run or leap out of the water, or it'll sound and bore for some rocks or snags. In the deeper water of quiet pools or lakes it may do most of its fighting below the surface, but

She's admiring smallmouth bass caught in the St. Lawrence River near Clayton, New York. These bass are found in many river systems from Maine to Tennessee. (New York State Chamber of Commerce Photo)

Floating down a river, casting as you go, is a good way to catch smallmouth bass. You can also get off the boat and fish from shore or from islands along the way. (Mercury Motors Photo)

even here it will show more speed, flash, and endurance than the largemouth bass.

Most smallmouth bass in rivers will run from one-half pound to about two or three pounds in weight. They may average somewhat larger in lakes, but any fish going four or five pounds is a big one in northern states whether caught in a river or a lake: In southern states such as Tennessee and Alabama they may reach larger weights because of the longer feeding and growing season and the abundance of shad minnows in the larger reservoirs and tailwaters below dams. The eleven-pound, fifteen-ounce rod-and-reel record smallmouth bass was taken in Dale Hollow Reservoir on the Tennessee-Kentucky border by David Hayes in 1955.

However, most of the southern lakes and reservoirs are usually better suited for largemouth bass than for smallmouth bass. If you want good smallmouth-bass fishing you're better off in our northern states and Canada. Michigan has excellent smallmouth-bass fishing in Lake Michigan and the Les Cheneaux Islands in Lake Huron as well as in many other lakes and rivers. In Minnesota, Lac La Croix, the Mississippi River, and the Quetico-Superior wilderness (to name only a few of the state's bass waters) are noted for smallmouth bass. In Missouri the Ozark region has many streams and impounded waters to fish. In Ohio, the Maumee River and central Ohio streams such as the Big and Little Darby, Big Walnut, and Whetstone are good. Pennsylvania has Lake Erie, Allegheny Reservoir, Kinzau Bay, the Susquehanna River, and the Delaware River. New York has the St. Lawrence, Finger Lakes, Niagara River, Delaware River, and many lakes and reservoirs in the Catskill Mountains region that contain smallmouth bass. In New England the state of Maine ranks high for smallmouth bass, with such noted waters as the Third Machias Lake, Big Lake, Scraggly Lake, Great Lakes Flowage, Spednic Lake, Pocomoonshine Lake, Crawford Lake, Meddybemps Lake, and the St. Croix River. The upper reaches of the Penobscot and Kennebec rivers are also good. New Hampshire has many lakes, rivers, and streams that contain smallmouth bass; among the best are Lake Winnipesaukee, Lake Wentworth, Connecticut River, Lake Winnisquam, and Sunapee Lake. Vermont has the Connecticut River and the White, West, Williams, Black, Missisquoi, Lamoille, and Winooski rivers. Lake Champlain also contains smallmouth bass. Maryland has several reservoirs in addition to the Potomac River. In West Virginia, the Summerville Reservoir and such streams and rivers as the Greenbrier, New River, South Branch of the Potomac, Shenandoah, Little Kanawha, and Ohio all contain smallmouth bass. Arkansas has the Buffalo and Beaver rivers. Kentucky has the Dale Hollow Reservoir, Center Hill Reservoir, Woods Reservoir, and Norris Lake. Bass in Alabama are concentrated in Pickwick Lake, Wilson Lake and Dam, Wheeler Lake, and Tennessee River.

There are also some smallmouth-bass waters in California, Oregon, and Washington. And, finally, Canada offers some great smallmouth-bass fishing, especially in Ontario, Quebec, and New Brunswick.

Chapter 4

ATLANTIC SALMON

Ask any expert fresh-water angler which fish he considers the greatest game fish in fresh water and chances are he'll say the Atlantic salmon. This big fish is esteemed by anglers not only in America but also in Europe and other parts of the world where it is found.

Through the centuries the Atlantic salmon has been highly prized both for sport and for food. In England, Scotland, and in this country, Atlantic salmon were once so plentiful that they were served to servants and workers nearly every week. Some of them complained if they had to eat salmon more than twice a week.

That, of course, was in the good old days when Atlantic salmon swarmed up coastal rivers as far south as the Connecticut River. But during the past century Atlantic salmon have been depleted by commercial fishing, heavy sport fishing, pollution, dams, and changing conditions of our coastal rivers.

Nowadays, Atlantic salmon are found in Maine, Canada, the British Isles, Norway, Sweden, Finland, Iceland, France, and Spain. Atlantic-salmon fishing can be expensive on most European rivers and some rivers in Canada. You can pay anywhere from five hundred to one thousand dollars a week to fish a certain stretch of river, not including the cost of a guide. After you add air fare or transportation, it becomes obvious that this is not a poor man's sport. But in recent years more sections of salmon rivers in Canada have been acquired by the provinces and have been opened to public fishing. This brings the cost down quite a bit, and the average angler can usually afford a few days of fishing on a public salmon river.

As almost everyone knows, Atlantic salmon ascend fresh-water rivers to spawn after spending from one to six years in the ocean. Those that return to the stream after one year in salt water

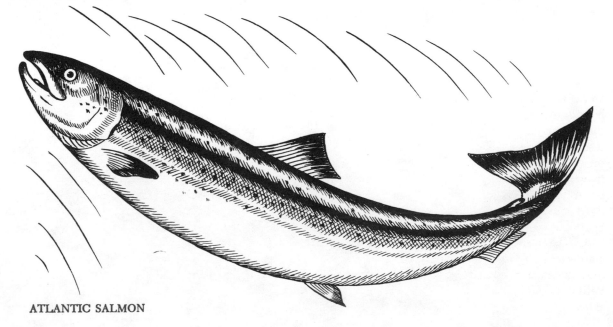

ATLANTIC SALMON

The more popular and productive spots on Atlantic salmon rivers can get crowded at times.
(*New Brunswick Travel Bureau Photo*)

are called grilse and range from three to six pounds in weight. The fish that spend two or three years in the sea are much larger when they return to spawn, sometimes reaching twenty to thirty pounds in weight. The longer a salmon lives and feeds in the ocean, the heavier it will be. Atlantic salmon do not die after spawning as the Pacific salmon do, but may return to spawn again.

An Atlantic salmon just entering the fresh waters of a river is a handsome fish. It has a dark steel-blue back, silvery sides, and white belly. Small black spots may cover the back and sides. After spending some time in fresh water

the salmon loses its silvery hue as its coat turns dull and reddish or gray. The spots grow larger toward spawning time. After spawning the fish-become even drabber and tend to lose weight. At this stage, they are called "black" salmon or kelts. These spent fish are often caught in the spring on their way back to the ocean. But most expert anglers consider them inferior in fighting ability and endurance to the "bright" salmon fresh-run from the sea.

Atlantic salmon can be caught in this country and Canada on fly-fishing tackle only. At one time, long, double-handed salmon fly rods from 12 to 16 feet long and weighing up to 26 ounces were used. A few such rods are still being used in Europe, especially Norway, for big fish in heavy waters. With graphite as a rod material you can now make long fly rods that have power but weigh much less than bamboo or glass fly rods. But the trend in recent years has been toward shorter and lighter fly rods from 8 to 9½ feet. The longer, heavier, more powerful rods are best for making long casts in big waters with big fish. They are also best for casting into strong winds. On the smaller rivers, for small fish and for dry-fly fishing, the shorter, lighter fly rods can be used.

The single-action fly reel used for salmon fishing should be larger than most trout reels. There are now many fine fly reels made for saltwater fly fishing that can also be used for salmon fishing. The reel should hold your fly line with at least 150 to 200 yards of backing line. This backing line can be braided Dacron line testing 15 to 20 pounds.

The fly line used will vary according to the flies you will be using, the river being fished, and the location of the salmon in the river. The usual lines for salmon fishing are No. 8-, No. 9-, or No. 10-weight, depending on the rod used and the fishing being done. A floating, weight-forward fly line is good for all-around salmon fishing and allows you to make long casts. But many salmon anglers prefer double-tapered fly lines for dry-fly fishing. Still others like sinking fly lines rather than the floating types for use with wet flies. In rivers with strong, fast currents or deep pools, where salmon are lying deep, the sinking fly line will get the fly down to where the fish can see it. They can also be more effective when the water is cold and salmon are sluggish and not inclined to rise or move far for a fly.

The fly leaders used for salmon fishing will usually run from nine to twelve feet long. Occasionally, in very clear and low water, you may have to use a longer leader. The tippet strength will vary from three to twelve pounds, depending on water conditions, the fly being used, and the size of the fish usually caught in a particular river. Tapered fly leaders are commonly preferred; shorter, heavier tapers are used for big fish, heavy waters, and wet-fly fishing, while the lighter, longer leaders are best for clear, low-water conditions, small fish, and dry-fly fishing.

For years Atlantic-salmon anglers used the old standby gaudy, wet patterns tied especially for salmon. They are still good, but in recent years anglers have started using the simpler, more subdued hair-wing flies. These are usually tied with squirrel, deer, bear, goat, or woodchuck hair. Such patterns as the Black Bear, Cigar Butt, Green Groundhog, Cosseboom, Butterfly, Hathaway Special, Bomber, Muddler Minnow, and the Rat series of flies have replaced the traditional flies.

But it still pays to carry the older-type flies for the days and conditions when salmon want them. Some of these are the Black Dose, Durham Ranger, Thunder and Lightning, Green Highlander, Silver Gray, Silver Doctor, Blue Charm, Jock Scott, Silver Wilkinson, Dusty Miller, Lady Amherst, and Mar Lodge.

The wet-fly patterns in the larger sizes from No. 3/0 down to No. 2 are used in the early spring when the water is fast, high, and roily. Later on, flies in size Nos. 4, 6, 8, and 10 can be used with the smallest sizes most effective when the river is low and clear.

There are also times on certain rivers when Atlantic salmon will take streamers and bucktails. Such patterns as the Governor Aiken, Mickey Finn, Tri-Color, Thunder Creek, Gray Ghost, and Warden's Worry have all been successful.

You can also try nymphs when salmon are present in a river during low-water conditions. Favorite patterns here include the Black Nymph, Brown Nymph, Gold Nymph, Leadwing Coachman Nymph, March Brown Nymph, and Olive Nymph.

The key to success in Atlantic-salmon fishing is to time your fishing trip to coincide with the runs of the fish upstream. It is important to be on the river when the fish are entering fresh water. The exact day when this occurs varies from river to river and from year to year. It depends on many factors such as the weather, water temperature, water level and flow, and time of year. Salmon like to move into rivers when they are high and the current is strong from recent rains. Then they move upstream fast from pool to pool, often covering many miles in a short time. When the river is low the salmon may not enter the river at all, but rather wait in the estuaries. Or they may move up to a deep pool or hole and wait there for the river to rise.

Good salmon fishing can be experienced as

On some of the larger rivers in Canada, anglers catch Atlantic salmon from boats. Guides with boats are usually available for this type of fishing. (New Brunswick Department of Tourism Photo)

early as April on some rivers and as late as October on others. The spring run is usually the best, with May and June being two good months on many waters. During the summer months of July and August the fishing may be fair to good if the river isn't too low. September may be a good month on many rivers, especially when the fall rains raise the level of the water.

Once you are on a salmon river and have established that the fish are present, you still have to locate the spots where salmon are lying in the river. Casting blindly, as is often done when fishing for trout, rarely pays off in salmon fishing. Most expert anglers like to locate a fish first and actually see it or at least have an indication of its presence before they start casting.

Naturally, the natives of the area or anglers who have fished a certain river for many years have a big advantage. They have seen many fish or have caught them in certain spots and know where to look for them. That is why an angler fishing a certain river for the first time will get much quicker results if he hires a guide. The guides are familiar with the river, know the habits of the salmon, and know where they are lying under various water conditions. On certain rivers in Canada you must hire a guide, especially if you fish from a boat. But even when fishing from shore, a guide can be a big help.

If you are on your own you can try to locate a fish in shallow water in depths ranging from three to eight feet. It is usually best to concentrate on the pools, especially the swift, shallow pools rather than the deep, quiet ones. Look for rocks or boulders around which the current flows. The eddies behind or below such rocks will often hold salmon. Or they may be lying alongside a rock or boulder that splits the fast current. The areas around gravel bars, the tails of pools, and along the deep-cut banks and ledges are also productive spots. If a river forms a lake, look for salmon at the inlets and outlets.

At times you can also see salmon leaping or rolling on the surface. High-leaping salmon are less likely to strike your fly than one that just barely shows its back or fins above the water. But when salmon show at all, at least you know that they are present and you have a good indication where they are lying—which means that you won't waste time casting over empty water.

Salmon can be caught throughout the day early in the season when the water is high and cold. Later on, during the summer months when the water is low and clear, better results are obtained early in the morning and in the evening.

The basic method of presentation of the wet fly for salmon differs somewhat from that usually used in trout fishing. Instead of casting upstream for salmon, anglers generally cast across and downstream, allowing the fly to swing in an arc. If you see the salmon or know which way he is facing, try to present the fly broadside to him. At the end of the drift the fly can be retrieved in short pulls against the current, or it can be picked up before a new cast is made.

When fishing a long pool where the exact position of the fish is uncertain or where several fish may be laying scattered in different spots, you can start with short casts and then lengthen them to cover all the water. Then you can move to a new position a few feet downstream and repeat the casts in a series of arcs to cover all the water.

As a general rule it is best to have the wet fly travel just below the surface or not too deep. However, there are times in deeper pools or runs when it pays to let the fly sink and drift closer to the bottom. This is especially true when the water is cold and big fish, which are more apt to take a fly that travels slow and deep, are present.

Atlantic salmon often lie alongside or behind a rock that splits the current.

Most of the time you let the fly drift naturally with little or no drag. You may have to raise or lower your rod tip to control the line. Or you may have to mend your line by rolling it upstream so that it makes a curve on the upstream side to enable the fly to drift without drag or an unnaturally fast swing.

Yet salmon will often take a fly that is retrieved rapidly just below the surface or is skated or skittered on top to create a small V-shaped wake or ripple. To do this you tie a riffling hitch or Portland Creek hitch by throwing one or two half hitches around and behind the head of the fly. This is tightened so that the fly is almost at a right angle to the leader. The fly is then cast across and downstream and skated on the surface just fast enough to leave a slight wake. To do this most effectively make short casts and hold the rod high so that most of the fly line is off the water.

When fishing wet flies from a boat with a guide, you will, of course, follow his instructions on what fly to use, where to cast, and how to work the fly. Casts from a boat are usually made on both sides, with the line being lengthened to cover most of the water. Then the boat may be moved downstream by the guide to a new spot, where the procedure is repeated.

During the summer months when the water is low, clear, and warm, salmon will often rise to a dry fly more readily than to a wet one. You can use such flies as the Wilkinson, Pink Lady, Whiskers, Irresistible, Hendrickson, Mackintosh, the Cahills, Wulffs, and the various bivisibles and spiders. Dry flies in size Nos. 6, 8, and 10 are usually used, but at times you may need a larger fly in size Nos. 2 or 4 to raise certain fish.

When using dry flies you should also cast across and downstream well above the fish so that the fly drifts over it. Salmon aren't as frightened as trout at seeing an angler nearby. So you don't have to sneak up on them or use too long

Portland creek or riffling hitch.

a line. However, it is wise not to get too close—or make unnecessary movements or create vibrations. The dry fly should be fished without drag most of the time. But here again, there are instances when you can deliberately skate a fly with a short twitch or pull to try to induce a strike. Salmon will often rise and play with a dry fly: Some will simply approach it, while others will move it out of the water with their head. When this happens keep casting and changing fly patterns or sizes; your chances of hooking the fish at this time are excellent.

The thing to remember is that Atlantic salmon feed little if at all in fresh water. So they aren't too interested in your offering. With luck you may get a strike early after a few casts—or you may have to make a hundred casts before a salmon suddenly decides to take it. Of course, in rivers where fish are plentiful and you have many spots to fish, you don't have to make too many casts over the same fish. You can make a couple of dozen casts with different flies and then move down to the next fish or hot spot. But in rivers where fish or productive fishing spots are scarce, you may have to spend a lot of time casting to one or two fish.

Salmon are slower and more deliberate than trout about taking a fly. So don't strike too fast when you see the fish rise or flash. Wait a second or two until you feel the pressure of the fish before you set the hook.

Once hooked, a salmon may make a long, fast run, leap high out of the water, or walk on its tail. Its acrobatics and long, powerful runs make him one of the top fighters to be found in fresh water. Fight a salmon directly from the reel instead of holding the line as you would do when fighting a small trout. And keep a light drag on the reel in the beginning to permit the fish to take line freely during its runs. Try to stay abreast or below the fish at all times. If the fish takes off downstream you will have to follow it until you come abreast of it again. Many big fish are lost in fast, shallow rapids when they tear off downstream and take all the line or break off altogether.

If there's a sand or gravel beach or bar, you can often beach the fish in shallow water and then pick him up under the gills. Nets are used by many guides when fishing from a boat or shore. A tailer that snares the fish around the tail by means of a wire noose is preferred by many

This angler is holding a beauty of an Atlantic salmon caught in the Margaree River, Nova Scotia. Most of the rivers in Nova Scotia are public, and several have good runs of salmon. (Nova Scotia Communications Centre Photo)

salmon anglers. Gaffs have also been used, but they may injure a fish that later escapes. Some expert anglers also grab a salmon around the narrow part of the tail with their hand.

Most of the salmon you catch will range in weight from 3 to 20 pounds. Big salmon from 20 to 50 pounds are not too plentiful in most rivers these days. The largest ones are usually caught in Europe, especially in Norway. The rod-and-reel record is a 79-pound, 2-ounce salmon caught in 1928 by Henrik Henrikson in Norway. One of the largest ever recorded weighed 103 pounds and was killed by Scottish poachers at the mouth of the Devon River in 1902.

Atlantic salmon make fine eating, but most anglers don't fish for them because of their food value. Salmon are sought after because most fresh-water anglers find them an unpredictable and difficult fish to hook and land. They offer a challenge to anglers not provided by other fresh-water fish.

In the United States the Atlantic salmon is found predominantly in the state of Maine. Here such rivers as the Penobscot Aroostook, Machias, Dennys, Narraguagus, Pleasant, Sheepscot, Tunk Stream, and Little Falls can be fished. The total take of salmon on all the Maine rivers is not too high—several hundred fish in an average season. Most of the salmon are caught by local fishermen, since not too many out-of-state anglers fish these waters. However, there is plenty of room and enough salmon in Maine waters to accommodate many more anglers during the season.

Atlantic salmon have also been stocked in the Connecticut River and in rivers entering Lake Michigan and Lake Huron, and fishing for them may develop in these waters in the future. They have also been stocked in some lakes in Oregon such as Mud Lake and Hosmer Lake, where they have been caught consistently from boats.

In Canada, New Brunswick offers some of the best salmon fishing in North America, despite its proximity to the United States. There the famed Miramichi River system is the most productive. Other salmon rivers include the Cains, Dungarvon, Renous, Tobique, Upsalquitch, Tabusintoc, Restigouche, Sevogle, Bartholomew, Hammon, Alma, Black, Jacquet, Bartibog, Big Tracadie, and St. John's. In New Brunswick most of the salmon waters are private or leased, but more and more stretches have been opened to the public in recent years.

Nova Scotia has over forty salmon rivers, all of them open to the public for the price of a fishing license. Such rivers as the Medway, Tangier, Gold, Margaree, Tusket, Moser's, Wallace, Phillip, French, Waugh, Stewiacke, Grand, and St. Mary's are best known.

In Quebec, until recently all salmon waters were private or leased, but now there are more public waters. You can fish the Matane, Port Daniel, Little Cascapedia, Petit-Saguenay, Laval, Moisie, St. Jean, Cap-Chat, Dartmouth, York, George, and Whale rivers.

In Newfoundland most of the rivers are open to the public, and the best ones are the Humber, Grand Codroy, Little Codroy, Serpentine, Portland Creek, Plancentia, Trepassy, Castors, Torrent, Highland, Exploits, and Gander Rivers. Most of the salmon caught in these rivers are the smaller grilse, which average about five pounds.

In Labrador, all the rivers are also open to the public, and the top waters here are the Forteau, Pinware, Eagle, Sand Hill Creek, and Adlatok rivers.

In foreign countries Iceland has about sixty salmon rivers. Salmon do not run too big here but are plentiful; the Laxa Grimsa, Langa, and Nordura rivers are favorites. There is also Atlantic-salmon fishing in the British Isles, France, Spain, and Norway.

Chapter 5

LANDLOCKED SALMON

Every spring, thousands of anglers in our New England states and in Canada eagerly await the cry, "the ice is out," on their favorite landlocked-salmon lake. Then regardless of the weather, which can be raw and cold in April, they converge on the lake and spend hours trolling or casting from small boats for one of their favorite fish.

The fish they are seeking—the landlocked salmon—is almost identical to the great Atlantic salmon, which runs up rivers to spawn from the sea. The main difference is that the landlocked salmon, as its name implies, is trapped in fresh water and doesn't migrate to the sea. Landlocked salmon are also smaller than the Atlantic salmon and never reach the weights of their seagoing relatives.

In appearance the landlocked salmon looks a lot like the Atlantic salmon except that it has larger eyes, longer fins, and double-X black spots on its back. It is blue-green on its back and has a reddish tint over its silvery sides.

Landlocked salmon are also called Sebago salmon, Sebago trout, Schoodic salmon, lake salmon, and ouananiche. The latter name comes from the parts of Canada where this salmon is found.

Landlocked salmon are most common in Maine, New Hampshire, Vermont, northern New York State, and Canada. They have been introduced into many waters in these states and as far south as New Jersey. But they thrive best in colder, northern lakes that are fairly large, deep, and contain plenty of smelt, on which salmon feed. They have also been introduced into South America, where they are thriving and reaching the heaviest weights, especially in Argentina.

But no matter where you find them, landlocked salmon rate among the top fresh-water game fish. They are fast, tough spectacular fighters guaranteed to provide plenty of thrills. The landlocked salmon is also one of the largest game fish to be taken in many waters, and it makes fine eating.

In choosing tackle for landlocked-salmon fishing, many anglers rely on the fly rod, usually a light-to-medium-weight rod from 7½ to 9 feet in length. It should have a fairly large reel with a good drag and a capacity to hold 100 to 150

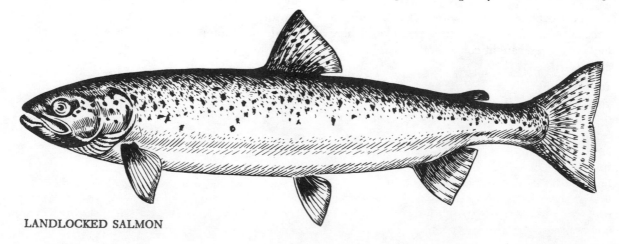

LANDLOCKED SALMON

In many lakes in Maine and Canada landlocked salmon are often caught by trolling streamer flies with fly rods. These were taken in Lac Brule in northern Quebec. (Canadian Government Travel Bureau Photo)

yards of backing line. Such a rod can be used for casting or trolling. For casting streamer flies, a weight-forward sinking fly line can be used. For fishing dry flies, a double-tapered fly line is needed. These lines can also be used when trolling from a boat, but actually you don't need a fly line when trolling; a reel filled with 10-to-15-pound-test monofilament line will suit your needs.

More and more landlocked-salmon anglers are using spinning tackle for trolling and casting lures. A medium fresh-water spinning rod and spinning reel filled with six-to-ten-pound-test line can be used to troll lures, flies, or smelt, or to cast them from a boat or shore. A few anglers prefer to use bait-casting rods and reels for trolling or casting. For deep trolling with weights,

somewhat heavier fresh-water or light salt-water rods are also used.

Lures used with a fly rod are mostly streamer or bucktail flies, wet flies, nymphs, and dry flies. The streamers and bucktails used for trolling from boats are large and are often tied on double or tandem hooks. The most popular and effective streamers and bucktails include the Black Ghost, Gray Ghost, Supervisor, Mickey Finn, Nine-Three, Silver Doctor, Highlander, Barnes Special, Brook Trout, Black-nosed Dace, Red-and-White Bucktail, Edson Light and Dark Tiger, Green Queen, and Green King. Marabou streamers with silver bodies or Mylar strips or tubing and white or yellow feathers can also be deadly. Streamer and bucktail size Nos. 2, 4, and 6 are the best ones to use.

Dry flies are preferred on certain days, waters, and seasons when landlocks are feeding on top. Such dry flies as the Gray Wulff, White Wulff, Green Drake, Black Gnat, Adams, Red Fox, Light Cahill, Quill Gordon, March Brown, and spiders and bivisibles in sizes from Nos. 8 to 14 should be carried for this fishing.

When casting or trolling with spinning rods or bait-casting rods you can use lures such as the Sidewinder, Dardevle, and Mooselook Wobbler spoons. Weighted spinners can also be used. In recent years the slim, minnow-type plugs such as the Rapala and Rebel have proven very effective when trolled shallow or deep. The Flatfish is an older favorite for such trolling.

Mooselook Wobbler for landlocks.

Landlocked salmon are also caught on smelt, alewives, or minnows sewn on a single- or double-hook rig. The commonly used smelt is bent slightly so that it wobbles and flashes when trolled behind the boat, anywhere from fifty to eighty feet from the stern. A light keel sinker is added a couple of feet ahead of the smelt to keep the line from twisting. You can also drift with a live smelt, alewife, or minnow by hooking it through the lips and then letting it out with a couple of split-shot sinkers on the leader. Keep the reel in free spool or with the bail off so that when a landlock grabs the bait you can let some line flow off the reel for a few seconds before setting the hook.

The best time of the year to catch landlocked salmon is, as stated earlier, just when the ice breaks up on a lake and for about two to six weeks after that. When the water temperature on the surface hovers between forty and forty-five degrees during the day, landlocks often go on a feeding spree. This may occur as early as April in the southern part of Maine and New York. But in the northern part of Maine and in most of Canada you have to wait until May before this happens.

When smelt are moving into streams to spawn, landlocks congregate to feed on them at the inlets, outlets, and mouths of feeder streams and the shallow water along shore. Later on, in late June, July, and August, when the water gets warm, the landlocks go down into deeper water and are harder to catch. In early fall, landlocks move into rivers to spawn, and good fishing can be had at times in shallow water at the mouths of the streams and in the rivers themselves if the season is still open at that time. In extreme northern waters in Quebec, Labrador, and Newfoundland, landlocks will often stay and feed on top and in shallow water all summer. Even in southern Canada and in Maine you can often have good fishing on top and in shallow water if you fish around daybreak and dusk.

When the season first opens and the ice breaks up on the lake, the weather is often raw and cold, and the water rough. But good landlocked-salmon fishing can be had on such wet, cold, windy days, despite the weather. In fact, most landlocked-salmon anglers agree that the days when the water is rough are better than when the lake is smooth and calm, since landlocked salmon come up to the surface when the water is rough and go down when the water is calm. In the latter situation, deep trolling is required. You can also have better luck on calm days if you fish early in the morning and toward dusk. If the water is choppy or rough you can often take salmon during the middle of the day. A dark, overcast day is usually better than a bright, sunny one.

As we have seen, landlocked salmon often congregate around the mouths of streams or rivers entering a lake. Troll for them along rocky shorelines, ledges, and wherever there are sharp dropoffs into deeper water. Rocky points, bars, and shoals extending well out into the lake and then dropping off into deeper water are also good spots to try. Landlocks tend to gather and feed on the side or shore where the waves pile up. At other times they may be scattered all over the lake and can even be caught in the middle of the lake. On certain occasions they can be seen chasing smelt or other small fish to the surface.

The most popular and productive method of catching landlocks is to troll streamer flies and lures such as spoons, spinners, or plugs behind a boat. This is usually done by two anglers in a boat with two or three rods. Two fly rods are placed in rod holders attached to each corner at the stern so that they spread out at an angle. Then a spinning or bait-casting rod is placed in the middle. The streamers usually used on the

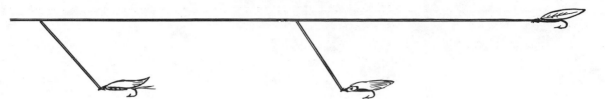

A three-streamer trolling rig for landlocked salmon.

fly rods are trailed from forty to one hundred feet behind the boat. The spinning rod or bait-casting rod in the middle can have the lure about twenty to thirty feet out. Landlocks are not boat-shy but rather seem to be attracted by the wake of a moving boat.

In trolling, you will, of course, cover the hot spots where landlocks are believed to be present or feeding. Or you can follow the contour of the lake by weaving in and out. One man can also cast toward shore from the moving boat. A landlocked salmon may follow his lure toward the boat, then see one of the lures on the other rods and grab it.

When the water is choppy no rod action is necessary to obtain strikes. But when the water is calm or when fish refuse to take a straight trolled lure, you can impart some rod action to tease the fish into hitting. Raising and lowering the rod tip is one way to do this. Another is to pull back and forth on the line to make the lure dart forward, then drop back. Usually a fast-trolling speed of four or five miles per hour is best. But you can also vary the speed of the boat to see which one brings the most strikes. Another trick you can try is to troll two or three flies on the same line rather than just one.

Many expert anglers prefer to cast rather than troll for their fish in the early spring when the salmon are on top. You can work the mouths of streams and the shorelines by casting streamers with a fly rod. Anglers using spinning or bait-casting tackle can cast spoons, spinners, and underwater plugs. Your chances are increased if you can find landlocked salmon feeding on smelt and chasing them to the surface. In a boat try casting all around, working different depths, and trying different retrieves. Later on, during the summer and the early fall months, good fishing for landlocks can sometimes be had with dry flies, wet flies, and nymphs. The best dry-fly fishing in lakes usually takes place early in the morning or evening when salmon are feeding on hatching insects. They can often be seen forming circles or rings on the surface as they rise to pick up an insect. At such times cast your dry fly toward the rings and let it lie motionless for a second or two. Then give the fly some action by skating it across the surface in short twitches or even short hops.

Some of the best fly fishing with streamers, dry flies, wet flies, and nymphs takes place in streams or rivers when the landlocked salmon enter such waters. Landlocked salmon will enter cool, well-aerated rivers even during the summer months. But the best fishing usually takes place during September, when they enter the rivers to spawn. Then a rising river will bring them in, and good fishing can be had below falls, rapids, and dams. You can work the various dry flies, wet flies, and nymphs in much the same manner as for trout, allowing the flies to drift or float through the pools, pockets, and runs. Streamers, of course, can be retrieved fairly fast in short spurts to simulate a frantic minnow.

During the hot summer months in most lakes, however, landlocked salmon go down deep and can be caught mostly by fishing with live bait or by deep trolling. This usually means using lead core or wire lines on fairly heavy tackle and trolling a series of spinners with baits such as smelt, minnows, or worms. Instead of the bait you can also troll a small underwater plug or a spoon. Monel lines testing about 20 pounds can be used and may have to be let out anywhere from 60 to 200 feet to reach the ledges, spring holes, and water temperatures preferred by the smelt and the salmon themselves. This means that the lure or bait will have to reach anywhere from 30 to 150 feet, depending on the lake being fished, the wind, the weather, and the depth with the preferred temperature. You have to experiment with various lengths and speeds of trolling and different depths until you get a strike. Of course, if you have a boat equipped with a depth finder or a fish finder, you can locate the bottom structure and even the bait and fish themselves. If you use a boat with

Anglers catch many landlocked salmon in Maine lakes by casting or trolling from boats near shore early in the spring, soon after ice-out. (Maine State Development Office Photo)

downriggers you can troll deep and still use light tackle to get the most fight out of the landlocks.

When hooked on top or near the surface a landlocked salmon is a fast, flashy scrapper that hits a lure hard, runs, leaps, twists, circles, and dives all around the boat. Many fish are lost during the fight, or right at the boat itself. A big, wide-mouthed net is best when boating a salmon, and even then, great care must be taken. The safest procedure is to fight the fish as long as possible, until it turns over on its side—then net it *head* first.

Landlocked salmon, which in most waters don't grow as big as Atlantic salmon, usually range from about 2 to 6 pounds. A 10- or 12-pound landlock is a big fish. The record taken on rod and reel is a 22½-pound fish caught in Sebago Lake, Maine, on August 1, 1907, by Edward Blakely. There are records of big landlocked salmon caught in weirs or nets weighing up to 36 pounds. But such big fish are extremely rare in this country and even in Canada. The biggest landlocked salmon caught nowadays are found in Argentina, where fish over 15 pounds are fairly common, and a few going over 20 pounds have been caught on rod and reel.

In Maine there are over 300 lakes and rivers containing landlocked salmon. Some of the best waters include Sebago Lake, Moosehead Lake, Mooselookmeguntic Lake, Grand Lake, Big Lake, Pococumas Lake, Pleasant Lake, Dobsis

Lake, Spednic Lake, Green Lake, Eagle Lake, Square Lake, Lake Chesuncook, Rangeley lakes, the Fish River chain of lakes, Moose River, Kennebec River, Union River, and the branches of the Penobscot River.

New Hampshire has Lake Winnipesaukee, Sunapee Lake, Merrymeeting Lake, Big Dan Hole Pond, Big Squam Lake, Bow Lake, Newfound Lake, Ossipee Lake, Pleasant Lake, Silver Lake, the Connecticut chain of lakes, and some of the rivers entering these lakes.

Productive lakes in Vermont are the Caspian, Willoughby, Big and Little Averill, Seymour, Dunmore, Crystal, Echo, Maidstone, East Long Pond, and Harvey's Lake.

Farther south, landlocked salmon have been stocked in Quabbin Reservoir in Massachusetts and in a few lakes in the Adirondack region of New York State such as Schroon Lake and Lake George.

Landlocked salmon are also found in Canada in New Brunswick, Ontario, Quebec, Labrador, and Newfoundland. Here, the more remote northern areas provide the best fishing both in lakes and rivers, even during the summer months.

Chapter 6

COHO AND CHINOOK SALMON

When the first edition of this book was published (in 1964), fishing for coho and chinook salmon in fresh-water inland lakes was unheard of. The introduction of the coho and chinook salmon into Lake Michigan and other waters is a success story in modern fish culture that has paid off very well: An entirely new sport fishery has been created in the Great Lakes area and other waters. Today vast armies of sport fishermen descend on these waters with one purpose in mind: to hook a big, wild, silvery coho or chinook salmon.

The amazing part of the whole story is that this fishery developed in only a few years—the first coho salmon were planted in 1966 in creeks and rivers entering Lake Michigan. The first chinook salmon were stocked in the same lake a year later. The results were almost immediate and quite surprising: Only 90 days after stocking, a 5-inch coho salmon had grown to 15 inches and weighed 1¼ pounds. In 18 months some of the salmon grew to 15 pounds!

Evidently both the coho and chinook found the deep, cold waters of Lake Michigan to their liking, and the abundance of alewives and smelt in the lake provided plenty of food for the new arrivals. Since then coho and chinook salmon have been stocked successfully in most of the other Great Lakes and in many other lakes, reservoirs, and impoundments in various parts of the country.

Neither the coho nor the chinook salmon are new fish; both have always been present in Pacific salt waters and are very popular game fish all along the West Coast of the United States and Canada. Actually there are five species of Pacific salmon that ascend the rivers of the coastal states to spawn. With the exception of a few specimens caught in fresh-water rivers during their spawning runs, most of these salmon were caught until recently almost exclusively in salt water. But now, thanks to human intervention, coho and chinook salmon provide good fishing (until they die after spawning) in fresh waters throughout the country.

The coho salmon, also known as the "silver" salmon because of its predominantly silvery color, has black spots on the back and upper part of the tail. The interior of the mouth is usually gray or black, with whitish gums. The body of a coho is usually smaller and more slender than that of the chinook salmon.

The chinook is also called the "king," "spring," and "tyee" salmon. It too has black spots on its back and on the top half of the tail, but the spots may also appear on the lower half of the tail and on the fins. The interior of the mouth is gray or black, with black gums. The body of the chinook is usually deeper than that of the coho salmon.

Coho- and chinook-salmon fishing varies with the seasons and with the water temperatures of a lake. In the southern part of Lake Michigan, off the shores of Illinois and Indiana, especially near Michigan City, the season starts in April as the water begins to warm up. This early fishing is usually close to shore and near rivermouths. By May the salmon start moving north along both shores of Lake Michigan and a bit farther offshore into deeper water. During June and July they move still farther out in the lake to colder and deeper waters. By August and September the salmon are in the central part of Lake Michigan. Then by October and Novem-

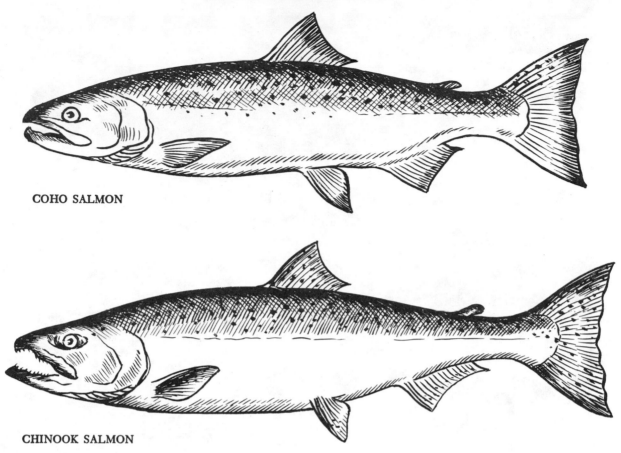

COHO SALMON

CHINOOK SALMON

ber they reach the northern part of the lake and start entering the streams and rivers for spawning.

The key to locating salmon is water temperature. Their movements from shore and from the surface to deep water will depend on the thermocline—that is, the layer of water whose temperature is most suited to the fish. This layer will rise and drop depending on the season, the weather, the wind, and the time of day. Both the coho and the chinook feed most actively when the water temperature is from 44° to 58° F—54° F is the ideal temperature. An electronic thermometer is a big help in finding the layer where the salmon are feeding. A depth sounder or fish finder also aids in locating salmon and baitfish in the open and deep waters of the lake.

In the spring of the year, when the salmon are smaller and can be caught closer to shore and near the surface, you can use lighter tackle. Here a trolling or spinning rod from 7 to 9 feet long is best. It should have a fairly limber tip; the reels should be filled with 8-to-20-pound-test line. The lighter lines can be used with spinning rods and reels, and the heavier lines can be used with bait-casting or light salt-water revolving-spool reels.

Since in the early spring salmon are in shallow water and in the upper 30 or 40 feet of water, you can troll with little or no weight on the line but can control the depth by letting out line or using lures that run deep. Occasionally you may have to add a light trolling weight or sinker to get down deeper. You can let out anywhere from 50 to 250 feet of line depending on the lure used, the location of the fish, and the water conditions on the day you are fishing. As a general rule you'll find the cohos feeding closer to the surface and less boat-shy than the chinooks. In fact, cohos will often rise up to the surface to feed on alewives or smelt. Chinooks will stay deeper and farther away; they hit best early in the morning and in the evening.

The lures used in the spring for salmon tend to be somewhat smaller than those used later on in the summer and fall. Spoons, both fresh-water

Anglers fishing from charter or private boats on Lake Michigan often take big catches of coho and chinook salmon. Note the downriggers on the boat and the salt-water tackle in the foreground. (*Michigan Travel Commission Photo*)

DODGER

Dodger or flasher trolling rig for salmon.

and salt-water types from 3 to 5 inches long, are very good in silver, gold, brass, and copper finishes. Fluorescent yellow, orange, pink, red, and green spoons are also effective. Spinners, either the single-blade weighted types or those rigged with tandem blades or in series, can also be used. Plugs such as the Flatfish, Tadpolly, Rapala, Rebel, Redfin, and Pikie Minnows are favored by many anglers. Most of these lures can be used behind attractors such as cowbells and metal dodgers or flashers. Streamer and bucktail or coho flies with Mylar strips can also be used.

During the summer months, when both the cohos and chinook are down deep, trolling in depths from 50 to 150 feet will be required to reach and catch the fish. One way to do this is by using wire lines, such as Monel, testing 20 to 30 pounds. Here you need a sturdy salt-water-type trolling rod with roller guides and a metal spool reel designed for wire lines. On the end of the wire line add a small barrel swivel. To this you attach a trolling weight (anywhere from 4 to 16 ounces, depending on the depth you have to reach) and then a 30- or 40-pound monofilament leader about 5 or 6 feet long. On the end of the mono leader you add your lure. Most of the same spoons, spinners, plugs, and flies mentioned earlier for the spring fishing can also be used in the summer, but should be a bit larger in size.

Some anglers also use a trolling plane that consists of a plastic or metal plane or fin, counterbalanced by a weight. This dives and pulls the lure down deep (some models can be adjusted for depth). When a fish is hooked the plane trips so that there is less pull or resistance when fighting a fish.

In recent years most serious coho- and chinook-salmon anglers, fishing guides, and charter-boat captains have started using downriggers on their boats to reach the depths where salmon feed. Downriggers are superior to other methods because you can locate and control the depth at which the lure travels. The big downrigger reel mounted on the boat holds a strong wire line with a round cannonball weight on the end that can be raised or lowered to the desired depth or level. The fishing line leading from the rod is attached to a release clip. The fishing line can be set so that the lure travels anywhere from six to two hundred feet behind the downrigger weight. For cohos, the lure or bait can usually travel a shorter distance from the boat than for the warier chinook. When a salmon takes the lure or bait, the fishing line is released from the clip and you can fight the fish without any weight. Lighter tackle can be used when fishing with downriggers than when using wire lines or weighted lines that do not release the sinker or weight.

For downrigger fishing, rods with limber tips and reels filled with fifteen- or twenty-pound-test line are popular. Some big charter boats and private boats have four downriggers each. Two are standard models for the stern, and two have swing-out arms for the gunwales or sides. But for the average small boat, two downriggers at the stern will suffice.

When salmon are down deep, you can also try drifting in a boat and jigging vertically at the depth where the fish are located. This can be done with a seven or eight foot spinning rod or heavy bait-casting or popping-type rod. Lures such as heavy bucktail or feather jigs, heavy spoons, and other metal lures can be lowered and then worked up and down to give them action.

When the salmon are in shallow water near shore in the early spring and again in the fall, they can often be caught from shore, in the surf, or from breakwaters and piers or docks. Here a long, light, salt-water, surf-fishing-type rod can be used to cast the heavy spoons, metal lures, spinners, and plugs that the fish hit.

As we have seen, Great Lakes coho and chinook salmon start moving in the fall into shallow water near shore at the mouths of streams and

In the spring and fall you can catch coho and chinook salmon from the shores of Lake Michigan or from its piers and docks. (Michigan Tourist Council Photo)

rivers, prior to entering them for spawning. They can then be caught by shallow-water trolling or by casting from boats and shore. You'll often see the fish concentrated around the stream outlets and "porpoising" on the surface.

Once the coho and chinook enter a stream or river for spawning they stop feeding, but will still hit a lure or take a bait. These are the big, mature fish that can be caught during October and November in the upper reaches of the streams and rivers in very shallow water. Here you look for individual fish on the spawning beds and wade in the water quietly below the fish until you are within casting distance. It is also possible to approach the fish from upstream until you can reach it with a cast.

Most anglers use spinning or bait-casting

Flies for chinook.

A fly-rod angler with a big coho caught during its spawning run in the fall. (Michigan Travel Commission Photo)

tackle for cohos or chinooks found in streams or rivers. They'll take such lures as spinners, spoons, plugs, or jigs, or baits such as salmon or steelhead eggs and worms. Other anglers use fairly heavy fly rods, 8 to 9 feet long, with No. 9 or No. 10 fly lines, and an 8- or 10-pound-test tippet on their leader. They cast gaudy steelhead flies, streamers, bucktails, or specially tied salmon flies on Nos. 4 to 1/0 hooks.

Big chinook salmon can also be caught in fresh-water streams and rivers along the coasts of California, Oregon, Washington, British Columbia, and Alaska. They will also hit spinners, spoons, cherry bobbers, plugs, and jigs. But here too, some anglers like to go after chinook with fly rods. The big chinook, up to 50 pounds or more, will hit special Pacific salmon patterns tied on No. 8 or No. 10 hooks. These have long tails and no wings and chenille or tinsel bodies. For most of this fishing, shooting, head-sinking fly lines are used to get down to the deep water in fast currents where the big salmon are lying. You also have to make long casts to reach the fish in many spots.

Most of the big chinook salmon in these Pacific Coast rivers are found in the deeper pools, when the water is low and clear. A rain that discolors the water a bit will make the salmon hit the flies or lure more readily. Often you can see the salmon lying in the pools or you will see boils on top. The best fishing is usually early in the morning or in the evening. The best approach here is to get above the spot where the salmon are lying or showing, cast across and slightly downstream, and let the current take the fly or lure down to the level of the fish. When it does reach the fish, start retrieving the fly or lure in short, quick jerks.

Both the coho and chinook salmon will enter Pacific coastal streams from June to November, depending on the particular stream or river and weather and water conditions. Usually the best fishing takes place during August, September, and October. During dry spells the salmon are often held up at the river's mouth in salt water and cannot enter the river itself until heavy rains raise the water level. Once in the river itself, the salmon become wary, moody, and unpredictable fish—difficult and challenging to catch.

But no matter where you catch them in fresh water—in a river or a lake—both the coho and chinook are big, powerful fish that make long runs, bore down, and do not give up too quickly. They also make good eating if caught in a lake or near the mouth of the river soon after entering it. Later on, when they reach their spawning beds and after spawning, their flesh turns soft and dark and they aren't very good for the table.

Most of the coho you will catch will range from about two to twenty pounds in weight. The smaller fish caught in the Great Lakes in the spring will run from about two to six pounds, though in the fall they will range from four to twelve pounds. Several coho salmon over thirty pounds have been caught in weirs in rivers during their spawning runs. The biggest reported was a thirty-nine-pound, two-ounce fish caught in the Manistee River in Michigan.

Chinook, which reach a much bigger size than coho, range from fifteen to forty pounds in weight. Chinook in the fifty- or sixty-pound class have been caught in fresh-water rivers along the Pacific Coast. Some of the biggest ones, going up to eighty or ninety pounds, have been caught in British Columbia, Canada, and Alaska. Chinook can reach over one hundred pounds in weight.

Many of the streams and rivers entering Lake Michigan, Lake Huron, Lake Superior, Lake Erie, and Lake Ontario are now stocked with coho and chinook salmon. Fishing is good along the lake shores of Michigan, Wisconsin, Illinois, Indiana, Ohio, Pennsylvania, and New York, and in many rivers entering these lakes. You can now find many lake ports where you can charter or rent a boat for this type of fishing. Or you can launch your own boat from many ramps found along the shores of the Great Lakes.

There is also some coho-salmon fishing in New Hampshire along its ocean coast and in the Lamprey and Exeter rivers. Massachusetts, Rhode Island, and several other states have been trying to introduce coho and chinook salmon into some of their lakes and rivers.

Chapter 7

BROWN TROUT

The brown trout is a relative newcomer to the American continent compared to the native brook trout and rainbow trout, which were on the scene long before the white man, or, for that matter, the Indians appeared. The first brown trout were sent to this country from Germany in 1883 by Herr F. Von Behr. At that time eighty thousand brown trout eggs were sent to Fred Mather at New York's Cold Spring Harbor Hatchery on Long Island. Some of the brown trout eggs were forwarded to the Caledonia hatchery in New York State. The rest were sent to the United States Fish Commission's hatchery at Northville, Michigan. During the following years additional shipments of eggs of a different variety of brown trout called the Loch Leven arrived from Scotland and England.

From the year 1886 the distribution of young brown trout expanded rapidly to various New York State waters. Later other shipments of brown trout were sent to other states and Canada. By 1900 brown trout had been introduced in the waters of thirty-eight states. Nowadays the brown trout is found in almost every state except some deep southern states, where it is scarce or absent. Actually, the brown trout is an international fish, found in most of Europe, parts of the Middle East, North and South Africa, North and South America, Asia, Australia, and New Zealand.

When brown trout first appeared in numbers in American waters they weren't welcomed with open arms by most trout fishermen. In fact, many protested loudly that the brown trout was ugly, not good to eat, and not much of a fighter on the end of a line. They also said that the brown trout was a cannibal that ate other trout and was responsible for the disappearance of the brook trout in eastern streams.

But as the years went by the genuine qualities of the brown trout revealed themselves, and today this immigrant is revered by countless serious fly fishermen. He's still not too popular with the casual fisherman or the clumsy, unskilled novice. They'd rather fish for the rainbow trout or brook trout, which are easier to catch. The brown trout is wild, wary, and soon learns to survive in hard-fished, civilized streams and lakes. As streams and rivers become warmer, more polluted, and more heavily fished, brook trout and even rainbow trout tend to disappear. But brown trout manage to survive and even

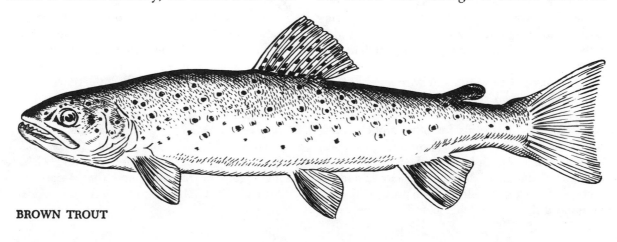

BROWN TROUT

thrive in many such waters. Brown trout are also more aggressive than the native trout and take over in most waters. The result is that more and more streams and rivers end up containing mostly brown trout.

This situation is welcomed by the dry-fly purists and serious trout anglers. To them the brown trout presents a challenge unmatched by other trout. He rises more readily to a dry fly than either the rainbow trout or the brook trout. He is also more selective in his feeding and thus harder to fool with ordinary flies, lures, or baits. Brown trout are now found in many waters near big cities and towns where other trout are scarce or absent. Catching a brook, rainbow, or any other trout is considered fun and sport, but catching a good-sized brown trout is considered an achievement.

At one time scientists used to differentiate among European brown trout, German brown trout, Loch Levens, and others, but today they are all lumped under the name of *Salmo trutta.* Most anglers call it the brown trout or brownie.

The name indicates the general color of the fish. This may range from a pale dirty yellow to olive brown or greenish brown. These colors become lighter toward the belly, which is a creamy white or yellowish. There are dark spots on the head, dorsal fin, and the back above the lateral line. Orange or reddish spots are often found along the sides. Brown trout that run to sea or live in lakes usually are bright silver. Large, old brown trout develop big heads and a hooked, undershot lower jaw.

Fly rods from short, light seven-footers to long, heavy nine-footers are used for brown trout depending on the waters being fished, the flies or lures used, and the size of the trout being caught. Brown trout are also caught in streams, rivers, and lakes on spinning tackle. Spin-casting and bait-casting outfits and even cane and glass poles have all been used by trout anglers. For trolling deep in lakes, even heavier rods and reels are used with weights or wire lines.

The angler who seeks brown trout with a fly rod has to carry a wider selection of fly patterns and sizes than he needs for other trout. A wise old brownie that has been approached on many occasions or has even been hooked and got away becomes "educated," highly suspicious, and selective. Even the smaller brown trout will often demand a fly that matches closely in size, color, and shape, the naturals they are feeding on at the time.

Some of the more popular and tested dry flies that can be used for brown trout include the Adams, Light Cahill, Quill Gordon, Blue Dun, Black Gnat, Hendrickson, Light Blue Quill, White Miller, Royal Coachman, Ginger Variant, Ginger Quill, Pale Evening Dun, Goofus Bug, Irresistible, Royal Wulff and others in the Wulff series, and the various bivisibles, spiders, and skaters. These can be carried in size Nos. 8 to 18.

During the summer and early fall, when brown trout are feeding on terrestrials (or land insects) such as ants, beetles, grasshoppers, and crickets, your flies should imitate these creatures. Some of the best patterns are the Letort Hopper, Letort Cricket, Michigan Hopper, Deer Hopper, Black Ant, Black Beetle, Crowe Beetle, Inch Worm, and the Jassids. These are tied in size Nos. 8 to 22.

There are also times when brown trout feed on tiny midges, which, again, should be imitated by your flies. The most popular and effective are the Black Midge, Brown Midge, Olive Midge, and Blue Dun Midge tied in size Nos. 20 to 28.

An assortment of wet flies such as the March Brown, Gray Miller, Cahills, Leadwing Coachman, Black Gnat, Ginger Quill, Wooly Worm, Quill Gordon, and Hendrickson should also be carried in sizes from Nos. 6 to 14.

Nymphs also take many brown trout early in the spring and throughout the year. There are many patterns on the market such as the Brown Stonefly, Ted's Stonefly, Brown Bomber, March Brown, Cream, Hare's Ear, Gray Nymph, Breadcrust, Dragon, and Caddis Larva that are good. Those tied on Nos. 8 to 14 hooks are most used. Some of these nymphs should be weighted types.

A good assortment of streamers and bucktails should also be carried when you fish for big brown trout, since they often feed on minnows or other small fish. In this instance, it's a good idea to use streamers that imitate the minnows and small fish found in the stream or river being fished. Some of the proven streamers and bucktails are the Mickey Finn, Black-nosed Dace, Brown and White, Black and White, Black Ghost, Gray Ghost, Golden Darter, Grizzly King, Muddler Minnow, and the Marabous in different colors. These can be tied on hooks size Nos. 2 to 10.

When you use spinning, spin-casting, or bait-casting tackle, various kinds of small lures such as spinners, spoons, jigs, underwater plugs, and plastic lures will take brown trout; these lures are especially effective for big fish in the larger rivers and lakes.

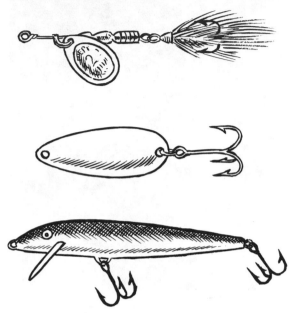

Lures for big brown trout.

Bait fishing for brown trout is done with such live natural baits as nightcrawlers or earthworms, minnows, crayfish, frogs, and various land and water insects.

Brown trout can be caught during most of the trout-fishing season, but certain times are better than others. The bait fisherman and spinning angler usually do best early in the year during April and early May. This is also a good time for fishing with streamers and bucktails as well as with wet flies and nymphs. Later on from about the middle of May until July, the dry-fly fisherman usually does best. But the farther north you go and the higher the altitude you fish, the better the fishing during the summer months. Many lakes and streams in our northernmost states and in Canada provide good brown-trout fishing in July and August.

Some big brown trout are also caught during the fall months when they move up streams and rivers to spawn. If the trout season is still open at this time you can have some great fishing in waters and pools below obstructions such as dams, logjams, and waterfalls. Brown trout will often gather in certain pools a month or two before spawning.

Early in the spring when the water is still cold, your best fishing will be during the middle of the day. This is also true in the late fall, when the water turns colder. Then as the water warms in the spring and insects begin to hatch toward evening, your best fishing will be during the late afternoon and toward dusk. During the hot summer months, early morning, dusk, and night provide the best fishing. In fact, big brown trout are noted for their night-feeding habits during the summer months. The best way to locate brown trout—or any trout, for that matter—is to live by the stream or visit it often, and spend many hours observing the fish and their favorite hiding and feeding spots. Brown trout especially are known for choosing a good spot and staying there. Big ones, particularly, will take over a pool and chase away or eat the smaller ones. Because of this, fishing some pools will often be a waste of time if the only resident is a big, wise old brownie that is hard to fool. But some pools may contain several good-sized fish, which can be caught at the heads and tails of the pool and sometimes even in the deeper water.

Brown trout like shade over their heads during the daytime. So look for them under rocks, ledges, logs, under cut banks, in the roots of trees or under the branches, and under bridges. Since these objects provide cover, safety, and security, trout will stay hidden in them most of the time when not actively prowling or looking for food.

Brown trout are usually found in the slower-moving stretches of water, such as shallow pools and runs where they do not have to exert themselves against the current. During the summer, however, they may be in fairly fast water or along the edges of the stronger currents. A brown trout likes to lie in front of a rock, boulder, or other obstruction that splits the current or in a deep pocket between two such obstructions. In the evening and at night brown trout often come out of their hiding places and venture into shallow water at the heads and tails of pools and along the banks.

Of course, the obvious, easy way to locate brown trout is to actually see them lying in the water on the bottom or rising for hatching flies or for insects falling into the water. You'll often see only dimples or wakes made by the feeding fish.

Many big brown trout, like this 6¼-pounder, are caught at night on big wet flies, bass bugs, streamers, bucktails, and small plugs. (Burke Lure Company Photo)

During the daytime big brown trout usually hide under rocks and boulders; under tree trunks, limbs, and branches; under overhanging banks, branches, and brush; and in other dark, shady spots. (Michigan Department of Natural Resources Photo)

Once the fish is located or a specific spot is suspected of harboring a trout, caution must be observed in approaching the fish. In shallow, clear water and in small streams, especially, you must keep out of sight, avoid casting a shadow, and move as slowly as possible. Try to avoid wading, and fish from shore, if possible, when working a narrow stream. If you do wade, move carefully, quietly, and slowly, and stand still for long periods of time so that you don't create waves or vibrations.

Dry-fly fishing is most effective when flies are hatching and brown trout are feeding on them, or when trout are in a feeding location and are waiting to see what the current brings their way. During a hatch it is important to match the size, color, and general shape of the natural insects the fish are feeding on. As a general rule the larger flies are better early in the year and the smaller ones later on, when the water is low and clear. Then long leaders, up to twelve feet, with fine tippets may be needed to fool the fish and make the fly drift naturally.

Proper presentation of the dry fly is important; it should be dropped lightly and accurately a few feet in front of the trout so that it drifts naturally with the current. The line should float and the leader should sink. The slack line should be gathered with your hand but not so fast as to cause the line to pull on the fly. This would create a drag and should be avoided because it gives the fly an unnatural movement and speed. In most dry-fly fishing you cast upstream and across. But if you see a fish or a rise or can pinpoint the location of a brownie, you can cast a few feet above it so that the dry fly drifts toward it. You can also cast downstream if you are standing directly above the fish's position. But here plenty of slack in the line is needed to allow the fly to drift down naturally.

However, there are times when brown trout will take a dry fly that is deliberately pulled or skated across the top of the water. Spider and Skater flies are best for this. You can cast them like any dry fly and let them drift naturally until they are downstream. Then you can retrieve them by holding the rod high so that the fly skims on top of the water or even hops occasionally. On big pools or quiet stretches you can cast across stream and begin, almost immediately, a smooth, even retrieve, causing the fly to skim on the surface.

In the late summer and early fall you can fish the terrestrial flies for big brown trout. At this time, especially along meadow streams on windy days, trout will often lie close to the banks waiting for land insects to be blown into the water. If you see fish rising, cast to them. At other times you can float the fly along the banks, under overhanging trees and bushes, and through rapids, riffles, runs, glides, and pockets.

Brown trout, especially the big ones, feed more underwater than on the surface, so day in and day out, wet flies or nymphs are usually more effective than dry flies. Both wet flies and nymphs can be fished by casting across and slightly upstream and then letting them drift naturally with no pull or drag during most of the drift. When the fly reaches the end of its drift or swing, let it pause and rise, then retrieve it in short, quick jerks. Often two wet flies or a combination of a wet fly and a nymph on the end of the leader will be more effective than just one. You have to develop a sort of sixth sense to detect a strike and to set the hook at the right moment. Some anglers attach a dry fly above the wet fly or nymph and watch the dry fly to detect a strike. You can also watch the floating fly line if you are fishing wet flies or nymphs not too deep. Or you can look for the flash of fish underwater and then set the hook. But wet flies and nymphs usually produce best when fished deep with sinking fly lines, in which case it is very difficult to detect a strike.

Streamers and bucktails are often deadly for brown trout and are usually best early in the spring or in the fall. In the summer streamers produce well right after a heavy rain or shower that raises a stream and discolors the water a bit. But they can also be used early in the morning, in the evening, or at night when brownies are chasing minnows in the shallows or tails of pools. At other times you can fish the deeper waters of pools, holes, deep pockets, and runs. A streamer or bucktail can be cast quartering upstream and allowed to drift down with the current on a fairly slack line. When it reaches the end of the drift let it pause and flutter a few seconds, then bring it back in spurts or short darts. You can also cast downstream and hold the streamer in the current in a good spot and work it back and forth. Or you can retrieve it on top of the water to make it look like a frantic minnow. At other times, in deep pools and in lakes,

Fly fishing for the wily brown trout requires skill, stream know-how, and the proper presentation and manipulation of the fly. (Pennsylvania Fish Commission Photo)

you can let the streamer or bucktail sink deep to the bottom and then retrieve it in slow, short spurts. Here weighted streamers and sinking fly lines are most effective for reaching the depths fast and holding the fly there.

The spinning or casting rod is a highly effective weapon for big brown trout, particularly on the larger streams, rivers, and lakes. With such a rod you can reach spots such as broad runs, pools, pockets, overhanging banks, deep-cut banks, and other spots where brown trout may be lying or feeding. Such lures as spinners, spoons, jigs, and small plugs can be cast at almost any angle and worked at varying speeds and depths. Sinking lures can be retrieved quickly near the surface or allowed to sink toward the bottom and retrieved slowly, in an erratic manner.

More brown trout have probably been caught on an earthworm or a nightcrawler than on any other natural bait. This is especially true during the spring of the year, but a skillful angler can take big brown trout throughout the year on worms. You can fish the worm with a fly rod or a long spinning rod, but whichever tackle is used, try to drift the worm deep and as naturally as possible under stumps, tree roots, fallen trees, logs, around boulders, rocks, ledges, and cutbanks. The best procedure is to cast the worm upstream above the spot to be fished and let it drift down with the current. In slow- or medium-flowing water you don't need a sinker or weight. But in faster, deeper water you may have to add a split-shot sinker or two on the leader to get the bait down.

A minnow sewn on a single or double hook is often deadly for big brown trout. The minnow is rigged so that it has a slight curve or bend and is cast across stream and allowed to drift and sink toward the bottom, then it is retrieved slowly with short jerks to make it dart, wobble, and flash. Split-shot or light-clincher sinkers are often added to the leader about eighteen or twenty inches ahead of the minnow to provide more weight for casting and to allow the bait to sink in the deeper pools and fast runs. The weight also makes the minnow rise when pulled, and allows it to sink down when you stop the retrieve. The result is an effective crippled action.

Some of the biggest brown trout are now caught in the larger rivers, lakes, reservoirs, and impoundments. On our larger trout-bearing rivers in Montana and other western states, float trips are popular to reach spots that are rarely or never fished by shore anglers. Here you can fish from the boat itself with fly tackle or spinning gear, or you can beach the boat and fish from shore and from islands or bars. The tailwaters below dams often contain big brown trout that can be caught on flies, spoons, spinners, and natural baits.

Brown trout can be caught in many lakes and reservoirs in the early spring, when they will often be seen feeding on alewives or minnows close to the surface in shallow water near shore. Anglers casting from shore, piers, docks, and breakwaters can use weighted spinners, small spoons, and small plugs to catch them. From a boat you can fish with a live alewife or minnow and cast it toward feeding fish or near the shore. Later on, when the water and weather warm up, you can fish the live baitfish in deeper waters from fifteen to thirty-five feet. In this case, you may need a weight or sinker to take your baitfish down and to hold it at those depths.

In the Great Lakes and other big lakes, trolling is a very effective method for taking big brown trout. Here you can use spinners, spoons, or plugs such as the Flatfish, Rapala, and Rebel, and troll these on long lines up to three hundred or four hundred feet out in shallow water near shore. The mouths of streams; areas over rocky shoals; sandbars; along dropoffs; off points; and over submerged trees, rocks, and boulders are especially productive. This shallow-water trolling is best in the spring, early summer, and fall.

During the summer months, as we have seen, brown trout go deep, which means that you will need lead core, or wire, lines or downriggers to get the lures or baits down to where the fish are. Lures such as spoons or plugs are trolled slowly most of the time, but, since big brown trout will often follow a lure and make passes at it, you can try speeding up the boat for a few feet every so often to provoke a strike. Or you can try to give the lure extra action with up-and-down sweeps of the rod. A zigzag pattern of trolling is often better than a straight course.

Anglers trolling in the Flaming Gorge Reservoir straddling Wyoming and Utah use sinking-type Rapala plugs, which they troll close to shore at 10-to-20-foot depths, with 200 to 250 feet of line out. The best fishing here has been found along shores with rockslides or steep, sloping banks, and off points or flats that run out into deeper water and have bottom cover such as rocks, boulders, sunken trees, or brush. Since the brown trout here run over thirty pounds in weight you need a sturdy trolling rod with a bait-casting or revolving-spool reel filled with fifteen-pound-test mono line.

Brown trout aren't spectacular fighters, although they'll occasionally leap out of the water. Usually they prefer to slug it out below the surface and try to snag your leader or line around a rock, log, or tree root. Big ones have the weight to give you plenty of trouble, but after the first run or two, they can usually be handled more easily.

In the smaller streams brown trout will run from about half a pound to several pounds in weight. In the larger rivers they'll often reach ten to twenty pounds. But the biggest ones are caught in our larger lakes and reservoirs. A thirty-one-pound, eight-ounce brown trout was caught in Lake Michigan by John Duffy on July 3, 1976. A thirty-three-pound, ten-ounce brown trout was caught in Utah's Flaming Gorge Reservoir by Bob Bringhurst on March 4, 1977. The official rod and reel record is a thirty-five-pound, fifteen-ounce fish caught by Eugenio Cavaglia in Nahuei Huapi Lake, Argentina, South America, on December 16, 1952. The Utah Division of Wildlife gill-netted a forty-four-pound brown trout in the Flaming Gorge Reservoir. There have been reports of brown trout weighing over fifty pounds, taken commercially or in nets in European waters.

Chapter 8

BROOK TROUT

When the first white men settled in North America the only trout they found in the East was the brook trout. This colorful trout was the true "native" trout and the only one known to these early settlers. Up until the time the rainbow trout and brown trout were introduced into eastern waters, the angler who went trout fishing caught only brook trout.

The brook trout was a great favorite of those early trout fishermen. Abundant in almost every river, stream, brook, and in many lakes and ponds, it provided both sport and food. Early accounts tell of the wonderful brook-trout fishing in many areas in New England, New York, and other eastern states. The brook trout ranged in those days from Labrador west to Saskatchewan and south through the Alleghenies to northern Georgia. Then it was introduced in the West from California to Alaska and later in the Rocky Mountain states.

Today the brook trout is still a popular fish in those areas where it is fairly plentiful. It is the most co-operative of the trouts, feeding on a wide variety of foods and almost always willing to take a properly presented fly, lure, or bait. The brook trout is usually caught in scenic, beautiful, wild, cool, clear streams and rivers.

Unfortunately, brook-trout waters are becoming scarce, and those that remain are often in remote wilderness areas, difficult to reach. With the advance of civilization, the growth of cities, towns, farms, factories, and lumbering, the accompanying clearing of land, as well as pollution and siltation, are all to blame for this situation. In addition, water temperatures in most streams and rivers have become too warm for brook trout. Of course, fish hatcheries keep producing millions of brook trout for the "put and take" fishing practiced in many states. But most serious trout fishermen want the natural, wild brook trout and leave the mass-production product for the casual trout fisherman.

Brook trout have been called eastern brook trout, speckled trout, native trout, mountain trout, red trout, squaretails, and brookies. The brook trout actually isn't a true trout but belongs to the char family like the lake trout and the Dolly Varden trout.

Anyone who has seen the brook trout in its fall spawning colors will admit that it is one of the prettiest of trouts. The back is usually blue-green or bronze-green. Other characteristics are wormlike markings on the back and sides up to the lateral line, and red dots outlined in blue on the sides. The fins have dark bands and are edged with pink blending into white. In small brooks, deep forests, and some big, deep Canadian rivers and lakes, the brook trout is very dark all over. Those that run to sea turn silvery, but soon revert to the original colors when they return to fresh water.

Brook trout can be caught on the same fishing tackle and outfits as the brown trout. Fly rods, of course, are best for casting the various dry flies, wet flies, nymphs, and streamers, and are also good for bait fishing. For fishing the smaller streams and brooks, where small brook trout predominate, you can use the lightest and shortest fly rods, from 6 to 7½ feet long, with Nos. 3-, 4-, or 5-weight fly lines. For fishing with lures you can use light-spinning, spin-casting, and bait-casting outfits.

Brook trout, especially in wilderness waters, often go for the more colorful, gaudier wet-fly patterns. You can use the Parmachene Belle, Silver Doctor, Red Ibis, Royal Coachman, Montreal, Grizzly King, Professor, Black Gnat, Gray Hackle, and McGinty in sizes from Nos. 6 to 14.

Of the dry flies, the Black Gnat, Royal Coachman, Light Cahill, Dark Cahill, Quill Gordon,

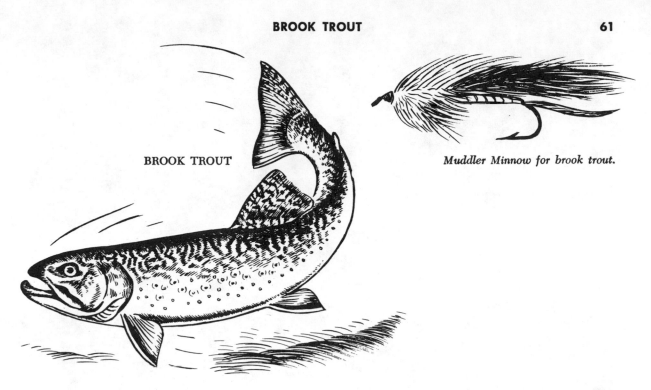

BROOK TROUT

Muddler Minnow for brook trout.

Hendrickson, Adams, Gray Hackle, Yellow May, Ginger Quill, Montreal, and the Wulff series are good. You can also carry some spiders and bivisibles and a few terrestrials. Dry flies in size Nos. 12 to 18 are usually used.

Streamers and bucktails used for brook trout include the Red and White, Mickey Finn, Black-nosed Dace, Dark Edson Tiger, Light Edson Tiger, Green Ghost, Black Ghost, Supervisor, Nine-Three, White Marabou, Yellow Marabou, and the Muddler Minnow. These can be carried in size Nos. 2 to 10, with the larger sizes best for big brookies in wilderness rivers and lakes, and the smaller flies for small brook trout in small streams and brooks in more heavily fished waters.

For spinning, spin-casting, or bait-casting tackle, you can use spinners, spoons, jigs, small plugs, and plastic lures. Brook trout are also one of the easiest trout to catch on natural baits such as worms, minnows, grasshoppers, crickets, and nymphs.

Brook trout start feeding early in the spring soon after the ice is out: April, May, and June are usually good months. In the colder northern lakes and in the mountain lakes and rivers of Maine, Canada, and our western states you can often have fairly good fishing in July and August; in more southern waters, however, the summer months are not too good.

Brook trout prefer the cool, clean, turbulent waters in streams and rivers. In small streams look for them along under cut banks, overhanging trees, brush, logs, tree roots, logjams, behind rocks and under ledges, and in the deeper holes and pools. They usually like to lie behind a rock, log, or other obstruction. During the warmer months they may be in the deepest pools in streams and rivers and around spring holes or the mouths of cool brooks. Many brook trout at this time will also move up into the cooler brooks and tributaries.

In lakes big brook trout will often be found close to shore in the early spring soon after ice-out or around the mouths of brooks and streams entering a lake. They feed on smelt, minnows, and other fish that congregate there. Later on, as the water warms up, they will often move into the cooler streams and rivers and into the running water connecting lakes or other large bodies of water.

During the summer months in the large, deep, clear lakes, brook trout will often be found in depths ranging from twenty to fifty feet; fifty-five to fifty-eight degrees is the preferred temperature range. Here they will usually hang out over structure such as underwater plateaus or islands, points sloping into deeper water, and along dropoffs and ledges. The cool underground springs entering a lake will also attract them at this time.

Beaver ponds, especially those in the more

Brook trout like clear, cold waters and are often caught in the picturesque rivers and lakes of our northern states and Canada. (Nova Scotia Communications Centre Photo)

remote forests, often contain brook trout. Some of these beaver ponds contain them in abundance and provide good fishing, while others may have few if any trout in them. You can locate beaver ponds by studying topographic maps or by following streams through the woods. Since most beaver ponds are on the small side and usually calm and clear, brook trout are very wary and easily spooked in these waters. So they have to be approached carefully and quietly. The best fishing in beaver ponds usually takes place in the spring, but if the water in the pond stays cool, they can also be caught during the summer months. Most of the action will take place around daybreak and a bit later, and then again toward evening and dusk. Rainy, overcast days are usually better than bright, sunny ones.

Heavy showers will often trigger good fishing in beaver ponds.

Brook trout from certain Atlantic coastal streams and rivers will migrate to the sea, live there in salt water for a few years, and then return to the same river or stream to spawn. The Canadian Maritime Provinces often offer good fishing for these sea-run brookies for a short period in June when they begin their run up the rivers. These fish often move in schools, and you have to find a spot where they stop for a day or two. Usually early morning and evening fishing is best for these sea-run brook trout.

In late August and September, big brook trout will leave the lakes and enter the tributary streams. You can often see them moving upstream, leaping over small falls and lying at the

Some of the best brook-trout fishing today can be had in the more remote lakes and beaver ponds in forested wilderness areas. Here you usually have to fish from shore or from a make-shift raft such as the one these anglers are using. (Idaho Fish & Game Department Photo)

head of rapids in pockets. They will often feed at this time and are partial to streamer flies.

Although brook trout will often hit flies or lures or take baits with abandon, they can also be a difficult fish to catch in our hard-fished waters, and must be approached with care and caution. Try to sneak up to each spot quietly and avoid wading in the water. Instead, fish from the bank and hide behind a tree trunk or a bush, or crouch low.

The brook trout is mostly an underwater feeder and can be caught on wet flies fished below the surface. You can cast the wet fly across and slightly upstream and, while keeping the slack line under control, let it drift naturally in the current. At the end of the drift, lift the fly out of the water for a new cast, or retrieve it up-

stream in short spurts. You can even try skitter-ing it on top of the water. If the shallow working fly doesn't produce, let it sink to the bottom and keep it moving deep. Here you may have to cast upstream more to get it to sink deep enough. In fast water you should add a split-shot sinker or two to get it down near the bottom. Of course, you can also use a sinking fly line in fast and deep waters. Nymphs will also take brook trout and can basically be worked in the same way as wet flies.

Brook trout will also take a dry fly at times, especially when they are feeding on hatching in-sects or those being blown or falling into the water. Here the fly is drifted naturally, with the current over the rising fish. Since most brook-trout streams are narrow with trees and over-

He's holding two big, beautiful brook trout caught on a fly rod in Ontario, Canada. It is still possible to catch such big brookies in the more remote fly-in rivers and lakes of Canada. (Ontario Ministry of Industry & Tourism Photo)

hanging limbs on their banks, long casts or false casting cannot be done. So you have to flip out the leader and a short length of fly line or even just dap the fly on the water a short distance from the tip of the rod. The fly should be a good floater and be dressed with a flotant.

Streamers and bucktails are often effective for large brook trout, especially on the big rivers and lakes. The trout here often feed on smelt or small fish running up a stream to spawn, and any streamers or bucktails resembling these baitfish will work. Give them an erratic, hesitant retrieve in two- or three-foot spurts and try them at different depths from top to bottom.

Some big brook trout are also taken at times on lures such as small spoons, weighted spinners, jigs, and underwater plugs. Here too, lures that resemble the small fish prevalent in the waters being fished are best. When using a spoon, cast it out and let it sink and flutter down a few feet; start reeling, then stop and let it flutter down again. Keep doing this all the way in. Big brook trout will often follow a spoon, and hit it as it flutters and sinks.

Brook trout can also be taken by trolling on the larger rivers and lakes. Trolling with fly rods and streamers or bucktails, in the same way as for landlocked salmon, described earlier in this book, is often effective in the spring near shore and in the mouths of streams. In fact, while trolling for landlocked salmon, many anglers often hook brook trout. You can also troll spoons, spinners, and small plugs near shore in the spring and fall. Later on, during the summer months, these lures should be trolled deep with weights or wire lines.

When brook trout are down deep in lakes you can also try jigging up and down close to the bottom. Such lures as the Swedish Pimple, the Ugly Bug, and other small jigs in the ¼-to-½-ounce sizes are good for such jigging. You can add a worm, a minnow, or a plastic worm to the jig to make it even more effective.

Live-bait anglers find the ordinary garden worm a fine bait for brook trout, especially in the spring of the year. At this time when the trout will be hugging bottom, the worm should be drifted deep enough to reach them. The worm used for brook trout can be hooked through the middle and drifted in the current along the edges of the fast water, under overhanging banks, around sunken trees and logs, and in the pockets and deep holes. Follow the drift of the worm with your rod and allow plenty of slack line for a natural drift. When a bite or pickup is felt wait a few seconds, then set the hook. Live insects such as grasshoppers and crickets can also be used for brook trout and are especially effective on the smaller meadow brooks. You can also use worms, minnows, crayfish, and small frogs for big brook trout in lakes.

A wild, good-sized brook trout in fast water puts up a strong, stubborn battle. They rarely leap out of the water like the rainbow trout or even the brown trout at times. And they are not noted for making long runs. But they usually bore deep, twist, roll, and try to foul your line around a tree root, rock, or log.

Unfortunately, most of the brook trout caught these days are small fish rarely going more than 10 or 12 inches in most small streams. In some tiny brooks and mountain streams they are fully grown at 7 or 8 inches. However, in the large rivers and lakes of the more remote wilderness areas, trout weighing up to 7 or 8 pounds are still caught. Though most of these waters are in the northern sections of Canada, some of the biggest brook trout are now caught in Argentina and Chile, where they were introduced. The world record on rod and reel is the 14½-pound brook trout taken by Dr. W. J. Cook on the Nipigon River, Ontario, Canada, in July 1916.

A wild, fresh-caught brook trout makes delicious eating. The flavor and texture of their flesh cannot be matched by the other trouts.

The best brook-trout waters in the United States are found in Maine, New Hampshire, Vermont, and other northern states. The mountain states along the Appalachians and the Rockies are noted for their brook-trout streams. Some of the best fishing is found in the brooks, streams, and ponds of the national forests and parks located in higher altitudes. Canada still has fair to good brook-trout fishing, especially for big fish, in the provinces of Quebec, Ontario, Manitoba, New Brunswick, and Nova Scotia, as well as in Newfoundland (especially in Labrador).

Chapter 9

RAINBOW TROUT

The spectacular rainbow trout is one of the most popular of trout species among fishermen, who pursue it avidly by fly casting, spinning, spin casting, bait casting, trolling or bait fishing. One of the most widely distributed of the trouts, it is found from Alaska to California, throughout our northern and western states, in Canada, Europe, Asia, Africa, New Zealand, and South America.

Rainbow trout are also known as California trout, Pacific trout, salmon trout, western rainbow, and steelhead. The last is a rainbow trout that goes to sea or into large lakes and then returns to the rivers to spawn. (See the next chapter for information on this seagoing rainbow trout.)

A rainbow trout is a colorful and beautiful fish when first removed from the water. The back is usually greenish or bluish, shading into silvery green on the sides. The whole upper surface of the body, head, fins, and tail are covered with small dark spots. A wide band of crimson or pink runs along the lateral line from head to tail.

This stripe is most evident in large mature fish and in males at breeding time. The female rainbow trout may lack this pink stripe and appear silvery all over. The rainbows that live in lakes or in large, deep bodies of water often turn dark steel blue on the back and silvery on the sides.

To catch rainbow trout, you can use the same fishing tackle that was discussed in detail in the chapter on brown trout. However, for the bigger rainbows on larger rivers and in big lakes you can use somewhat heavier fly rods as well as bait-casting, spinning, and spin-casting outfits.

Although rainbow trout do not rise to a dry fly as readily or as often as the brown trout, they can be taken on many of the same dry-fly patterns used for the brownies or brookies. Of the dry flies, the Grizzly Sedge, Green Sedge, Quill Gordon, Light Cahill, Ginger Quill, Adams, Fanwing Royal Coachman, Hendrickson, and Black Gnat are most effective. On western waters when the salmon flies hatch, you can use the Bailey Salmonfly, Kolzer Orange, and Sofa

RAINBOW TROUT

Small spoons and spinners are highly effective lures for catching big rainbow trout and steel-head in rivers and lakes. (Worth Fishing Tackle Company Photo)

Pillow. The various bivisibles, spiders, and variants are also good at times. Dry flies in sizes from Nos. 10 to 18 are best suited to the rainbow trout.

In wet flies you can stock such patterns as the Brown Sedge, Green Sedge, Coachman, Royal Coachman, Alexandria, Skykomish Sunrise, Parmachene Belle, McGinty, Gray Hackle Yellow, Black Gnat, Mosquito, and Wooly Worm. The various yarn flies in white, yellow, orange, pink, red, and green fluorescent colors, or combinations of these, are highly effective in discolored or murky waters and for the rainbows that run up rivers to spawn. The wet flies in size Nos. 8 to 16 are most effective.

Nymphs are very good in low, clear-water rivers and in many lakes. The different patterns used for other trout often work for rainbows too. Special nymphs tied for western rainbows include the Montana Nymph, Troth's Black Stonefly, Bird's Brown Stonefly, Box Canyon, and the Orange and Girdlebug. Some of these are gaudy and, as a result, are good in murky water, but in clear water the plain, simple nymphs, such as those tied by Ted Fay and called the gray nymph, cream nymph, yellow nymph, burlap nymph, and fuzzy nymph, are better. In mountain lakes, nymphs with fur-dubbing bodies are effective. Weighted nymphs that go down deep are better than those that ride high. Nymphs in size Nos. 4 to 12 are the most popular and effective.

Streamers and bucktails, among which are the Mickey Finn, Red and White, Brown Bucktail, Black-nosed Dace, Gray Ghost, Black Ghost, Warden's Worry, the Marabous, and the Muddler Minnow, will also take rainbow trout.

And various grasshopper, cricket, and beetle

imitations can be carried for late-summer and early-fall fishing when land insects are falling on the water.

For use with spinning, spin-casting, or bait-casting tackle various lures such as spinners, spoons, jigs, small plugs, plastic worms, and other plastic lures are good. They are especially effective on the larger rivers and lakes for big rainbow trout early in the season when the water is cold, but can be used throughout the year. Lures are also deadly for spawning "steelhead" rainbows that enter the rivers and streams from large lakes.

Rainbow trout are also caught on various natural baits such as salmon eggs, worms, crayfish, hellgrammites, grubs, and minnows. Where salmon eggs are illegal anglers often use substitutes such as pink or red yarn on a hook, cooked tapioca dyed red, and tiny balls shaped from Vaseline, cheese, marshmallow, or dough, and rubber or plastic imitations of fish eggs.

Rainbow-trout fishing is usually best early in the spring right after ice-out. Late March, April, and May are usually good months in most areas. During this time the big rainbows will head up the streams and rivers to spawn. Another good period is during September, October, and November, when big rainbow trout return to the rivers from the larger lakes. But the smaller rainbow trout can be caught during the summer months in many waters that remain cool. There is often excellent fishing in our extreme northern states, in Canada and Alaska even during the hot summer months.

The time of day when fishing is best for rainbow trout will depend on the season, water conditions, and water temperatures. Early in the spring and late in the fall the fishing is often good during the middle of the day. In colder climates and in high-altitude mountain lakes, the middle of the day is a productive time through most of the fishing season. In warmer climates and during the summer months in our more southerly states, early morning and evening hours are usually better.

Rainbow trout like the faster portions of rivers and streams. Thus you'll often find them in the rapids, riffles, fast glides, runs, and pockets. The white water at the heads or tails of pools and under waterfalls will also attract them. But even in this fast water they like to lie along the edges of strong currents and around obstructions: in front, behind, and alongside a rock, boulder, stump, log, or tree trunk. Fast water running along under cut riverbanks or shorelines will also hold them. Big rainbows can often be seen on their spawning beds in the shallow water, especially early in the morning and evening. During the day they will often hide in the deeper water and pools. And, of course, you can also look for rainbow trout rising and feeding on hatching insects.

In lakes look for rainbow trout early in the spring cruising the shallows near shore and gathering at the mouths of streams and rivers prior to entering them. Later on during the warmer months they will hang out in deeper water along dropoffs and rocky points sloping into the lake. In clear, mountain lakes, you can often spot rainbows cruising near shore from your vantage point on shore or in a boat.

Rainbow trout are mostly underwater feeders but will rise to a dry fly on many occasions, especially when insects are hatching. Then you can drift a dry fly on top in the same manner described in the chapter dealing with brown trout. Dry flies will also take rainbow trout in lakes when they are feeding on hatches of flies in the evening. Here you try to cast as soon as you see the rise or dimple on the water.

For lake-dwelling rainbows, wet flies and nymphs can be fished deep by using a sinking fly line and weighted flies. Let the flies sink and retrieve them in short pulls. Most of the time you have to cast blind, trying different depths until you start getting the fish to hit. But in clear, calm, mountain lakes, you can often see individual rainbows cruising near shore. Then you can cast a wet fly or nymph anywhere from ten to fifteen feet ahead of the fish, let it sink slowly until the trout gets close enough to see it, then start retrieving it with short pulls of the fly line.

When fishing with streamers and bucktails, try stripping in a streamer on top across the stream so that it leaves a tiny wake on the surface. But most of the time you have to get down deep to interest rainbow trout. Sinking fly lines are best for this. Some anglers also make up a rig with a tiny three-way swivel: A two-foot leader and the fly are tied to one eye of the swivel; the line is attached to the second eye; and a short six-inch dropper with two or three split-shot sinkers is tied to the third eye. The rig is cast out and allowed to sink to the bottom, where it can move

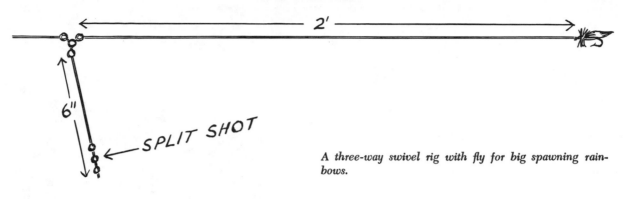

A *three-way swivel rig with fly for big spawning rainbows.*

along the rocks, with the lead weights keeping the fly just above the bottom.

This same deep fishing can be done with lures, especially for the big rainbows called "steelhead" that run up rivers from lakes in the spring and fall. Here a spinning or bait-casting outfit can be used with such lures as spinners, spoons, cherry bobbers and drifters, small plugs, and plastic lures. These are cast across and upstream and allowed to tumble, drift, and sink in the current. They should travel as close to the bottom as possible without fouling. When the lures reach a point downstream from the angler they can be retrieved slowly and erratically against the current. Lures can also be used in lakes; here you cast from shore or a boat and retrieve the lures at various depths until you locate a feeding fish.

Instead of fishing from shore, you can use a boat on the larger rivers, anchoring it about fifty or sixty feet upstream from the spot you want to fish. Your tackle should include spinners, spoons, or small plugs like the Tadpolly, Flatfish, or Lazy Ike, a rod eight feet in length, and a bait-casting reel filled with fifteen- or twenty-pound-test line. Let the lure out in the current for about fifteen or twenty feet and hold it in one spot for a while. Then let out a few more feet of line and hold it in that spot for a time. You should feel your lure working in the current at all times, even when it is just being held in one spot. When the lure reaches the spot where you think steelhead are lying, hold it there for quite a while. You can try moving the rod from left to right, or else lift the rod quickly to make the lure dart forward, then let it drop back again.

You can also float down a river in a boat and cast flies or lures toward likely spots for rainbow trout. This is especially productive in the fast,

cool tailwaters below dams in the rivers of Arkansas and Tennessee. These rivers rise and fall as the water is released from the dams, and fishing spots will change with these fluctuations.

Bait fishing is very effective and can often be deadly for rainbow trout in many streams and rivers. Anywhere from one to five salmon eggs or a cluster or spawn sac can be used for bait. Nightcrawlers and garden worms are also good, especially in the spring of the year. These baits should be cast upstream and across and allowed to drift along the bottom with the current. You can fish these baits with a fly rod without any weight, but a sinking fly line, or two or three split-shot sinkers can be added to the leader to get the bait down.

However, the most effective rig for big rainbows when you are bait fishing or even using lures consists of a short two-foot leader tied to a small three-way swivel and a small sinker on a short dropper tied to another eye of the swivel. Slim, lead-pencil-type sinkers are also used because they hang up less often than other styles. This rig is bounced along the bottom with the baited hook on a tight line so that you can feel a bite or change in movement and set the hook accordingly. See the next chapter, "Steelhead," for more details on how to fish baits and lures deep, near the bottom.

Trolling is a good way to take rainbow trout on the larger rivers and in most lakes. You can use wet flies, streamers, and nymphs on a sinking or lead-core fly line and troll them at slow or moderate speeds. Extra rod action and pulls on the line can be imparted to give the flies a more lifelike action. In the spring and fall this trolling can be done in shallow water close to shore and around the mouths of streams and rivers entering a lake.

Good fishing for rainbow trout can be had in the tailwaters below dams in many states. The trout thrive in the cool waters released from the lake or reservoir above. (Massie-Missouri Commerce Photo)

Later on as the water warms, you can use spinning rods, bait-casting tackle, and fresh-water trolling outfits for trolling in deeper water. Here one of the most effective lures is a series of spinners in front of a worm or minnow on the hook. You can also troll weighted spinners, spoons, and underwater plugs. When rainbow trout are down deep you may have to troll with weighted lines, wire lines, or downriggers to reach the depths where they are lying or feeding.

In the smaller streams and lakes, rainbows will average from 1 to 5 pounds, but in the larger rivers and lakes they often reach much heavier weights. The rainbows that have access to a big body of water with plenty of alewives, smelt, or other small fish will often grow to 15 or 20 pounds or more. The Kamloops rainbow found mostly in Idaho and British Columbia reach a giant size. One of the largest taken on rod and reel went 37 pounds and was caught in Lake Pend Oreille, Idaho, on November 25, 1947. Many other fish in the 30-pound class have been taken from these and other waters. Even bigger Kamloops rainbows have been reported from British Columbia, where fish going over 40 pounds have been trapped by the game commission for eggs. Two huge rainbows weighing 48 and 52½ pounds were reportedly taken from Jewel Lake, British Columbia, back in 1931 and 1933.

Rainbow trout taken from wilderness streams and lakes make excellent eating. The hatchery trout are not as good but after they live in a lake or stream for a few months they improve. Many rainbow trout are raised for the market and sold to the public.

Rainbow trout are found in so many waters in

High-altitude mountain lakes in the Rocky Mountains, in our northern states, including Alaska, and in Canada offer some of the best rainbow-trout fishing to be had anywhere. (Alaska Department of Economic Development Photo)

this country, and in Canada that it is impossible to list even a few of the best waters in this book. The best fishing and the largest number of rainbows are found in our northern states such as Washington, Oregon, northern California, Utah, Montana, Michigan, Wisconsin, Minnesota, and New York. There is excellent rainbow-trout fishing in the Great Lakes region and in the many streams and rivers entering the lakes. Many rivers and lakes in Canada offer fine rainbow-trout fishing, with British Columbia tops for big fish. Rainbow-trout fishing in Alaska is fabulous. Argentina, Chile, and Peru, in South America, have some huge rainbow trout in mountain lakes and rivers. The same is true of Australia and New Zealand.

Chapter 10

STEELHEAD

As we have seen, the steelhead is a rainbow trout that migrates down a coastal river to the sea, spends a few years there, and then returns up the river to spawn. Anglers along the Pacific Coast from California to Alaska have no Atlantic salmon in their rivers, but are perfectly content with the steelhead as a good substitute. In fact, since both fish are very similar in appearance, habits, and fighting ability, it is difficult to determine which is superior.

More anglers fish for steelhead than for Atlantic salmon because steelhead are much more numerous and are found in many more rivers. Most of the steelhead rivers are open to the public, and the fishing seasons are long. (You can actually catch steelhead most of the year.) In addition, you are not restricted to the kind of tackle you can use, as is the case with Atlantic salmon, which can only be taken on fly rods.

All this makes the steelhead highly popular with Pacific Coast anglers, who seek this fish in rain, snow, sleet, and freezing weather during the winter months. But while steelhead are much more numerous than Atlantic salmon, they are not always an easy fish to catch, and they offer a challenge to most anglers, whether novice or expert. It takes skill to locate steelhead, to cast and present the bait or lure, and to hook and fight them successfully. In the rushing rivers where they are found they are really tackle-busters. And to complicate things even more, steelhead reach a good size. So you can consider yourself lucky if you land more than half of the steelhead you hook.

A steelhead looks like a rainbow trout except that a steelhead may be bigger, longer, more streamlined, and different in color when it first comes in from the sea. Fresh from the ocean, a steelhead, as its name implies, has a steel-blue or greenish back, silvery sides, and some dark spots on the back and tail. After it has been in fresh water for a while it reverts back to the original rainbow-trout colors.

Steelhead are caught with a variety of fishing outfits, from dainty light fly rods to heavy surf-fishing rods. Years ago, the most popular outfit was a long bait-casting or two-handed rod used with a bait-casting reel or small salt-water revolving-spool reel for drifting baits and lures with the current. Such outfits are still used, but most of them have been replaced by spinning rods, ranging from 6½ to 8½ feet in length. The

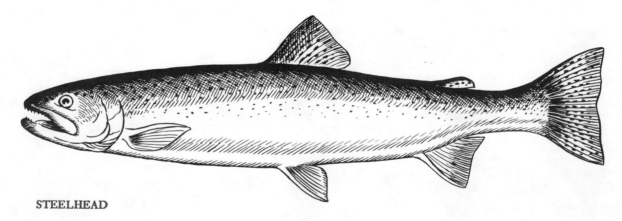

STEELHEAD

shorter, lighter spinning rods are used with the smaller spinning reels filled with 8-to-15-pound-test lines. The longer, heavier spinning rods similar to surf rods are used with the larger spinning reels filled with 12-to-20-pound-test lines. The longer, heavier rods are used where the rivers are wide and at the mouths of rivers or for "plunking" with bait and sinkers on the bottom of such rivers.

For fly fishing, a good, powerful, graphite rod, from 8 to 9½ feet or even longer, that can handle Nos. 8 to 10 weight-forward or shooting-head fly lines, is needed. Floating fly lines are used with dry flies, but most of the time you need a slow-sinking, medium-sinking, or fast-sinking fly line, depending on the depth you are fishing and the speed of the current. Tapered leaders from 9 to 12 feet tapering down to 8-, or 6-, or, at times, 4-pound-test tippets are most practical for the tough, fighting steelhead.

The angler who prefers to use artificial lures for steelhead should carry spoons in various sizes, colors, and weights. Silver, gold, and brass spoons, as well as those painted in bright fluorescent yellow, pink, orange, or red, are all good. Weighted spinners are also good for casting and probing the bottom where steelhead lie. The Cherry Bobber spinner, which has a balsa body to keep it from sinking, can be used with a sinker rig, often to deadly effect. Equally good are various other lures with imitation egg clusters such as the Oakie Drifter and the Spin and Glo. Various types of jigs can also be used to get down deep. Underwater plugs such as the Flatfish, Rapala, Rebel, and other small minnow-type plugs are used mostly with sinkers in order to reach bottom.

For the fly-rod angler, there are numerous, productive wet flies and streamers, many of which are standard trout patterns, though some flies are tied especially for steelhead. These include the Royal Coachman, Silver Doctor, Gray Hackle, Queen Bess, Van Luven, Skykomish Sunrise, Polar Shrimp, Umpqua, Silver Ant, Orange Optic, Thor, Silver and Golden Demons, Harger's Orange, Comets, Governor, Burlap, Babine Special, Skunk, Fire Fly, and Kalama Special. Atlantic salmon flies will also take steelhead at times. Another variety of steelhead fly is made from yarn tied around the hook. These flies are often a bright fluorescent color such as yellow, orange, pink, or red. Some are wrapped in the shape of a small ball to look like a big salmon egg or a small cluster. Called "Glow Bugs," they are highly effective, especially in cold and murky waters. Wet flies tied on size Nos. 4, 6, and 8 hooks are usually the most effective.

When steelhead take dry flies you can use patterns such as the Gray Wulff, Black Wulff, March Brown, Adams, Royal Coachman, Light Cahill, and the Pink Lady in size Nos. 6, 8, 10, and 12. But you can also use many of the other trout patterns used for brown trout and brook trout.

Steelhead are also caught on natural baits such as salmon eggs fished singly, in groups of two or three, or in clusters or spawn sacs on a hook (size Nos. 4 or 2 for clusters; a smaller No. 10 for one or two eggs). The eggs of a fresh-caught chinook salmon are especially popular since they are smaller, firmer, and stay on a hook longer than those of other species. Fresh eggs taken from a female steelhead are also very good. These eggs are made up into clusters with tiny bags of thin maline netting in the following manner: Place the eggs in the centers of three-inch squares of netting, gather the corners together, and tie them with thread to form a small bag. Steelhead will also take crayfish tails or nightcrawlers drifted along the bottom or allowed to lie still in a quiet pool.

The key to success in steelhead fishing is to time your fishing trip to coincide with the run of fish up the river. Since this may vary from river to river and from year to year, it requires constant checking to see if there are fish in the section or stretch you plan to fish. Some rivers have only one main run of fish, such as the summer run, which may start in April in some rivers or as late as August or September in others. Other rivers may have a summer run and then later on a winter run, which may begin in October or later and last until February and March on some rivers. On still other rivers there are continuous runs of fish from early spring to winter as fish keep entering at various times. Before planning a trip it's a good idea to get in touch with someone who is right on the river and can tell you if the steelhead are running.

On short rivers the runs may only last a few weeks, with the fish moving upstream rapidly and not spending much time in any spot. On the longer rivers, the runs spread out over a greater period of time, with different sections of the river producing fast fishing as the steelhead move upstream. Here you have to follow the fish or intercept them if you want to catch them. Large stretches of the river may be barren of fish or contain only a few strays, while other sections will provide hot fishing.

Even when the steelhead are moving in the river there is no guarantee of good fishing. A sudden storm, prolonged rain, or drop in water temperature may put a stop to the fishing. It has been found that when the water temperature is below thirty-nine degrees Fahrenheit the steelhead are inactive and feed little. Also, a rapidly rising river that becomes discolored is usually unproductive. But after the river starts to clear and the water becomes a milky green or blue, the fishing picks up again.

After a heavy rain, the upper portions of a river clear first, then the lower portions. It may take two, three, or more days for the fishing to return to normal in some rivers. In others it may take several days or a week or two before it pays to go fishing. At such times, try fishing some of the smaller tributaries or streams entering the main river. These are usually clearer or clear faster than the big river itself.

Native anglers who live near the river have a big advantage. They can wait and watch the river to choose the best fishing periods. But anglers some distance from the river can check the weather reports to find out if it has rained there recently or if any rains are expected. Some of the tackle shops near the river you plan to fish can also give you a report on river conditions and let you know if steelhead are biting.

During the summer you can fish for steelhead in the daytime on overcast, cloudy days. But if it is sunny, bright, and hot, your chances are best early in the morning and again in the evening. During the winter months if the weather and water are cold you can fish in the middle of the day and afternoon when the water may have warmed up a bit.

Even after you arrive on a river and are assured that the fish are present, there is another important hurdle to overcome. You have to locate the fish in the river itself so that you can present the bait or lure to them. If you have fished the river before and know the locations and spots where steelhead like to lie or rest, this is not a big problem. But if you are fishing a strange river or are a beginner, then you have your work cut out for you.

The main point to keep in mind is that steelhead are usually found in "holding" or "resting" spots, where they are protected from the main force of the current. So in a riffle or rapid, they will be found along the edges of the fast water at the head or tail of the run. If there are boulders or rocks, look for the fish in front, behind, or along the sides of such obstructions. Along the banks of a river they may lie behind rock outcroppings, rock ledges, under cut banks, or overhanging trees, or behind logs, tree trunks, or driftwood. In pools look for them at the tails or heads rather than in the deeper, quieter middle portions. Pools should be fished from the shallow side, with casts made toward the deeper side.

Steelhead anglers look for holes where up to a dozen or more fish bunch up and rest before moving upstream to the next favorable spots. During the summer months, when the water is low, the fish tend to concentrate in the deeper runs, holes, and pools, in water from four to eight feet deep. They also seek shade from overhanging trees, under cut banks, brush, and bridges. Bottoms lined with big rocks and boulders that slow the force of the current are favorite spots for steelhead to lie. Another good summer spot is at the head of a pool where the white-water rapids enter the pool.

Most expert steelhead anglers study their favorite river during the low-water periods. They memorize and pinpoint the location of every boulder, rock, log, hole, depression, and obstruction that may harbor a steelhead later on when the river rises. They they can cast their lure or bait into these spots even though they cannot see the configuration below the surface. Once they take some fish from these spots they know they can return and catch some more as new fish replace those that have been caught or have moved upstream.

The method usually used to catch steelhead is to drift a natural bait such as salmon eggs or an artificial lure such as a spinner, spoon, or salmon-egg imitation close to the bottom. One of the best rigs used by present-day steelhead anglers is simple but effective. To make it, slip a one-inch length of surgical tubing on your line, and tie a barrel swivel on the end of the line. To this, tie a 15-inch leader with the hook or lure on

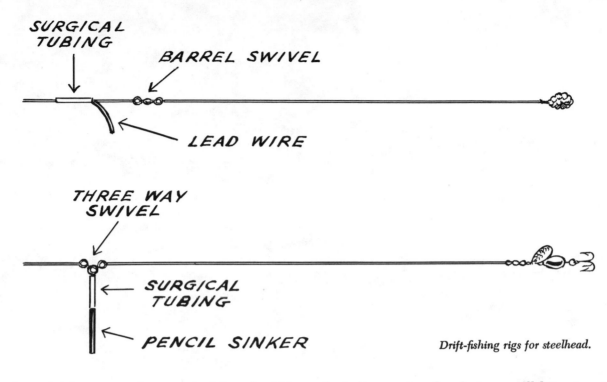

SURGICAL TUBING
BARREL SWIVEL
LEAD WIRE

THREE WAY SWIVEL
SURGICAL TUBING
PENCIL SINKER

Drift-fishing rigs for steelhead.

the end. Then insert about a 3-inch length of ⅛-inch-thick lead wire into the tubing. The length and thickness of the lead wire will depend on how much weight you need to reach and stay on the bottom in a fast current. The surgical tubing with lead weight can also be shifted up and down the line to give you a shorter or a longer leader as needed. The beauty of this rig is that if the lead gets caught you can give a hard yank to pull out the lead and free the rest of the rig. However, since you will probably still lose some rigs, it pays to make up a couple of dozen in advance and take them with you to replace those that are lost.

The rig described above is often used with egg clusters for drift fishing; the proven technique is to cast across and somewhat upstream and let the bait drift downstream on a tight line so that the sinker bounces bottom at all times. That's the main secret—keep the sinker rolling or bouncing on the bottom so that the bait passes through the resting or holding spots where steelhead are lying. Keep taking up slack line, raise and lower the rod tip, feed some line as the situation demands, and always be on the alert for the slightest stop, pause, or nibble indicating a pickup or bite. Then raise the rod tip smartly to set the hook. It may only be fouled on

the bottom or in a log, but you still have to set the hook at every indication of a bite in order not to miss a genuine bite.

Carry plenty of lead wire or sinkers and keep changing lengths and weights to match the current and depth you are fishing. Either trim the lead or add a longer length until your bait or lure moves a little slower than the current and keeps hugging the bottom.

Although natural baits such as salmon eggs and worms are used a lot, artificial lures such as spinners, spoons, jigs, imitation eggs, plastic lures, and plugs can also be used for drift fishing. Natural baits are usually best when the water is high and somewhat roily or discolored. Lures work better when the water is clear and lower. The heavier lures such as spoons and jigs are often fished in many spots along the bottom without the help of a sinker. But the lighter lures can be fished with the same rig and lead wire used with natural baits.

Lures can be worked by casting upstream and across and letting the current take them down deep along the bottom. Steelhead will often hit the lure as it is swinging in the current if it has some action or flash. At other times you can reel the lure slowly and even give it additional jerks with the rod tip. If you can wade out above a

On the larger rivers you can catch steelhead from a boat by casting or trolling, or by anchoring the boat and letting out a lure or bait down deep in the current. (Mercury Motors Photo)

good holding spot, let your lure down with the current and hold it there while working it back and forth in a small area.

On certain big, wide, and deep rivers, the best steelhead spots are reached by boat, and here steelhead are taken by drift fishing and trolling. If you can hold the boat in one spot or anchor it, let your bait or lure move down with the current into holes or other spots where steelhead may be lying. In such situations, you may also need a sinker or weight to get the bait or lure down close to the bottom.

Some sections of steelhead rivers, especially the lower portions, are wide, slow-moving, and have deep pools. Or they may be muddy from recent rains. Here still fishing or "plunking" is the most effective method. A plunker chooses a spot on the bank and stays there most of the time. From there, he casts out his salmon eggs, worms, or crayfish tails on a bottom rig with

sinker and lets the bait rest on or near the bottom. Then he puts his rod in a holder or forked stick on the bank and sits down to wait for a bite. A fairly long, heavy bait-casting or spinning rod with lines testing from fifteen to twenty pounds is generally used for this type of fishing.

For real sport nothing beats hooking and fighting a steelhead on a fly rod. Unfortunately, this fishing is usually restricted to certain rivers and certain seasons. It is most effective during the summer and early fall months when the water is low and clear. However, with the modern sinking fly lines it is now possible to catch steelhead on flies even during the cold winter months.

Wet flies and streamers can be used in much the same manner as for trout fishing. You can cast across and upstream and allow the fly to sink close to the bottom as you take up slack line. If you see a steelhead or know where one is

Big steelhead like this one can be caught during the late fall and winter months in many rivers in Oregon. (Oregon State Highway Photo)

lying, keep casting so that the fly drifts and swings in front of its nose. Steelhead will often ignore the fly or even move out of the way, but suddenly may decide to take it after several casts. Usually the fly is taken at the end of the swing. While steelhead will hit a fly drifting naturally, you'll get more strikes if you give it some action with short pulls or jerks.

To cover the most water, start fishing upstream with short casts and gradually progress to longer ones until you have covered most of the holding spots. Then you can move downstream a short distance and repeat this procedure. It is important to have the fly moving as close to the bottom as possible during the drift or swing. This may mean changing fly lines often to match the speed of the current and the depth of the water. Weighted flies are more effective than unweighted ones for this fishing.

At times, you can also catch steelhead on dry flies on the surface. This is usually possible when the water is low and clear in the summer or early fall, when the steelies are feeding on hatching insects. The late-afternoon and evening hours are usually the best times for this fishing. The dry fly is allowed to drift naturally in the current, but steelhead have been known to take a fly that is skated or skittered along the surface.

Once you hook a steelhead on any kind of tackle you can look forward to a fast, spectacular fight. The smaller fish will leap out of the water again and again. Steelies of all sizes will make long, fast, powerful runs, often forcing you to follow them downstream in a strong current. The safest way to land a steelhead is to beach it on a sloping rock, gravel bar, or sandbar. When you are fishing from a boat or shore with deep water at your feet, a wide-mouthed net or gaff can be used.

Steelhead caught during the summer range in weight from two to eight pounds or so. The winter fish are much larger, often going up to fifteen or twenty pounds. Steelhead up to thirty pounds are caught in many rivers. The rod-and-reel record is a big forty-two-pound, two-ounce steelhead caught in Alaska on June 22, 1970, by David White.

In California steelhead are found in such rivers as the Klamath, Trinity, Sacramento, Russian, American, Yuba, Feather, Smith, Matole, and Guatuala. Oregon has many steelhead rivers, among which are the Rogue, Umpqua, Destuches, Coquille, Siletz, Siuslaw, Sandy, Alsea, Wilson, Big Nestucca, and Columbia. The last also flows through the state of Washington, whose other productive rivers include the Duckabush, Kalama, Stillaguamish, Snoqualmie, Washougal, Wind, Quinault, Dosewallips, Green, Lewis, Puyallup, Skagit, Skykomish, Nisqually, Chehalis, Cowlitz, Puyallup, Wenatchee, Rogue, Queets, Naselle, Willapa, Nooksack, Bogachiel, and Toutle. In British Columbia such rivers as the Fraser, Kispiox, Cowichan, Skeena, Cooper, Sustut, Babine, Dean, Thompson, Vedder, and Bella Coola offer great steelhead fishing as does the famed Campbell River on Vancouver Island. Alaska also has many rivers in its southeastern section that can be fished for steelhead.

Of course, many other rivers and streams in the areas listed may have steelhead runs. Some may be good one year and a flop the next. Some may be blocked by sandbars that form at the mouth and prevent the steelhead from entering. When heavy winter rains open these rivers to the steelhead, the fishing is good. For the latest information on the rivers, it's a good idea to contact local fishermen, sporting-goods and tackle stores, the outdoor writers of local newspapers, and your state fish and game department. It also pays to visit the river yourself to see firsthand if water conditions are right and to find out if fish are being caught.

Chapter 11

LAKE TROUT

The lake trout is unfamiliar to many anglers and not too popular as a game fish, mostly because their range is limited and good fishing for them usually takes place during seasons when few anglers are on the water. Another factor is that the best lake-trout fishing is found in remote northern, wilderness areas accessible only by float planes. And even here the fishing season may only last about two months. So only a small percentage of fresh-water anglers have had firsthand experience with lake trout. But for those anglers who live in areas where lake trout are found and who spend time seeking them or traveling to the best spots, there is fine sport to be had with these large fish.

The lake trout is a char like the Dolly Varden trout and brook trout. It is also called the Mackinaw, togue, Great Lakes trout, forktail trout, gray trout, salmon trout, namaycush, and laker.

In color it varies from gray to light green, brown, and almost black. The whole body is covered with lighter, irregular spots, and its belly is cream-colored or white. The laker has a large head, a large mouth with strong teeth, and a forked tail.

Originally the lake trout was found from Labrador to Alaska, throughout the Great Lakes, and in northern New England. But it has been introduced into many other states as far south as Connecticut and New York. However, lake trout thrive best in the large, clear, cold, and deep northern lakes, where the best fishing takes place from spring to fall.

The fishing tackle used to catch lake trout will vary depending on the season, the depth being fished, the lures and weights being used, and whether the angler is casting or trolling. Spinning, spin-casting, bait-casting, and even fly rods have all been used. For trolling with weights, wire lines, or in deep water, heavier musky-type or trolling rods or even light, salt-water trolling rods and reels are brought into play. You can also use heavy spinning-type rods and reels for some kinds of trolling. When solid wire lines such as Monel stainless steel in 20-to-30-pound-tests are used, a strong salt-water-type reel with a metal spool holding up to six hundred feet of line may be needed. Anglers can use braided lines, lead-core lines, and monofilament lines with heavy sinkers or trolling weights to get the

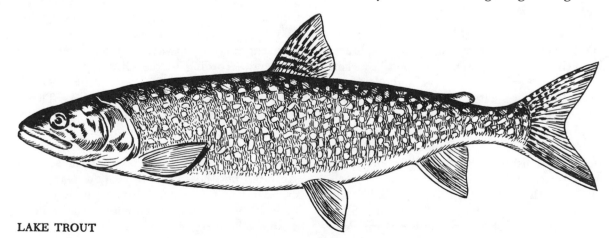

LAKE TROUT

lure or bait down deep enough. Fairly heavy tackle is needed for this type of fishing. In recent years downriggers used with lighter tackle, have become popular for deep trolling. With this method, you get more fight from the fish because the weight is released when a lake trout is hooked.

The lures used for lake trout include spoons of various shapes, sizes, and weights and lengths up to five or six inches. These can be silver, chrome, or gold, or painted in fluorescent yellow, pink, orange, red, green, or blue. The heavier, thicker spoons can also be used for casting when lake trout are in shallow water or near the surface. Heavy spoons can also be used for jigging. Spinners, either used singly, in pairs, or in series are also used for trolling. The long, light, large plugs such as the Rapala, Rebel, and similar underwater types are very effective for trolling near the surface or down deep. And when using a fly rod for casting or trolling you can use the big streamer and bucktail flies such as those used for landlocked salmon or coho salmon. Various kinds of jigs are also used for casting, trolling, or jigging.

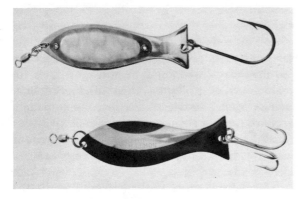

Worth Demon spoons used for lake trout.

Lake trout feed on smelt, ciscoes, tullibees, whitefish, yellow perch, sculpins, suckers, darters, alewives, chubs, shiners, and other small fish and minnows. These can all be used as bait or for trolling behind spinners or flashers. You can also use strips cut from fish or even nightcrawlers or worms behind spinners or on jigs.

Lake-trout fishing is best early in the spring soon after the ice is out and then again in the fall when the fish return to the shallows to spawn. So in most areas of the United States you'll find the best fishing during April, May, early June, and then again during October and November. During these months, the trout will be in shallow water and close to the surface. During the summer months, when lake trout are deep, the fishing is slow, except farther north in Canadian and Alaskan waters, where the ice may not break up until June or even July, and good fishing is often had during July, August, and early September. Lake trout are also caught through the ice during the winter months, but more on this later.

Lake trout can be caught on almost any day, but many anglers prefer windy, rainy, cloudy days for the fastest fishing. This is especially true when the lake trout are in shallow water. When they are down deep you can often catch them during the middle of the day.

Finding lake trout in the spring is easy because they are usually feeding near shore at the mouths of inlets and streams entering the lake and along the reefs and shoals extending from land. They prefer shoals or reefs with deep water nearby and a bottom strewn with rocks or boulders. The smaller fish will venture into the shallows, but the larger ones usually prefer somewhat deeper water. At this time the waters are cold inshore and at the surface throughout the lake. Lake trout usually follow regular predictable routes when they move about a lake. These routes can provide fast fishing if you are there when the lakers are moving through.

During the summer months locating the lake trout presents more of a problem, since they are in very deep water at this time. You may find them in some lakes only 50 feet down, while in others they may be down 100, 150, and even 200 feet deep. They like a water temperature ranging from 42° to 55° F, so a thermometer is a big help in finding the level where they are lying. This layer with the preferred temperature and sufficient oxygen will vary in depth from lake to lake and according to the changing seasons. If this thermocline lies over a reef, shoals, rocks, or a hole, you have a prime spot for lakers. That is why a depth finder is also a must for locating such bottoms and even finding the fish when trolling or jigging in deep water.

In the extreme northern lakes of Canada you can often find lake trout in shallow water near shore and in the upper layers even during the summer months. They even enter some rivers in these northern regions and can be caught, as we have seen, during July, August, and September.

When lake trout are in fairly shallow water near shore you can catch them by casting either from shore or from a boat. A boat is best because you can move around, trying different spots and covering more deeper water by casting in all directions. Spoons and underwater plugs and spinners are best for this fishing and should be retrieved at a low or medium speed with plenty of action. You can also try a few casts with the lure traveling just below the surface. If you get no strikes let it sink a bit deeper, reel it in, and work it at that level. On the next cast let it sink still deeper and retrieve it at this level. Keep doing this until you find the level at which the fish are lying or feeding. You can also move the boat around and cast over a reef or shoal from different angles.

When lake trout are in shallow water or near the surface in lakes (or if you are fishing the northern Canadian rivers), you can have great sport catching them with a fly rod. Here big streamers or bucktails with Mylar strips or silver bodies fished on a sinking fly line is the best combination. And instead of casting, you can try trolling the streamers behind a boat along shore or over shoals and reefs.

For deep-water trolling the same spoons, spinners, and plugs mentioned earlier can be used at different depths and different speeds until you find the right combination. You can also troll a smelt, alewife, or minnow with a curve in its body. Use a lead core or wire line when deep trolling with bait or lures. Let it out until you feel it hit bottom, then reel in a couple of feet and troll at that depth. Once you locate the depth where the fish are, you can mark your line with plastic tape so that you can let out the same length every time. Even when using lead core or wire line you usually need trolling weights or sinkers to get down deep enough. These can be used with a triangular trolling rig or a three-way swivel rig. Or you can attach the trolling weight between the wire line and the monofilament leader.

The best trolling speed for lake trout is very slow and against or across any current. You'll get more strikes and hook more fish if your raise the rod in a quick, short sweep and then lower it at regular intervals. This causes the lure or bait to rise and dart forward and then settle back toward the bottom, giving it a crippled action. If you bump bottom with the weight every so often, you will know that you are deep enough.

Although the plain lures or baits will catch lake trout, they often become more effective if used behind a series of spinners called "cowbells" or behind a metal dodger or flasher. These act as attractors, giving off vibrations, flashing, and imparting an extra action to the lure or bait. They work especially well when used with a sewn smelt, alewife, or minnow behind them.

In recent years the older methods of deep trolling for lake trout have been replaced by the use of downriggers. Anywhere from one to four of these can be mounted on a boat so that you can then lower and control the lure or bait at exactly the level you want. The depth is measured by a mechanical counter or by the number of turns of the handle on the wheel. The fishing line is attached to a heavy weight that takes the lure down, but the line is released when a lake trout strikes. In this manner, you can fight the fish without any weight, use much lighter tackle, and have more fun and sport.

And, nowadays, more and more anglers are also jigging for lake trout rather than trolling. For this, you can use fairly light spinning and bait-casting rods, reels, and lines. Almost any heavy, sinking lure can be used for jigging, but a white or yellow leadhead jig weighing about two ounces is usually employed. Heavy spoons or the Hopkins lures are other alternatives. A strip of fish can be added to the jig as an extra attraction. Jigging can be done from a boat drifting over the rocks, shoals, or reefs where lake trout like to lie or feed. Send the lure down to the bottom and, when it hits, reel in a couple of turns and start working it up and down. Or, after it hits bottom, jig for a while near the bottom, then start reeling it toward the surface as you work the rod tip.

Lake trout can also be caught in the winter through the ice. Here, too, jigging is the best method. Use a short bait-casting rod and a bait-casting reel filled with 20-pound-test mono line.

Jig with strip of fish for lake trout.

Lake trout can also be caught through the ice during the winter months with live or dead minnows as bait or by jigging with spoons. (Michigan Travel Commission Photo)

18"

Two-spoon jigging rig for lake trout.

A silver or gold spoon can be used plain or dressed with a dead minnow or a strip of fish on the hook. Some anglers use a combination rig with two spoons. The spoon can be lowered to the bottom, then raised a few inches and worked up and down. You have to develop the right jigging speed to get strikes—neither too fast nor too slow. The spoon should rise and then flutter down in an attractive manner.

Lake trout can also be caught by fishing live minnows or other small fish on the bottom throughout the season. Here a live smelt or alewife, small sucker, or chub from four to six inches long can be hooked through the back. For this fishing you need a bottom rig with a sinker just heavy enough to reach the bottom. Let the minnow or small fish swim around until a lake trout comes along and swallows it.

A lake trout hooked on or near the surface on light tackle can provide an exciting battle. They run fast and occasionally kick up a fuss on or near the surface. But a laker hooked on wire line or rigs with heavy weights or sinkers at great depths is another thing. A disappointing fight usually ensues, with the fish giving up long before it reaches the surface. Then you just have the dead weight to raise to the top. Nowadays, downriggers that release the weight when a fish is hooked are a big improvement, since you get more fight and have more sport with lakers using lighter tackle.

Of course, if you catch the really big lake trout found in the Far North you'll get a long, stubborn fight even on fairly heavy tackle. But big lakers are rare in most waters of the United States, and most of those you'll catch will go from about 5 to 15 pounds. However, in parts of Canada and Alaska, lake trout up to 20 and 30 pounds are fairly common. The rod-and-reel record is a 65-pound lake trout caught by Larry Daunis in Great Bear Lake in Canada. A few others in the 60-pound class have also been caught by sports fishermen. But lake trout grow much larger, and there have been reports of fish going 80, 96, 102, and 104 pounds caught on hand lines or in nets.

The lake trout has a fine-flavored flesh that can be fried, baked, broiled, or smoked. The Eskimos in Alaska prefer lake trout over rainbow trout when it comes to eating, and in Canada lake trout appear regularly on restaurant menus. Lake trout used to be caught commercially in large numbers in the Great Lakes until they became scarce thanks to the lamprey eel, a creature that attaches itself to the fish and sucks out its blood and body fluids. Now that the lamprey eels have been brought under control, there is good fishing for lake trout in the Great Lakes once more.

As stated earlier, lake trout are found in many lakes in Alaska. In Canada, Saskatchewan is noted for its lake-trout waters, among which are Waterbury Lake, Kingsmere Lake, Lac La Ronge, Black Lake, Little Bear Lake, Cree Lake, Reindeer Lake, and Lake Athabasca. In Manitoba, God's Lake, Nueltin Lake, Reed Lake, Clearwater Lake, and Lake Athapapuskow are productive but can only be reached by plane. In the Northwest Territories, Great Bear Lake and Great Slave Lake are noted for their big lake trout. In Alberta, you can fish Cold Lake, Gris Lake, Wentzel Lake, Peerless Lake, and Swan Lake. In Quebec, Lake St. John, Lake Wakonichi, Lake Mistassini, and Chibougamau Lake can be fished as well as most of the extreme northern part of the province bordering Hudson Bay and Ungava Bay. There is also some lake-trout fishing in Newfoundland, Labrador, Nova Scotia, and New Brunswick. For information about a certain area in Canada, write the Canadian Government Office of Tourism in Ottawa, Canada.

In this country, Maine has many productive lakes, including Beech Hill Pond, Moosehead

These two huge lake trout were caught in God's Lake in Manitoba, Canada. This is fly-in territory, with only a short summer fishing season. (Manitoba Department of Tourism & Recreation Photo)

Lake, Branch Lake, West Grand Lake, East Grand Lake, Schoodic Lake, and Sebec Lake. In New Hampshire you'll find lake trout in Big Greenbough Pond, Silver Lake, Tarlton Lake, Squam Lake, and Newfound Lake. Wisconsin's Green Lake is well known for its lake-trout fishing, and in Michigan you can try Torch, Elk, Crystal, and Higgins lakes. In Idaho, lake trout are found in Priest Lake. Utah has Fish Lake and Bear Lake. And in New York they can be caught in Lake George and in Seneca, Raquette, Cayuga, Keuka, and Canandaigua lakes. In Massachusetts, Quabbin Reservoir contains lake trout.

Chapter 12

MUSKELLUNGE

Most fresh-water anglers would like to catch a muskellunge because it is big and makes a real trophy. It also puts up a tough fight that strains the tackle and provides plenty of thrills. But not many anglers are willing to pay the price of catching a muskellunge. The musky is a moody, temperamental, unpredictable, tricky fish that is rarely easy to catch. It takes a lot of patience, persistence, and know-how to hook one, and plenty of skill and a bit of luck to boat or land one. Many big muskies manage to cut or break the line or straighten a hook and are therefore lost to the angler. You may have to fish for days or even weeks before you get so much as one solid strike from a musky. Even the expert musky anglers and guides claim that it usually takes a week of hard fishing to catch one or two fish. Many anglers who have pursued muskellunge for years have yet to catch their first fish.

Yet there are some anglers and fishing guides who have acquired reputations for their musky catches. These men and a few women catch dozens of big muskies each season, often winning contests for the biggest fish. Some of these anglers have even caught two or three fish in one day and several fish in one week. These skilled anglers are usually the musky "specialists" who fish only for these big fish and waste little time on other species. Most of them live close to the waters they fish and concentrate on the lakes or rivers that they know contain plenty of big muskellunge. They put in many hours, days, weeks, and even months casting or trolling for muskies.

The average fresh-water angler has to confine his fishing to a weekend or a brief vacation period, usually during the poorest time of the year. This may be sufficient time to catch some trout, bass, panfish, and other fish. But to catch a musky you'll have to allow plenty of time and make repeated trips to your fishing site throughout the season (from spring or early summer to late fall). To be frank, if you can't spend the time or don't have the patience and persistence to seek out muskellunge you're better off if you confine your fishing to other easier-to-catch species. With luck you may eventually hook a musky, and with still more luck you may land or boat him. In the meantime, you would have had a lot of fun and sport with smaller but more numerous and more co-operative species.

Let's take a close look at the muskellunge, which, as most anglers know, is a member of the pike family, related to both the pike and the pickerel. It has the same, big, alligatorlike jaws, sharp teeth, and long, slim body. The back is green or olive fading into gray, and the belly is white. There may be darker spots or stripes on

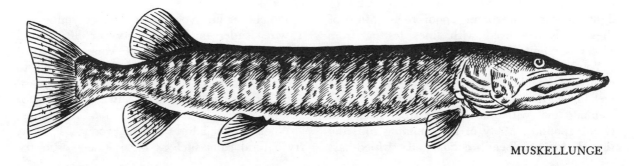

MUSKELLUNGE

the sides and tail, but these are often indistinct in the larger fish.

The muskellunge is known by many different names, which are usually spelling variations of the more popular one. Thus you'll see them called maskinonge, masquenonge, masquealonge, muskalonge, muskallonge, moskallonge, etc. They are also called the great pike, lunge, and musky. Most anglers like to use the last name.

Muskellunge are found in the Great Lakes region north to Canada. They are also found in the St. Lawrence River system (including parts of western New York) and in the Ohio River and Tennessee River systems. Many waters in Wisconsin, Minnesota, Michigan, and Pennsylvania also have them. Although they have been stocked as far south as Virginia, North Carolina, Kentucky, and Tennessee, muskies prefer cold northern lakes and rivers.

Many muskies are hooked each season on light tackle by bass fishermen, but only a small percentage of these are landed or boated. The majority of the big muskies hooked on such light tackle are lost. Yet too many anglers insist on using their regular light-bass tackle for this king of fresh-water game fish with a reputation as a tackle buster.

If you are really interested in catching some big muskies, you should get special tackle for them. Special bait-casting-type rods are labeled "musky" rods. These are stiffer and heavier than the bait-casting rods used for most bass fishing. In recent year the "worm" rods designed for plastic worm fishing have been used increasingly for musky fishing. These are stiff rods with plenty of backbone. If you plan to cast very heavy lures or suckers, a "popping"-type rod, from six to eight feet long with an eighteen- or twenty-inch handle, is best since you can cast it with two hands. Similar rods can also be used for trolling for muskies. These rods can accommodate either heavy-duty bait-casting reels or light salt-water revolving-spool reels. Most of these rods are used with lines testing from fifteen to twenty-five pounds.

You can also use a stiff spinning rod with plenty of backbone, ranging from six to eight feet in length. Such a rod calls for a good-sized spinning reel with lines testing from twelve to twenty pounds. Many of the spinning rods designed for steelhead, coho, and striped-bass fishing will serve equally well for muskies.

Muskies have also been caught on heavy fly rods, but since musky fishing usually requires a lot of continuous casting and a fast retrieve, the fly-rod user is handicapped. You can save your wrist and arm and fish longer hours by using a bait-casting or spinning rod.

The rods used for muskellunge are on the stiff and heavy side for several practical reasons. First, the musky has a tough mouth and usually holds a lure broadside in its strong jaws. This makes it difficult to move the lure in order to set the hooks if you are using a soft, limber rod and a line with a lot of stretch. Also, the large hooks used on most musky lures are harder to bury or set in the fish's mouth. In addition, you often have to use large, heavy lures to entice muskies to strike. Casting such lures requires a fairly stiff rod. Finally, you often have to turn, stop, or at least slow down a big musky heading for weeds, a log, or a rock. You can do this more readily with a stiff rod and a strong line.

When it comes to lures used for muskies, the old-time fluted spoon with feathers is still a good choice. So are the spinner and big bucktail combinations, especially those with black hair. In recent years anglers have been achieving excellent results with large-sized spinner baits. Spoons up to seven or eight inches long are also old-time favorites that still catch fish.

Various types of surface plugs such as poppers, swimmers, gurglers, crawlers, and crippled minnows with propellers will raise a lot of big muskellunge. Underwater plugs up to seven or eight inches long in solid or double-jointed models also take many muskies each year. The larger sized crankbaits used for bass will often work well on muskies. So do the jerk baits such as the Suick, Teddie Bait, and Bobby Bait, which are specially made for musky fishing. In recent years, the large-sized jigs and plastic worms (curly tail or grub tail) have proven very effective.

Whichever lure you use, make sure you attach a wire leader or heavy forty- or fifty-pound monofilament to the end of your line. Most musky fishermen who troll use leaders up to three feet long. If you find this difficult to cast, you can shorten it to ten or twelve inches for casting.

When artificial lures fail to produce a strike, try natural baits such as big minnows, suckers,

This musky was hooked on a spoon in an Ontario lake. Muskies will also hit spinners, plugs, plastic lures, and jigs. (Ontario Ministry of Industry & Tourism Photo)

carp, yellow perch, small walleyes, or other fish. The big salamanders called water dogs also make good musky baits. But the favorite natural bait is a live or dead sucker from eight to twelve inches long.

You may be able to catch muskies as early as March or April along their southern range if the legal season has started at the time. But farther north fishing doesn't usually begin until May or early June. June is a good month in most areas to start fishing for muskies. July and August have traditionally been the top months for musky fishing, probably because that is when most anglers get their vacations and can spend the most time on the water. But some of the best fishing occurs during September and October when the largest fish are taken. But a good musky fisherman who can locate the fish, knows which lure or bait to use and how to use it, and fishes hard, can catch muskies during most of the season from spring to fall.

Though muskies have been caught at almost every hour of the day, the optimum time will vary with the seasons and the waters being fished. Most anglers fish from early morning to late afternoon or evening, a period during which many muskies have been caught. But when the day is sunny and bright and the lake is flat and calm, especially during the summer months, you'll usually do better if you fish around daybreak and near dusk. Night fishing can be very good in some waters soon after the sun sets and for a short time after. Muskies have also been caught later at night, with or without moonlight.

Most expert musky fishermen and guides agree that the best fishing usually takes place on overcast, dark, rainy days when the surface of the water is rippled or choppy. Fishing can be excellent before or after a storm, but a cold front, while it lasts, will often kill the fishing. A wind from the south, southwest, or west is favored over an east wind, which can also result in poor fishing. Any sudden changes in the weather pattern should be watched, and after several days of fine weather, the change to rain or the approach of a thunderstorm can make the muskies hit.

The main secret in musky fishing is to locate the fish first, then concentrate your efforts on making them strike or take the bait. Your chances are increased if you can locate several good musky spots and spend the day giving each one a good workout. That is why a professional guide is a big help to the beginner or even to an experienced angler fishing a strange lake for the first time. The guide knows his waters and the habits of the fish under varying weather and water conditions. He can take you straight to the spots where he caught muskies before or knows that they are present.

For many years it was believed that muskies were all loners, shunning the company of their own kind. But this has been disproved in recent years, and it is now known that muskies will often gather in small schools. Such groups may consist of two or three fish or as many as a dozen or more. Homer LeBlanc, a great musky fishing guide on Lake St. Clair, Michigan, has caught as many as eleven muskies in one day from a patch of underwater weeds no larger than a room. Of course, muskies do separate and often feed alone; the biggest ones, especially, do not tolerate intruders into their favorite feeding spots or hangouts. They'll eat the smaller fish and chase away the bigger ones. While some big muskies will stay put in one spot for long periods of time, others will migrate daily from one spot to another. Other movements will be from deep water to shallow water, followed by a return to the deep water. Muskies will often spend a lot of time in deep water not too far from the shallower feeding areas. In fact, in recent years more and more musky fishing has taken place in deep water up to thirty or forty feet. However, most fishing for muskies is still done in the shallower water from four to twenty feet.

Favorite musky hangouts in a lake include coves, sunken trees, brushpiles, logs, stumps, rockbars, sandbars, sloping points of land, underwater islands, dropoffs, lily pads, overhanging trees, and any other cover, obstruction, or structure. One of the most dependable and productive spots is an underwater weedbed in water from six to twenty feet deep and near shore or even some distance from shore. Most of the muskies will be caught over the weeds or along the edges of the weeds, especially those bordering deeper water. Weeds attract and hide small fish, minnows, suckers, salamanders, frogs, and other aquatic creatures that muskies eat. For the same reason muskies will also gather at streams, rivers, inlets, or outlets to a lake.

But muskies migrate with the seasons in pursuit of food. In the spring, they will be close to their spawning grounds near channels, backwaters, rivers, and shallow, muddy bottoms. Then in the summer they will often be in deep water where ciscoes, whitefish, yellow perch, and walleyes are plentiful. In the fall muskies often return to feed in shallow water, again following the smaller fish that move into the shallows when the water cools.

Locating muskies in rivers or streams is somewhat easier because you have less water to cover and can concentrate on the deeper, quieter pool, holes, channels, long, deep stretches, logs, submerged trees or boulders, sharp bends, and mouths of feeder streams. In rivers you have to watch for heavy rains that raise the water level, muddy the water, and spoil the fishing. Wait until the water starts to clear and muskies start hitting again.

Another way to locate a musky is to see one break water or boil on top in order to catch a fish, frog, rat, mouse, muskrat, chipmunk, squirrel, duckling, gosling, or other small animal. (All these creatures have been found from time to time in musky stomachs.) You can also try casting a surface plug at random and watch for swirls or followups behind the lure. Muskies have the exasperating habit of following lures, only to refuse them near the boat. But at least you will know they are present and can keep returning to the same spot in the hope they'll grab the lure or bait on another occasion.

The best way to better the odds and catch more muskies is to choose the best lake or lakes to fish. Those with large musky populations, adequate spawning grounds, an abundant food supply, and a lot of water are usually the most productive day in and day out. The fish and game department of the state you plan to fish can supply this information. So can outdoor writers for newspapers, other musky fishermen, and musky fishing clubs. If you can find one to three good lakes in your area, fish them often, and learn the right waters and spots, you will have a big advantage. Then if one lake doesn't produce you can always drive to the other lake or lakes and try them.

Casting is a favorite and productive method of catching muskies in lakes and rivers. This is usually done from a drifting boat moving with the wind or current. You can cast toward weedbeds, rockbars, lily pads, sunken trees, logs, sloping points, underwater islands and reefs, and other cover and structure. It is best to cast ahead of a drifting boat or well to one side. Make casts about six feet apart in a semicircle, or if you prefer, in a circle all around the boat. If you raise a musky or see one following the bait or lure, drop anchor and work that spot thoroughly.

Spinner-bucktails and spinner baits can be retrieved in shallow water just below the surface by holding the rod high and reeling fairly fast. In deeper water hold the rod down, reel more slowly, and try different depths. Surface lures and plugs are most effective during the summer

Worth Musky Fin spinner-bucktail.

and early fall when the water is warm and muskies are most active. One good way to use a surface plug is to whip your rod up and down in short, fast jerks, reeling all the while so that the plug splashes, weaves, and sways on top. Then start reeling fast so that the plug dives and swims below the surface. Usually a musky will hit the plug soon after it submerges. Jerk baits can be worked in a similar fashion with long three-foot sweeps of the rod to make the plug submerge and dart forward; let it rise to the surface before you pull it under again. Or you can use the heavier or weighted jerk baits and work them below the surface for most of the retrieve. Surface plugs are especially good when used at dusk and at night.

Crankbaits—underwater plugs with big lips that make them dive and travel deep—are excellent when muskies are lying near the bottom over weedbeds, along dropoffs, bars, submerged

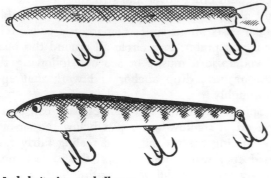

Jerk baits for muskellunge.

islands, and other structure. Here you make a long cast and reel in fast so that the plug travels along the bottom. When the plug is directly below the boat, quickly lift the rod tip high overhead. This makes the lure shoot upward, and any muskies following it will often hit it before it escapes.

Another good lure to use when casting for muskies is a jig weighing from ¼ to ½ ounce. Add a curly-tail plastic worm or grub to the hook on the jig. This can be reeled fairly fast in shallow water with an up-and-down jigging motion. In deeper water let the jig sink and bounce it along the bottom, especially along the edges of weedbeds.

As a general rule, it is best to retrieve the lures fast for muskellunge, especially during the summer and early fall months. Later on, when the water gets cold, you can slow down the retrieve. Surface plugs should be worked fast so that they throw plenty of splash and make a big commotion. But you have to experiment since there will be times when a medium or even slow retrieve is better. At other times, an erratic retrieve will interest the fish. But whether your retrieve is fast, medium, or slow, the lure should look alive and be moving at all times.

Muskies will often follow a lure up to the boat, then turn around or sink without striking. Or you may get a swirl behind the lure as it travels on or just below the surface. When this happens, speed up your retrieve and then, when it gets near the boat, don't take the lure out of the water. Instead, swish the lure around alongside the boat in a circle or figure-eight pattern. Or when the lure is about twelve feet from the boat, swing your rod quickly to one side so that the lure changes direction. This will often trigger a strike. If muskies continue to follow your lure without striking, try changing lures to find one that may interest them.

Trolling is often more effective than casting for catching muskies. This can be done in shallow water with anywhere from 50 to 125 feet of line out and with large spoons, spinners, spinner-bucktails, underwater plugs, and jigs. You can work your boat over and along the edge of weedbeds, alongside lily pads, around islands, over sunken points, and along the edges of channels, coves, or rivermouths. In shallow water, use a regular mono or braided line without a weight.

For trolling in deeper water, you can use the same lures as in shallow water, but with lead-core line, Monel wire line, or downriggers. Working the edges of weedbeds where the water drops off from six to twenty feet is a good way to take muskies during the summer months. Although lines without weight can be trolled up to a hundred feet behind a boat, muskies are not boat-shy in deeper water and will often hit a lure trolled a few feet behind the boat. Here you can use lead weights from four to six ounces between the line and leader to get the lure down. But in some lakes muskies have been caught as deep as thirty or forty feet; to reach such depths, you have to let out more line, unless you are using downriggers. Trolling fast (anywhere from four to seven miles per hour) has been found to be more effective than slow trolling.

Although the rods can be left in rod holders on the boat while trolling, you will usually get more strikes if you work your lure by raising your rod slowly, then letting it drop back quickly. This can be done as you let out line, as you reel it in, or every minute or two while trolling. The lure worked in this manner will often trigger a strike, whereas a lure moving on a straight line will not. This rod movement is especially effective with spoons or jigs.

When artificial lures don't work, try natural baits such as a sucker. This small baitfish can be hooked once through the head or harnessed around the head and then cast into likely spots. Since the sucker is dead it must be given action with the rod tip so that it spurts, dives, darts, and even surfaces. You can also try letting it sink to the bottom, then retrieve it toward the surface in short jerks. Dead suckers can also be trolled slowly behind the boat.

Another technique is to hook a live sucker, big

This muskellunge was caught by trolling in Chautauqua Lake, New York. Muskies are also caught by casting lures or suckers or by still fishing with live baits. (New York State Department of Commerce Photo)

minnow, or small fish through the back and let it swim around with or without a float until a musky grabs it. But no matter how you use suckers, small fish, or minnows, you must give the musky plenty of time to swallow these baits. A musky will grab the small fish in the middle, then swim off to swallow it. You must give slack line when this happens so that the fish doesn't feel the pull on the line. Keep feeding line and wait until a musky makes up its mind to swallow the baitfish. This might take a few minutes or much longer.

When you set the hook, either with lures or baits, come back hard with your rod tip. Some anglers even strike two or three times. Muskies clamp down on a bait and hold it firmly. They also have tough jaws. All of this means that you have to move the lure or bait and penetrate the jaws for the hooks to sink in and hold.

A musky puts up a spectacular fight at times, leaping, lunging, rolling, and splashing around on top of the water. At other times he sulks and make short runs below the surface. A big musky has plenty of endurance, staying power, and weight, and a fight may last a half hour or more. They will often head for a sunken log, rocks, trees, or other obstructions. Many big fish are lost near the boat when the musky makes a last, sudden surge or thrashes around wildly on top.

A musky should be played until it gives up— and turns over on its side. Then you can use a wide-mouthed net to scoop up the smaller fish. If the fish is large it is better to gaff it through the lower lip or jaw. Some expert anglers and guides grab a musky in the eye sockets or under the gill covers. But this should be done only with fish that will not be released. A big musky can also be beached on a sloping shore if the

Fred Kohler caught this big musky in Lake LeBoeuf in Pennsylvania. (Photo by Bob Chandler)

angler is fishing from land or gets out of the boat in shallow water.

It is believed that muskies reach over one hundred pounds in weight, but the largest taken on rod and reel weighed sixty-nine pounds, fifteen ounces. This fish was caught in the St. Lawrence River, New York, by Art Lawton on September 22, 1957. Through the years many other muskies in the forty-, fifty-, and sixty-pound classes have been caught. But in most waters you're lucky to catch a musky in the 15-to-30-pound class. Some outstanding catches of muskies have been made with light, spinning tackle by Len Hartman of Ogdensburg, New York, the holder of many musky records. His biggest fish was a sixty-seven-pound, fifteen-ounce musky caught in the St. Lawrence River on eleven-pound-test line!

Some of the best muskellunge waters \are found in Canada, particularly in Ontario, where the Lake of the Woods, Vermillion Lake, Eagle Lake, Kawartha Lake, Pigeon River, Pigeon Lake, Red Lake, and Lake Nipissing can be fished. As for the United States, Wisconsin has more than five hundred lakes and rivers containing muskies. Some of the most productive are Chippewa Flowage, Wisconsin River, Eagle River, Eagle Lake, Pelican Lake, Lac Vieux Desert, Lac du Flambeau, Grindstone Lake, Hayward Lake, Lac Court Oreilles, Moose Lake, Ghost Lake, Deer Lake, and Big Arbor Vitae Lake. In Michigan, Lake St. Clair, Gun Lake,

Thunder Bay, Munusconong Bay, Tahquamenon River, and Detroit River are noted for musky fishing. Minnesota's Leech Lake, Cass Lake, Rainey Lake, Battle Lake, Belle Taine, Mantrap, and Winnibigoshish lakes all have muskies. In New York, Chautauqua Lake, the St. Lawrence River, the Niagara River, and the Finger Lakes chain are fished for muskies, as are Pennsylvania's Pymatuning Lake, Tionesta Dam, Allegheny River, Susquehanna River, Delaware River, Juniata River, Conneaut Lake, Lake LeBoeuf, and Lake Edinboro. In West Virginia, the Little Kanawha River, Elk River, Big Coal River, Mill Creek, West Fork, Middle Island Creek, Salt Lick Creek, Cedar Creek, Hughes River, Leading Creek, and East Lynn contain muskies. Virginia has Smith Mountain Lake, Clayton Lake, and the Shenandoah, Clinch, and James rivers, while in Kentucky, Licking River, Red River, Kentucky River, Green River, Barren River, Obed River, and Kinniconick Creek can be fished. In Tennessee, muskies are found in Crab Orchard Creek, Dale Hollow Reservoir, and Woods Reservoir. Some waters in Ohio, Vermont, North Carolina, and Indiana also contain muskies.

But no matter where you see them, muskies offer a challenge and require plenty of skill and know-how to catch them consistently. If you catch only one big musky or a few good-sized ones, you have accomplished one of the more difficult feats in fresh-water fishing.

Chapter 13

PIKE

At one time very few anglers in this country or in Canada fished for pike deliberately. In the early days there was such an abundance of trout, bass, salmon, and other fresh-water fish that the pike was overlooked or scorned in favor of these supposedly more desirable fishes. Today, there are still a few diehards who consider the pike unworthy of the title of "game fish" and prefer other species. And in Canada and Alaska, where pike, along with other game fish, are very plentiful, they are still hated or ignored by native anglers.

Many anglers who despise the pike point to the fact that it destroys other fish and young waterfowl. They claim that many good trout and bass waters have been ruined by the introduction of pike. These greedy fish are supposed to have eaten up most of the trout and bass in those waters. In Saskatchewan and Manitoba pike do devour hundreds of thousands, if not millions, of ducklings.

But a look at the other side of the picture shows that in many waters, trout, bass, walleyes, and pike have lived together for ages and each species is plentiful. In certain waters, trout and bass may decline in numbers when pike first appear. But in many other waters biologists claim that pike actually improve the fishing by keeping down the numbers of yellow perch, sunfish, and other panfish. True, they'll also eat trout and bass, but the fish that are left grow larger in size in the lakes or rivers where pike are present. In waters lacking pike, panfish and even bass often become plentiful but are stunted in size.

But whether you admire the pike or hate him, you are missing some good fishing and sport if you don't try to catch this slim, toothy predator. Except for coloring, the pike looks like a smaller replica of its close cousin—the muskellunge. However, pike are more numerous and are found in more waters than the musky. They are also less temperamental and not so fussy about taking a lure or bait as the lunge. In recent years, more and more anglers have deliberately started fishing for pike and are enjoying some fine sport.

The pike also goes by other names, such as the great northern pike, northern pike, jackfish, jack,

PIKE

grass pike, and snake. The term "pickerel" is also used in some areas, but this, of course, is a misnomer, since the two fish are not identical.

The pike has a long, slim body with the dorsal fin set way back near the tail. The mouth looks like a big duck's bill or an alligator's snout. Most pike are olive or greenish in color with an occasional bluish cast. The color becomes lighter toward the belly, which is yellowish or white. Most pike have many yellow-white, bean-shaped spots along the sides of the body. However, there is also a "silver pike," which is bluish-gray in color and lacks the lighter spots. This variant is found in some waters in Minnesota and Wisconsin.

The pike is one of the most widely distributed fish in the United States, Canada, Alaska, Europe, and Asia. Although in this country the pike has been introduced into many waters as far south as North Carolina and Texas, it is mainly a fish of the colder, northern waters.

For small pike in open waters, you can use your regular bass- or walleye-fishing tackle such as a light or medium bait-casting rod, spinning rod, spin-casting rod, or fly rod. For larger, northern pike, the same tackle used for muskellunge (see preceding chapter) will be most practical. This is especially true when fishing around weeds, rocks, logs, sunken trees, brush, or other obstructions. A good all-purpose outfit is a spinning or spin-casting rod of medium or heavy weight, 5½ to 7 feet long, with a good-sized reel filled with lines testing from 8 to 20 pounds. The lighter lines are best for light lures, small fish, and open waters and for use with spinning rods. The heavier lines can be used for heavy lures, big fish, and snag-filled waters. Heavier lines are also used with the closed-face spin-casting reels.

For the utmost in thrills, try a fly rod, fly reel, and weight-forward fly line. The type of rod used for black bass, steelhead, or Atlantic salmon is fine. Streamer and bucktail flies are the best lures to use with a fly rod, although at times big popping bass bugs or minnow-type bugs also work when pike are hitting on the surface.

Lures used with casting rods or spinning rods include surface plugs, underwater plugs, spoons, and spinners. Spoons in silver, chrome, gold, nickel, and copper, as well as those with red-and-white finishes, are favored. Large spinners with feathers or bucktail, weighted spinners, and spinner baits can also be used. Most of the lures above can also be used for trolling. Another good trolling combination is a June-bug spinner with a minnow impaled on a tandem or double hook.

Pike will also take various natural baits such as frogs, minnows, chubs, alewives, suckers, yellow perch, whitefish, ciscoes, and other small fish.

Whether you use artificial lures or natural baits, it is important to have a wire leader or a heavy forty- or fifty-pound monofilament leader on the end of the line. For casting, this leader can be as short as ten or twelve inches, but for trolling, it should measure two or three feet. Pike, like muskies, have sharp teeth, which often sever an ordinary fishing line or light leader.

The top months for catching pike in most waters are May, June, September, and October. Most pike are caught during the daytime, but in some waters there is good fishing for them at night. Stormy, dark, rainy days are on the average more productive than bright, sunny ones.

The early spring is a good time to go pike fishing because at this time the fish are spawning in shallow water (from two to fifteen feet deep) near shore. Even before ice-out, pike will prepare to spawn by entering streams, shallow bays, sloughs, weedy coves, and marshes. When feeding or hiding in shallow water, pike love to lie in or near weedbeds, around stumps, lily pads, sunken trees, logs, rocks, and other cover. In lakes, look for them around the marshy coves, weeds, reeds, points of land, submerged islands, sandbars, rockbars, or gravel bars, and where creeks and rivers enter the lake. In rivers, they are found in the deeper pools, eddies, quieter backwaters, pockets of slack water, below falls or rapids, and on the downstream side of stumps, driftwood, logjams, rocks, and boulders. Pike prefer sluggish rivers and the slower-moving sections of fast rivers rather than strong, fast currents.

When summer comes, pike, especially the big ones, move into deeper waters (from twenty to fifty feet deep), where they remain for most of the day, returning to shallow waters from dusk to daybreak. (Small pike, on the other hand, remain in shallow waters throughout the summer months.) Pike seek out deeper waters during the summer not only to escape the heat, but also to feed on alewives, ciscoes, whitefish, or tullibees, which also move into deeper water at this time. In these deeper waters, pike will usually be found over or along some kind of structure or breakline, over submerged islands or humps, and off a long point or dropoff. Though the summer is a slow time for pike fishing, you can still catch good-sized pike by fishing deep or by going up to the colder lakes in our northern states and in Canada.

In the fall, pike return to their spring habitats in shallow waters. It is in the period immediately following Labor Day that the best pike fishing of the year takes place in most waters.

Not too long ago it was believed that pike were mostly solitary fish, spending much of their time in one spot. But this has been disproved in recent years when it was found that pike often move great distances in search of food. In the spring when spawning they will often gather in large numbers (up to two hundred or three hundred) in a bay or cove, and big catches can then be made in a small area. Later on, even when they move into deeper water, pike may travel in small schools or groups, which often move from deep water to shallow water to feed. These movements usually occur early in the morning or late afternoon and evening on bright days. On overcast or rainy days they will occur during the middle of the day.

It is often easy to catch pike, even big ones, in northern wilderness waters where they are plentiful and unsophisticated and where there is competition for food. In some of these waters in Canada anglers fishing in a single cove or bay have caught fifty to a hundred pike in one day! But in the more heavily fished lakes near the larger population centers pike soon learn to avoid most lures and even baits. Then you have to locate the fish and know how to work your lures or present the bait to get strikes. You will also have to spend plenty of time casting or trolling to land a big pike or two.

One of the best methods is to cast a spoon from an anchored or drifting boat outside weedbeds or lily pads or toward logs, driftwood, sunken trees, and other pike hangouts. In shallow water you can cast the spoon out and start reeling it back fast as soon as it hits the water. Make it skitter and travel on top for several feet. Then let it sink and flutter down. When fishing over a weedbed, cast your spoon out, let it sink, and then retrieve it just fast enough to clear the weeds. In somewhat deeper water outside the edges of the weedbeds and lily pads or along dropoffs you can let your spoon sink to the bottom. Wait a few seconds and quickly lift your rod tip high so that the spoon jumps off the bottom. Then let it settle back and repeat. Since pike will often hit a spoon that is sinking and fluttering toward the bottom, you have to watch your line carefully to detect a hit and set the hook. You can also catch pike in deep water by letting the spoon down to the bottom and then jigging it up and down.

Pike can also be caught on large weighted spinners, spinner-bucktails and on spinner baits. Spinner baits can be retrieved on the surface fast so that they buzz and sputter and create a commotion. Use a tandem or double-bladed spinner bait and cast it right into the thick weeds. You can also retrieve the spinner bait just below the surface or even deeper.

Great sport can be had with pike in shallow water when they are in the mood to hit surface plugs. Then you can use poppers, chuggers, swimmers, and crippled minnows, working them on top so that they kick up a splash and create a turbulence. Pike will hit such top-water plugs hard with a big splash, but often fail to get hooked. Nonetheless, it is exciting fishing and can provide a lot of action, especially toward evening when the water is calm and flat.

Instead of using spinning or bait-casting tackle, try using a fly rod with a big streamer up

Red-and-white Dardevle spoon for pike.

to 5 or 6 inches long. White, yellow, or combinations of red or blue and Mylar strips are productive flies to use. The big bass bugs or deer-hair bugs with thick bodies and Nos. 5/0 or 6/0 long-shanked hooks are also effective. When using bugs or poppers, cast one out and let it lie there a few seconds, twitch it to make it quiver, then give it a hard, sudden pop and retrieve it fast for a few feet. A stop-and-go action or erratic retrieve with a variety of speeds works best with the bugs.

When pike are in deep water use a bucktail or marabou jig in the ⅜-to-1-ounce size and add a strip of pork rind or a plastic worm to the hook. An even better combination is a jig and a minnow. Small suckers, shiners, alewives, chubs, and smelt from 3 to 6 inches can also be used on the hook. In the spring you can fish this minnow-jig along the edges of weedbeds in water from 6 to 18 feet deep. Work the jig pretty fast in long sweeps, letting it drop back toward the bottom at regular intervals. Later on, in the summer when pike are in deeper water, you can drift in a boat or backtroll very slowly, letting the jig and minnow sink to the bottom. Then raise it off the bottom about 3 or 4 feet in a series of quick, short jerks, let it drop back toward the bottom, and repeat the series of jigging motions. Most strikes will come as the jig and minnow are sinking, so you have to keep a tight line while the jig is dropping and keep an eye on the line at all times. Any sudden movement, slack, or strange action of the line that occurs is a signal to set the hook hard.

Jig and minnow for pike.

Trolling is a good way to locate and catch pike when casting doesn't produce. You can use the same casting lures mentioned above for trolling. In the spring and fall when pike are in shallow water you can troll close to shore. Early in the morning and evening you can troll over weedbeds. During the middle of the day troll along the edges of the weeds and along dropoffs and points of land. Pike are not too boat-shy and are often attracted by the wash of a propeller, so you can let one or two lines out only thirty to fifty feet behind the boat.

During the summer months when pike are in deeper water from twenty to fifty feet, you can troll with weighted lines, wire lines, or downriggers. Spoons, deep-running underwater plugs, spoonplugs, spinners and crankbaits can be trolled so that they travel close to the bottom. Here fast trolling will often produce more strikes than slower speeds.

Natural baits will also catch pike, especially during the hot summer months in deep water. Frogs can be used in the morning and evening in shallow water near shore and cast around weeds and lily pads. Minnows and suckers from four to eight inches long also make a good bait. These can be hooked through the back and allowed to swim around under a float in shallow water. In deeper water use a sinker to take the minnow down to the bottom. Minnows can also be hooked through the lips, cast out, and then reeled in slowly.

Pike will also bite well during the winter months and can be caught in many lakes and rivers where there is some open water near shore. Late winter when pike are schooling up at the mouths of rivers prior to spawning is usually best. Pike can also be caught through the ice during the winter months. Here live minnows make the best bait, but dead minnows can also be used. Lower the latter to the bottom and slowly give them some movement up and down to attract pike.

A pike usually smashes a lure hard and often hooks itself, but it's a good idea to set the hook with the rod to make sure. A big pike, like a musky, has tough jaws, and large or dull hooks require force to set them properly.

On light tackle pike will put up a good fight, with the smaller fish, up to ten or twelve pounds, often jumping out of the water. These smaller fish are also faster and more active. Larger pike are slower and do most of their battling below the surface. Pike also have the habit of allowing themselves to be brought up to the boat without too much fuss—then suddenly they go into a frenzy, leaping or thrashing around on top or making a short run. This will often take the angler by surprise, and the sudden strain may break the line or straighten a hook.

Pike should be played until they give up completely and turn over on their side before an at-

Pike put up a good fight, often splashing around on top; big ones especially can give you a lot of trouble on light tackle. (Ontario Ministry of Industry & Tourism Photo)

The biggest pike are caught in Canadian waters. This slim beauty was taken in Mistassini Park, Quebec. (Government of Quebec Tourist Branch Photo)

tempt is made to land them. A large, wide-mouthed net can be used for the smaller fish. The larger fish can be gaffed through the lower jaw. Experienced anglers and guides sometimes grab the pike in the gills or by placing a thumb and forefinger into the eye sockets. But this shouldn't be done with fish you plan to release.

It's also a good idea to have a billy or club handy so you can bop the pike on the head to stun him and stop him from thrashing around in the boat or on shore. A pair of long-nosed pliers are also good for removing the hooks from a pike's mouth.

The world-record pike caught on rod and reel is a forty-six-pound, two-ounce fish caught in the Sacandaga Reservoir, New York, by Peter Dubuc on September 15, 1940. In Canada, where pike from thirty to forty-two pounds have been caught, fish in the twenty-pound class are fairly common. Some big ones have also been caught in Alaska. Even larger pike, some going over fifty pounds, have been reported in European waters, especially Ireland. They are believed to grow up to sixty or perhaps seventy pounds.

Although pike are somewhat bony, they make good eating if you fillet the smaller ones and fry them. They can also be baked or smoked.

The best pike fishing is found in Canada, especially in Manitoba, Saskatchewan, and Ontario. In Ontario, Lake Nipissing, Lac Seul, Eagle Lake, Lake Abitibi, Lake of the Woods, Lake Huron, and Nipigon River are all productive. In Saskatchewan, Lake Athabasca, Rein-deer Lake, Cree Lake, Black Lake, Middle Lake, and the Fond du Lac River and Churchill River have some big pike. In Manitoba, the Little Churchill River, God's Lake, Island Lake, and such lakes as South Knife, Nueltin, Tadoule, Nejanilini, Kississing, and Reed can be fished. Of course, there are hundreds of other lakes and rivers in Canada that contain pike.

In the United States, you'll find some good pike waters in Michigan's Lake Superior, St. Clair River, Diamond Lake, and Paw Paw Lake. In Wisconsin, you can fish the Mississippi River, Grinstone Lake, Big Twin Lake, Forest Lake, Couderay Lake, and Megontonga Lake. Minnesota's pike waters are Minnetonka, Gull, and Pelican lakes. In Nebraska, pike were originally found in the Missouri, Niobrara, Loup, Elkhorn, and Platte rivers, but have also been stocked in many reservoirs such as Lewis and Clark. In North Dakota you can try Lake Metigoshe, Lake Darling, Garrison Reservoir, and Oahe Reservoir. Oahe Reservoir extends into South Dakota, where you can also fish for pike in Randall Reservoir, Lake Sharpe, and Lake Francis Case. In New York State, pike are found in the Thousand Islands area, St. Lawrence River, Lake Oneida, Seneca Lake, Finger Lakes, and Sacandaga Reservoir. In recent years pike have also been stocked in many other states throughout the country as far south as New Mexico, Arizona, and Texas. They acclimate easily and grow faster in the warmer waters. In Alaska pike are plentiful in many lakes and rivers in the heart of the state.

Chapter 14

PICKEREL

On the days when black bass aren't hitting, many anglers in our eastern states settle for pickerel. This smallest member of the pike family fills a niche somewhere between the black basses and the panfishes. He's not quite as desirable as the black bass, yet he's bigger and more of a true game fish than most of the panfishes. But to a surprising number of anglers the pickerel is more than just a "fill in" fish. Thousands of anglers go fishing for pickerel on purpose throughout the year. In New Jersey, when a vote was taken to determine the most popular fish in the state, the pickerel came out ahead, ranking high with still fishermen, fly fishermen, spin casters, and bait casters. Yet in many other states, especially in Maine, the pickerel is an underrated fish.

But in recent years the pickerel's fortunes have picked up considerably as more and more anglers turn to it for fun and sport. One reason for this development is that the pickerel is able to withstand a wide range of water temperatures. He's found in warm, sluggish streams and ponds and in the colder lakes and rivers. So if you live in one of the eastern states you'll probably find a pickerel pond, lake, or river nearby that you can fish. And the pickerel is a willing striker—almost always ready to hit a lure or take a bait.

There are actually three species of pickerels found in the United States: the chain pickerel, the redfin or barred pickerel, and the grass or mud pickerel. As far as anglers are concerned the chain pickerel is the only worthwhile species because the redfin and grass pickerels rarely grow over twelve inches in length.

The chain pickerel has many names, such as the banded pickerel, common pickerel, eastern pickerel, reticulated pickerel, eastern pike, grass pike, green pike, chain pike, jack, jackfish, swamp jack, and snake.

Once you've seen a few pickerel you can't mistake them for young muskies or pike. They have dark-green or brownish-green backs shading into lighter green and yellow on the sides. The belly is white, and chainlike dark markings cover the sides of the fish from the gill cover to the tail.

The pickerel is found in Canada in Nova Scotia, New Brunswick, and southeastern Quebec. In the United States its range extends from Maine south to Florida and Alabama and west to the Mississippi Valley, Texas, Missouri, and the Tennessee River system. However, pickerel have been introduced widely and are now found in at least thirty-six states.

Pickerel can be caught with a variety of tackle. Cane or glass poles are used for fishing with minnows or other baits or for skittering a

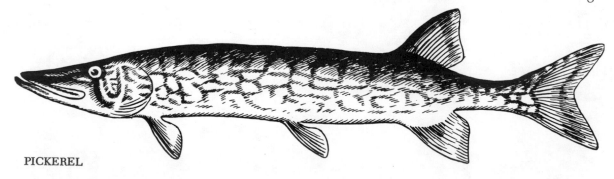

PICKEREL

Minnow on double hook and spinner for pickerel.

lure or bait on top of the water among lily pads and weeds. Bait-casting and spin-casting rods can also be used for casting or trolling. Many anglers, however, are turning to fly rods both for bait fishing or fly fishing, since they find that this light tackle provides the most fun and sport. However, the most popular pickerel outfit these days is a light spinning rod with 4-to-8-pound-test line. A somewhat heavier spinning rod can be used with the 8-pound-test line when fishing in heavy weeds.

Small spoons in red-and-white, silver, chrome, gold, brass, or copper finishes are old-time favorite lures that are still effective. Weedless spoons are best for casting into heavy growth or open pockets and holes among the weeds. The various types of weighted spinners with treble hooks and hair or feathers on them are also productive, as are the newer spinner baits in the smaller sizes. Unweighted spinners can be used with worms, minnows, or pork rind on the hook for trolling. The smaller surface plugs such as the poppers, swimmers, gurglers, and crippled minnows will all catch pickerel. So will the smaller silver or gold minnow-type underwater plugs such as the Rapala and Rebel. The shorter plastic worms, grubs, or curly tails on a weedless hook can also be used for pickerel. Jigs with bucktail, feather, or plastic tails have proven effective. Fly-rod anglers can select from a number of streamers and bucktails, including the Mickey Finn and White or Yellow Marabou. Those with Mylar strips or tinsel bodies are best. Bass bugs, hair frogs, and other fly-rod bugs are also effective.

The top natural bait is a minnow from about 2½ to 3½ inches long. This can be a small sucker, chub, shiner, dace, or other minnow or small fish. In coastal tidal waters or brackish waters the salt-water killifish often makes a good bait. Big pickerel will take small frogs, earthworms, or nightcrawlers, especially if they are given some motion in the water.

Pickerel will start biting early in the year and continue to do so well into the fall. The top months are usually April, May, June, September, and October. But in many cold, northern lakes there is often good fishing during the summer months too. Winter fishing through the ice is excellent in many lakes in our northern and New England states. Actually, the pickerel is really a year-round fish in most waters and can be caught in warm and cold weather.

In the spring and fall you can usually catch pickerel throughout the day. But during the summer months on bright, sunny days, the early morning or late afternoon and evening are best. However, if the day is overcast, cloudy, or rainy, you can often have good fishing during the middle of the day even in the summer. Windy days are particularly good for fishing with live bait or underwater lures. But for top-water plugs or bass bugs, the calm water toward evening provides faster action.

Pickerel usually prefer shallow, quieter waters and the heavily weeded areas of lakes and rivers. Look for the shallow bays and coves with heavy growth of reeds, lily pads, hyacinths, and any other vegetation. Look also for logs, stumps, sunken trees, rocks, boulders, brush, and any other cover and obstructions. Pickerel prefer to lie alone in such cover waiting to ambush a minnow, small fish, or frog. They will often come into extremely shallow water a few inches deep, with their dorsal fins protruding above the surface. However, when the water warms or cools too much, pickerel will often move out into the deeper holes, channels, and underwater weedbeds in water from eight to twelve feet deep.

In rivers you'll find pickerel in quieter, slower pools, eddies, backwaters, and shallow coves. Small, sluggish winding streams, canals, and rivers attract them more than fast rivers. There is good fishing for pickerel in some of the tidal rivers and estuaries along the Atlantic Coast. Here they will usually be found in the brackish and fresh water with weeds, reeds, or other vegetation. In some of these rivers fishing is best when the tide is high, while in others low tides are more productive.

Thousands of pickerel are caught by still fishing with a cane pole, a bobber or float, and a minnow on the hook. But you'll have more fun and sport if you use a light spinning rod or fly rod when fishing with minnows. Minnows can

Pickerel will hit most of the lures used for black bass, but somewhat smaller lures are best.
(Florida Game & Fresh Water Fish Commission Photo)

be hooked through the back or lips with a No. 1 or 1/0 hook. You can cast the minnow into likely spots and allow it to remain there a few minutes. Usually, a pickerel will swim over soon after the bait is cast and grab it. If not, wait a while, then reel in and cast to a new spot. Or you can drift along the edges of lily pads or weeds or along the shoreline, letting your minnow swim around behind the boat about thirty or forty feet away. In still fishing with minnows it is important to give the pickerel plenty of time to swallow the bait. They usually grab the minnow crosswise in their mouths, swim away a short distance, and then stop to swallow it. When they start moving once more, set the hook.

You can also use a minnow on a weedless hook and cast it into thick cover such as pads or weeds, then reel it back slowly on top, letting it sink down a short distance in open spots and pockets. The same thing can be done with a small frog on a weedless hook.

Skittering was a popular and effective way to take pickerel years ago. It is still used by some anglers and is a deadly method if practiced cor-

rectly. A long cane or glass pole about fourteen or sixteen feet long is used, and on the end of the line a minnow, frog, strip of pork rind, or the belly and two fins of a yellow perch or sunfish are impaled on a hook. This is flipped out and skittered or jerked along the suface in short spurts. It is most effective in the open pockets among lily pads, weedbeds, reeds, and around stumps and logs.

Pickerel will also hit worms, but some movement should be imparted to them by sinking or retrieving them in short jerks. A still worm doesn't interest pickerel, but if the bait is moving they will often take it.

Casting lures such as small spoons, spinners, plastic worms, and surface and underwater plugs can be very effective for pickerel, which will also hit a surface popper, swimmer, crippled minnow, or other plug that makes a commotion on top. Pickerel will streak after such a plug and hit it hard. Underwater plugs that travel just below the surface also work well. And, of course, they'll hit spoons and spinners as often as any other lures. Along weed shores, cast into any

Many big pickerel are caught through the ice during the winter months in our northern states. (Pennsylvania Fish Commission Photo)

narrow openings or pockets and coves that you see; also next to logs, stumps, and rocks. From shore or from a boat positioned next to the weeds or a bank, cast your lure so that it travels parallel to the shoreline.

Pickerel are usually scattered along a shoreline, so it is best to walk along shore and try different spots. If you are in a boat, use oars or an electric motor and move along the shore casting into likely spots. In very shallow water don't get too close but make a long cast well beyond the fish, and reel in the lure a few feet in front of it. Pickerel are very skittish in shallow water, and a big commotion or movement or the sight of a man or boat will frighten them, causing them to leave the shallow water and head for deeper water.

Pickerel will hit a fast-moving lure but will often miss it, so a somewhat slower retrieve is better for hooking more fish. A lure with plenty of movement and an erratic stop-and-go action will bring more strikes and hook more fish than a fast, steady retrieve. Pickerel will often follow a lure for a long distance, then suddenly decide to strike just as the lure leaves the water.

Fly-rod anglers can catch pickerel on bright streamers, bucktails, or bass bugs. The first two should be worked in long, fast strips or pulls, while poppers or bass bugs can be worked on top with plenty of splash and commotion to attract pickerel from a distance.

Trolling also accounts for many pickerel during the summer months or cold months when they are in open, deep water. But you can also troll along a shoreline where the water drops off sharply and along edges of lily pads, weeds, or other vegetation. Trolling over submerged weedbeds or along the edges of such weeds is another alternative. Some of the biggest pickerel are caught by trolling this way in deeper water. Spinners, spoons, or underwater plugs can be used for trolling. Or you can use a spinner and worm or minnow combination. In shallow water near shore let out plenty of line while trolling and have the lure travel just below the surface. In deeper water you can let the lure travel a few feet down and even along the bottom.

Winter fishing through the ice, popular with many fishermen on many lakes and ponds, accounts for more and bigger pickerel than are often taken during the summer months. Most anglers use tip-ups and wait for a bite in a shanty, behind a windbreak, or around a fire on shore. But you can also use a short, stiff rod to lower the bait into the hole. Live minnows make the best bait, but pickerel will also hit spoons, spinners, and jigs worked up and down in short jerks. Though the best fishing usually takes place over submerged weedbeds not too far from shore, it pays to drill several holes in different spots until you locate the fish.

A pickerel on the end of a line will put up a good fight if given a chance on light tackle. Sometimes it will come in with little resistance, but usually when the fish sees the boat it will suddenly break loose with a series of wild leaps, twists, and surface acrobatics that will surprise and delight the angler. But since a pickerel doesn't have too much endurance, it soon quits and can be netted. The hook tears out of its tender mouth easily, so don't horse the fish or try to lift it out of the water.

Most of the pickerel caught will run from about one to three pounds in weight. In some waters they may reach five or six pounds, but such big ones are not caught often. Several pickerel over nine pounds have been recorded; the present rod-and-reel record fish, going nine pounds, six ounces, was caught in 1961 by Baxley McQuaig, Jr., in Georgia.

Pickerel have a sweet, white, tasty meat but are quite bony. They should be cleaned and scaled soon after being caught or the flesh gets soft. The big ones can be baked or cut into steaks or fillets and fried. Smaller ones can be split open and fried.

If you live in one of the states where pickerel are found you'll probably know of or can locate waters containing these fish near your home. They are especially plentiful in New England, New York, New Jersey, Pennsylvania, Delaware, Maryland, Virginia, North Carolina, Georgia, and Florida.

Chapter 15

WALLEYE

In some northern states the walleye is the most popular of game fish, primarily because it reaches a good size and makes delicious eating. In addition it is often easier to catch than trout, bass, pike, or muskies. But don't get the idea that walleye fishing is simple, merely a matter of dropping your bait in the water or casting out your lure and just reeling it back. Walleyes are often difficult to locate at certain times of the year. And you have to present the bait or lure at the right level and give it the right action to get strikes.

Walleyes are known by a variety of names, including pike-perch, yellow pike, jack salmon, golden pike, yellow pickerel, Susquehanna salmon, opal eye, pickerel, and dore. (The last two names are used in Canada.) There is also a subspecies of walleye known as the blue pike, blue walleye, and blue pickerel found mostly in Lake Ontario and Lake Erie. Another fish, called the sauger (or sand pike or gray pike), is smaller than the walleye, though the two resemble each other considerably.

The true walleye varies in color depending on where it is found, but it is usually a dark olive or brassy color, mottled with yellow. The fins may be yellowish or pinkish, with a dark spot at the rear of the front dorsal fin. The walleye has a large mouth and strong canine teeth. The eye is large, whitish, and glassy.

Walleyes are found from Canada southward and eastward to North Carolina, Georgia, Alabama, Arkansas, and Tennessee. They are especially plentiful throughout the Great Lakes region, in Wisconsin, Minnesota, and Michigan, and in many Canadian waters.

You don't need any special tackle to catch walleyes. Almost any bait-casting, spin-casting, or spinning outfit suitable for black bass will do for walleyes. Light tackle will provide the most sport and fun, and only when fishing in certain waters and for extremely big walleyes do you need somewhat heavier tackle. Fly rods can be used when the fish are in shallow water near shore.

Not too long ago most walleyes were caught on spinners such as the June-bug type with a double hook and a minnow, worm, or lamprey eel behind it. Although these are still used to some extent, nowadays such lures as jigs, weighted spinners, spoons, and deep-running or sinking underwater plugs have become more

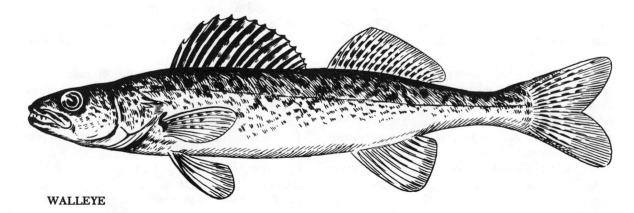

WALLEYE

popular. Walleyes will also take plastic worms or grubs, but these are usually used with jig heads or weights to get them down deep enough.

Natural baits such as minnows and chubs from three to six inches long can also be fished alive or dead behind a spinner or on a jig. Big nightcrawlers were often used behind a spinner, but now they are fished along the bottom with a sliding sinker rig for walleyes. Leeches, fished deep on a bottom rig, have also become popular in recent years. Walleyes will also take soft-shelled crayfish, lamprey eels, and frogs.

The walleye is mostly a cold-water fish, active during the spring, fall, and winter months. In southern waters such as those of Kentucky and Tennessee, the fish move up rivers to spawn as early as February, and good fishing continues into March. Farther north, the spawning run takes place in April and May. Good fishing in most areas generally takes place during May, June, September, October, and November. But walleyes can also be caught during the summer months, especially in the colder northern lakes and farther north in Canada. There is often good fishing for walleyes through the ice in many of our northern lakes.

In the spring and fall you can catch walleyes during most of the day. But during the summer months the early-morning, late-afternoon, evening, and night hours are best. In fact, walleyes do a lot of feeding at night from spring to fall, and you stand a good chance of catching them in the dark. If you fish during the day in summer, do so on cloudy, rainy, dark days rather than on bright, sunny ones. And windy days are usually better than flat, calm, windless days. Walleyes are extremely sensitive to light, and the brighter the sun and day, the deeper they go.

Locating walleyes may be easy and simple at times or very difficult depending on the area, season, weather, water depth, and time of day. Walleyes are also great wanderers, moving about in schools to different sections of a lake or river. In the spring when the walleyes move up rivers to spawn they are concentrated in smaller areas and are easier to locate. They tend to move into shallow water closer to shore during the fall months and at night. In Canada, walleye fishing is often good in rivers and running water connecting lakes during the entire season from spring to fall.

In rivers, look for walleyes below dams, falls, rapids or riffles, around rocks, boulders, and in the quieter pools and eddies. The tailwaters below dams and impoundments are especially productive. Toward evening and at night they may move into shallow water around rock ledges, sandbars, gravel bars, shoals, points of land, and mouths of tributary streams. Look for concentrations of minnows in the late afternoon and evening in shallow water or coves. Walleyes often come in to feed on them, and great sport can be had.

In lakes, fish around rocky points, dropoffs, rockbars, gravel bars, sandbars, ledges, reefs, mud flats, and deep water bordering rocky shores or cliffs. The mouths of streams or rivers entering a lake are often hot spots. Underwater islands and humps or shoals in deep water are good structure to fish during the summer months. Rocky bottoms are especially productive if there is deep water around them. But in lakes that are fairly shallow you'll often find walleyes spending much of the season feeding over weedbeds in water from five to ten feet deep.

As a general rule, fish the shallow inshore waters early in the morning around daybreak, in the evening, at dusk, and during the night. Fish the deeper waters in the middle of the day. Though walleyes are usually found in water from three to twenty feet deep, in some lakes, especially during the summer, they may be found in depths from twenty to sixty feet. In such deep water they are often found in schools several feet off the bottom. A depth finder or a fish finder is a great aid in locating these schools. Otherwise, try various depths until you locate the fish, and continue fishing the rest of the lake at that depth.

A good way to locate walleyes is by slow trolling. The most popular rig for this is a three-way swivel on the line about eighteen inches above a bell or dipsey sinker. To one of the eyes, add a three-foot leader with the lure or hook for the bait at the end of it. The line, of course, is tied to the remaining eye. You can use a spinner and minnow, or a spinner and worm or lamprey eel for such trolling. Spinners, spoons, or underwater plugs are also effective. To reach bottom and keep the rig and lure or bait away from the boat it's a good idea to let out anywhere from 100 to 250 feet of line while trolling very slowly.

Some of the best walleye fishing is found in rivers below dams, rapids, and falls, especially if there is a pool or deep water just below. (Johnson Motors Photo)

Lindy Rig for walleyes.

In recent years anglers have been making great catches of walleyes on the "Lindy Rig." This consists of a curved slip sinker with a hole, slipped on the fishing line, at the end of which is tied a barrel swivel. (The sinker will rest against the swivel.) Then tie a two-foot leader with a small hook on the other eye of the swivel. The hook can be baited with a whole big night-crawler hooked through the head. Or you can hook a leech through the head or a minnow through the lips. The rig is then let down to the bottom from a boat moving backward with a regular small outboard motor or forward with an electric motor. Or you can just drift in a boat if there is a wind or current to move the boat along at a slow but steady pace.

When you use a spinning reel with a Lindy Rig, fish with an open bail, or else have the reel in free spool if you are using a bait-casting reel. Then you can feel the tug on the bait and let the line slide freely through the hole in the sinker by letting out line. When you feel that the walleye has the bait well back in its mouth, set the hook. You have to develop a sense of "feel" to know when the sinker is bouncing bottom or sliding along the bottom. After some experience, you'll be able to tell whether you are over rock, gravel, mud, or sand bottoms.

Most trolling for walleyes is done very slowly, but some anglers have also had good results by trolling fairly fast to very fast with lures that bump bottom. The crankbaits are good for this and so are the metal "Spoonplugs." Trolling, of course, is done over the usual walleye structure or hangouts. Extra rod action every half minute or so will bring more strikes. Raise the rod tip fast, then drop it back.

Once you locate a school of walleyes by troll-ing or drifting in water that isn't too deep, you can drop anchor and cast to them. One of the deadliest lures you can use for such casting is a lead-head jig, in white, yellow, brown, or black, and dressed with hair or feathers. Or you can use one of those plastic tail or grub jigs. Jigs with hair or feathers are more effective if you add a strip of pork rind to the hook. Still other anglers prefer a plain jig head and add a minnow to the hook.

Any jig you use should be fished deep and slow along the bottom. From a boat you can cast out over structure and let the jig sink and settle on the bottom. Walleyes will often pick up a jig with a minnow or plastic tail when it is lying still on the bottom. After hitting bottom wait a few seconds and then start reeling in slowly in a series of short jerks, bouncing bottom every so often to know that you are deep enough. When the jig is directly under the boat, work it up and down, lifting and lowering the rod tip so that it has some action. You have to try to detect a bite and watch the line closely when using jigs, espe-cially in deep water. Walleyes usually hit the lure lightly so that it is hard to notice or feel when it has been taken.

When fishing a river you'll find the jig one of the best lures for getting down into the holes, pockets, or channels where walleyes are lying. The jig can be cast upstream and across to get down deep enough and then allowed to swing from the fast current into the slower spots and eddies. The strike usually comes as the jig reaches the hole or spot where the walleye is waiting. Spoons and weighted spinners can be fished in the same manner by letting them sink deep to the bottom and then retrieving them slowly along the bottom.

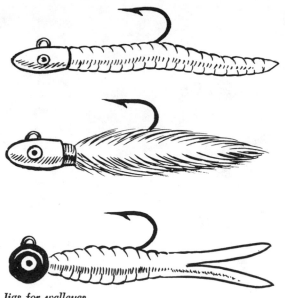

Jigs for walleyes.

Walleyes have also been known to hit surface plugs such as the Jitterbug and Hula Popper in certain waters at certain times. This usually happens around daybreak, at dusk, or at night when walleyes come into shallow water to feed on minnows. But most of the time you'll do better with deep-running or sinking plugs of the minnow type that can be reeled or worked right along the bottom.

Many walleyes are also caught by still fishing with live minnows. In fast rivers you can use a bottom rig with sinker and a two-foot leader with hook to hold the minnow. The rig with minnow can be cast into the river and allowed to drift down with the current into pools, holes, and deep spots. When it hits bottom let it rest for a few minutes, then lift the rod tip and let it drift to a new spot farther downstream. Let it rest again in the new location, before repeating the procedure. By doing this you cover more area and keep the bait moving. You can do the same in a lake, only here, with no current to activate or move the bait and rig, you have to cast out as far as you can. Reel in the slack and let the rig and minnow lie there a minute or so. Then lift the rod tip high and drop it back again as you reel in the slack. Keep doing this every minute or so until the rig is under the boat.

In a lake you can also still fish from a boat by letting the minnow down to the bottom. If the water is fairly shallow you can just add a split

shot or two to get the minnow down deep enough. In deeper water you can use a bottom rig with a light sinker to get it down to the bottom. The minnow should be raised up and down every so often to activate it and prevent if from hiding in the weeds.

A big nightcrawler can also be fished in a river by hooking it through the head once and then turning the hook around and burying the barb and point in the body of the worm. This is used on light spinning tackle with no weight unless the current is very fast, in which case you can add a split shot or two above the hook. The worm is cast out and allowed to sink all the way to the bottom where it can drift and roll over the rocks and into holes and crevices. You should try to feel it bumping bottom all the time. When walleyes grab and take the whole worm (as they do most of the time, you can set the hook immediatcly. At times, however, they'll be in a cautious or playful mood, and then you have to let them run and take line before setting the hook.

Walleyes are spooky fish in shallow water during the day or at night. Even in deep water avoid all unnecessary noise, vibrations, or splashing. Troll with an electric motor, drift quietly, or anchor for best results. When you fish at night, avoid all lights shining on the water. And when you fish in shallow water, troll with long lines. Big walleyes in schools tend to leave when a fish is hooked and runs around. Then it's usually a good idea to move on to a new spot.

Walleyes can be caught through the ice in many northern lakes in January, February, and early March. Drill several holes over rocks, sandbars, or reefs and shoals, and fish them with tip-ups. Live minnows from three to five inches long and hooked through the lips or the back make the best bait. Instead of one hook you can try fishing with two hooks at different levels. While fishing close to the bottom is usually best, there are times when the walleyes will be found suspended at a higher level.

Once you hook a walleye on a lure or bait, you'll have some sport and action but don't expect the speed and flash of a trout or bass. Walleyes don't jump or make long or fast runs, nor do they have much endurance. But a good-sized fish on light tackle can provide a good fight, especially if hooked in a fast-moving river.

A wide-mouthed net is best for boating a big

Canada produces some big walleyes, like this specimen caught in the Albany River in Ontario. But no matter what the size, walleyes make good eating. (Ontario Ministry of Industry & Tourism Photo)

walleye. Watch out for their sharp teeth when removing lures or hooks from their mouths.

Most of the walleyes that are caught will range from two to ten pounds, and any fish over that size is considered a big one. However, in some areas and during certain seasons, big walleyes are commonly taken. Rivers in Kentucky and Tennessee commonly yield fish from eight to fifteen pounds during the spawning run. Fish over twenty pounds in weight have been caught from time to time in these southern waters. The world record on rod and reel is a twenty-five pound walleye caught in Old Hickory Lake, Tennessee, by Mabry Harper.

No matter what their size, most anglers agree that the walleye is one of the best fresh-water fish for the table. They have a firm, sweet, tasty flesh that can be fried, baked, broiled, or boiled.

The walleye is widely distributed in North America, but some spots are more outstanding than others for the size or number of fish caught. You can't beat Canada, where they are found from Lake Athabasca across Alberta and Saskatchewan, down into the Hudson Bay basin, through the Great Lakes drainage basin, and over into Quebec, Ontario, and Labrador.

In the United States they are especially plentiful in Wisconsin, where such waters as Lake Winnebago, Red Cedar River, Wapogasset Lake, Balsam Lake, Half Moon Lake, Yellow River, St. Croix Lake, Eau Claire Lakes, Whitefish Lake, and Lac Court Oreilles are fished. In Minnesota they are stocked in over eight hundred lakes, the best of which are Fish Hook Lake, Mille Lacs, and Red lakes. In Michigan, the Menominee, Michigan, and Muskegon rivers are good, as are Gratiot Lake, Lake Bellaire, and Hubbard Lake. In Illinois, the Mississippi River and Kankakee River are noted for walleyes. In Ohio, Lake Erie and rivers such as the Sandusky, Maumee, and Portage contain walleyes as do Pennsylvania's Susquehanna and Delaware rivers. In New York, the St. Lawrence River, Lake Champlain, and the Delaware River (also in New Jersey) have produced many walleyes. In Tennessee, Center Hill Lake, Dale Hollow Lake, Norris Lake, Old Hickory Lake, Watts Bar Lake, and the Tennessee River are popular walleye waters, as are Kentucky's Lake Cumberland, Cumberland River, Rockcastle River, Laurel River, Green River, Kentucky Lake, Rough River Lake, and Nolin Lake.

Naturally, there are many other states and waters that provide walleye fishing. Write to your state fish and game department for a list of lakes or rivers containing walleyes in your area.

Chapter 16

YELLOW PERCH

Next to the sunfishes, the yellow perch is the most popular panfish found in the United States. It lives in many ponds, lakes, and large, slow-moving rivers, and may even descend to brackish water in coastal rivers. Usually abundant in most waters, the yellow perch travels in large schools and is a willing biter. All this makes the yellow perch popular with many fresh-water anglers. You'll be convinced of this if you ever go down to a lake or river in the early spring and see the thousands of yellow-perch fishermen gathered where the perch are running. Anglers of all ages and both sexes line the shore, piers, bulkheads, jetties, bridges, and shores of small creeks and rivers. Others are out fishing in boats of all kinds, from canoes to big yachts. And all these anglers on shore or in the boats are busy pulling in the yellow perch.

Yellow perch are found in the Hudson Bay drainage of eastern Canada south to Kansas and northern Missouri, Illinois, Indiana, and Penn-sylvania. Along the Atlantic Coast they range from Nova Scotia to the Carolinas. Yellow perch have also been introduced into many other states in the Midwest and along the Pacific Coast.

The yellow perch has been called the red perch, raccoon perch, ringed perch, zebra perch, lake perch, striped perch, and convict. It is easily identified by its six to eight broad, dark stripes over a yellow body. The back is an olive or drab-green color. The ventral and anal fins are a reddish orange.

You can catch yellow perch on most of the tackle used for other panfish, such as the cane or glass pole, spinning or spin-casting rod and reel, bait-casting rod and reel, and the fly rod. The cane pole is best for fishing from shore when the perch are in shallow water or from fishing from boats in shallow water. The fly rod, too, is used mostly for shore fishing or from boats in fairly shallow water. For deep-water casting or still fishing, a spinning rod and reel or bait-casting

YELLOW PERCH

When yellow perch come into shallow water to spawn in the spring, anglers catch millions of them from shore, piers, docks, and breakwaters. (Michigan Conservation Department Photo)

outfit is more practical. Of course, these bait-casting outfits can also be used when fishing in shallow water. Spinning and spin-casting outfits as well as bait-casting outfits are all good for trolling.

For casting with any of the outfits above you can use weighted spinners, spoons, spinner and worm combinations, spinner and fly combos, jigs, and tiny plugs. Small plastic worms and lures are also effective. Many of these lures can also be used for trolling.

Fly-rod fishermen can use wet flies such as the Silver Doctor, Yellow Sally, Parmachene Belle, Western Bee, McGinty, Red Ibis, Montreal, and Professor. These can be fished alone but are usually more effective behind a tiny spinner. Various nymphs can also be used. And such streamers and bucktails as the Gray Ghost, Mickye Finn, Black-nosed Dace, and White or Yellow Marabou have proven successful in the very small sizes.

However, most anglers seeking yellow perch use natural baits, and among these the live minnow is tops. Small minnows, no bigger then two inches in length, are best, and these should be used on small No. 6 or No. 8 hooks. Millions of perch have also been caught on worms (the smaller garden worms are better than the big nightcrawlers). Other baits include the tail of a small crayfish, beetles, grasshoppers, crickets, grubs, nymphs, and most other land and water insects. You can also use the small grass shrimp that live in bays and tidal creeks near salt water. Two or three of these shrimp on a hook are offered to the perch.

The yellow perch is one of the first fish to bite early in the spring. Soon after ice-out they run up rivers and creeks into shallow bays, along shore, and over hard bottoms, to spawn. This usually occurs during March, April, and early May, depending on the weather, water termperature, and latitude. But perch can be caught throughout the year from spring to late fall, and even in the winter months they are often taken through the ice.

There is really no special time of day to go yellow-perch fishing. You'll catch them all day long in the spring and fall in shallow water near shore. During the summer months when the perch are in deeper water, the fishing may be better early in the morning and in the evening. They will often go on a feeding spree toward dusk and bite right up until dark. Though some are caught at night, perch do not usually bite very well at this time.

In the spring, during the spawning season, yellow perch are often easy to locate, since they come in close to shore into shallow bays or along shorelines and run up rivers and streams. Later on, when they have finished spawning, perch may spread out more and wander about in schools of varying sizes. At this time, you'll find the best fishing in deeper water over underwater weedbeds, rocky bottoms, and sunken islands, along dropoffs and channels, and in the larger coves and bays. In rivers yellow perch are found in the larger, deeper, quieter pools, below dams, waterfalls, around old piers, bridges, and sunken trees, and near pilings and logs.

During the hot summer months a few small yellow perch may be caught in shallow water near shore during the day. But most of the larger ones go into deeper water seeking cooler temperatures and oxygen. The depth will vary with each lake but will usually range from twenty to fifty feet in most lakes. In very deep lakes they may be down as deep as seventy or eighty feet. Yellow perch will also suspend several feet above the bottom, but the best fishing most of the time is usually close to the bottom.

Since yellow perch are school fish, once you locate them you can usually catch them quickly one after another as long as they remain in the area. They tend to move in toward shore in the evening and remain on the bottom all night, then at daybreak they rise off the bottom, gather in schools, and move toward deeper water. Sometimes you can see them in the morning or late afternoon near the surface in large schools. Most of the time, however, you have to try different depths and spots until you find them.

One good way to locate yellow perch is to drift with the wind in a boat, slowly towing a hook baited with a minnow or worm down deep near the bottom. Or you can troll very slowly (from a rowed boat, or one propelled by an electric motor) with a spinner, spoon, or spinner and worm or minnow on the end of the line. When you catch the first perch, drop the anchor, and fish all around the boat.

Still fishing with bait is the most popular way to catch yellow perch. A light, sensitive float or bobber is attached to the line, at the end of which a No. 6 or No. 8 hook can be baited with a tiny minnow, worm, cricket, grasshopper, grub, or nymph. The bobber or float should be high enough on the line so that the bait almost reaches bottom or the top of the weeds. The bait should be lively to attract the perch. It also helps to keep moving the bait up and down or back and forth slowly to catch the attention of the fish. The yellow perch is a great bait stealer, or else it swallows the bait deep, so don't give him too much time when you get the first nibbles. Wait a few seconds and then set the hook.

One of the best baits for big perch is a belly strip cut from the perch itself or from a sunfish or other fish. This should be cut in a triangle about 1½ inches long and ½ inch wide in the front part. The hook is inserted into the widest part by running it into the flesh and out through the skin. Then add a split-shot sinker on the leader above the bait and let it out from a slowly drifting boat. Let out enough line so that the strip of fish moves just above the bottom or the weeds. Twitch the rod tip up and down slightly to make the bait dart and flutter. You'll catch big perch this way if you drift over structure such as edges of weedbeds, over beds of milfoil, through thin spatterdock, along drop-offs, and over submerged trees, stumps, logs, rocks, humps, and islands.

Fish belly strip for yellow perch.

Yellow perch will also hit tiny spoons, spinners, jigs, plastic worms and grubs, and plugs cast to the edges of weedbeds, over sunken weeds, along lily pads, and anywhere else they hang out. When they are down deep let the lure sink almost to the bottom and then reel it in as slowly as possible.

With a fly rod you can use small, wet flies, nymphs, tiny streamers, and bucktails. Cast these out, let them settle just below the surface, and retrieve them slowly in short jerks. If you get no strikes, let the flies sink deeper and work them at that level. If the fish are still deeper you may have to add a split shot or two on the leader to get the flies down. Of course, you can also use a sinking fly line to get them down.

When trolling, you usually have to let out a lot of line and add a clincher sinker to the leader to get the bait or lure deep enough. When yellow perch won't hit the plain lure try adding a thin sliver of pork rind or a worm to one of the hooks on the lure or fly. The main thing to remember when using lures for yellow perch is that they are slow, lazy, and cannot catch a fast-moving lure. So work the lure as slowly as you can with short jerks, twitches, and alternate pauses to give the perch time to catch and grab it.

Yellow perch are great winter fish, and many are caught by fishing through the ice. On some lakes catches of fifty to two hundred perch by a single fisherman in one day are common. For ice fishing, a short rod or stick from thirty to forty inches long can be used. The line should be a fairly heavy twenty- or twenty-five-pound-test monofilament for easy handling in the cold weather. You can also use a line on a spool attached to a tipup. To the end of the lines attach a No. 6 or No. 8 hook baited with a small live minnow from one to two inches long. Other baits that can be used are goldenrod grubs, mousies, waxworms, nymphs, corn borers, salmon eggs, or even a strip cut from the perch or the eye of a perch.

Yellow perch will also hit tiny ice flies, spoons, jigs, plastic bugs, or grubs fished through the ice. To make these even more effective add a natural bait on the hook. You can also rig two lures on the same line and add a light bell sinker to take them down. With lures, use light two-, three-, or four-pound-test lines on a short jigging rod. Work them up and down in short jerks, letting them sink and flutter.

Locating perch can be easy during the winter if you see anglers out on the ice fishing and catching them. Or you can try the spots where others have already drilled holes, then left to go home. Usually the best fishing will be in water from twenty to fifty feet deep in midwinter, especially on bright, sunny days. On cloudy days and toward evening try fishing closer to shore in shallower water. Perch will often gather over weedbeds or near them, off the ends of sloping underwater points or reefs. Underwater springs, creeks, brooks, and rivers entering a lake are also hot spots. Toward spring perch move closer to shore into shallow water prior to spawning.

The yellow perch is not much of a fighter on

Yellow perch bite readily through the ice in winter; the lake waters of our northern states are particularly productive at this time. (Pennsylvania Fish Commission Photo)

the end of a line. He pulls feebly and slowly and gives up too quickly compared to other panfish and game fish. The big ones reaching 2 or 3 pounds may provide some fun on ultralight spinning tackle or a fly rod. But, unfortunately, in many lakes perch are on the small side rarely going over a pound in weight. In some waters they are so numerous that they never reach more than a few inches in length and a fraction of a pound in weight. The largest yellow perch caught on rod and reel weighed 4 pounds, 3½ ounces and was caught at Bordentown, New Jersey, in May 1865 by Dr. C. C. Abbot.

Even though yellow perch fight poorly, many anglers will spend hours fishing for them be-cause of their eating qualities. The yellow perch, with a white, sweet, flaky flesh, is one of the tastiest fish found in fresh water. They are tough to scale, however, so keep them wet, and clean them as soon as possible.

If you live near the Great Lakes you can go fishing for yellow perch in Lake Michigan, Lake Erie, Lake Ontario, and Lake Huron. They are also common throughout eastern Canada. The New England states, especially Maine, have them in abundance in most lakes, ponds, and in deeper rivers. They are also found along the Atlantic Coast to the Carolinas and have been introduced in many western and Pacific states.

Chapter 17

BLUEGILL

Every country boy who has fished for sunfish has a warm spot in his heart for these small but colorful fishes. Even in later years many an older angler turns to sunfish for a day's sport and fine eating afterward. For the sunfish are obliging little critters, almost always willing to bite. To add to their appeal, they are widely distributed in this country; chances are that most rivers, creeks, lakes, and ponds near your home will contain them. The result is that millions of anglers pursue sunfish avidly; more of them are caught than any of the so-called game fishes.

The large sunfish family includes the black basses, crappies, warmouth, rock bass, and the various species of sunfish—the bluegill, pumpkinseed, redbreast sunfish, redear sunfish, longear sunfish, green sunfish, and spotted sunfish. Most of the information here concerns the bluegill sunfish, which is the largest and most popular. But all the techniques outlined in this chapter can be used to catch the other kinds of sunfish too.

The bluegill sunfish is also called bream (pronounced "brim" down South). Its other names are blackear sunfish, blue bream, blue sunfish, blue Joe, blue-mouthed sunfish, blue perch, copperhead bream, coppernosed bream, coppernosed sunfish, dollardee, polladee, and sun perch.

The bluegill has a blue-green to olive-green back, which becomes lighter on the sides. The breast is orange-yellow or orange-red. The younger specimens usually have vertical bars on the sides, while older and larger bluegills have a dark purplish back, a dull orange breast, and may lack the vertical stripes. It can usually be distinguished from other sunfish by its dark ear flap on the lower end of the gill cover and a dark blotch on the lower end of the second dorsal fin.

Originally native to the Mississippi River region, Great Lakes, and the eastern seaboard, bluegills have been widely introduced and can now be caught in most of our states. They prefer warmer, fertile lakes and ponds rather than the clear, deep, colder waters. They are especially

BLUEGILL

big and plentiful in our southern states with their longer growing seasons. And they do well in farm ponds, where they are commonly stocked with largemouth black bass.

More bluegills are probably caught on cane poles, glass poles, and poles cut from saplings or branches of trees than on any other tackle. The cane or glass pole from ten to twenty feet long is still a popular fishing tool used by many bluegill fishermen, women, and kids from shore and boats. A light monofilament line testing about eight or ten pounds can be tied to the end of the pole, with small thin floats or bobbers slipped on the line. The hook, tied to the end of the line, can be size Nos. 6, 8, or 10. This outfit is usually used with some kind of live or natural bait.

Spinning rods and reels and spin-casting tackle in the lighter weights also make ideal bluegill-fishing outfits. For bait fishing, you can use your regular fresh-water spinning and spin-casting rods and reels. But for casting small lures or very light baits, an ultralight spinning rod and reel with thin lines testing only from about two to four pounds are best.

Many anglers believe that a bluegill should only be caught on a fly rod for the most fun and sport. The shorter, lighter fly rods (7, 7½, or at the most, 8 feet long) are best. The fly reel, either single-action or the automatic type, can be filled with monofilament line testing 6 or 8 pounds for fishing with bait. For casting lures or flies a regular floating fly line is better. You can also use a sinking fly line when bluegills are deep and you want to reach them in a hurry.

Lures used for bluegills include dry flies such as the Wulff flies, bivisibles, the Gray Hackle, Black Gnat, Light Cahill, Adams, and other trout flies in size Nos. 8, 10, 12, or 14. Wet flies such as the Coachman, Black Ant, McGinty, Western Bee, Professor, Cowdung, Brown Hackle, and the Wooly Worms can be used too in size Nos. 8, 10, and 12. Nymphs of various patterns, sizes, and colors also catch many bluegills. So do the tiny streamers and bucktails. When using flies for bluegills choose the larger sizes for big bluegills and the smaller sizes for small fish.

Various small bass bugs and panfish bugs such as the poppers are also very good fly-rod lures for bluegills. Sponge-bodied spiders with long rubber legs in black, white, yellow, tan, gray, and light-green colors have also proven effective.

These can be made to float by squeezing them to remove the water, or they can be made to sink by pressing them underwater until they absorb all they can. Sponge-bodied spiders should be tied on No. 8 or No. 10 hooks for best results.

When it comes to lures, tiny spoons in silver or gold can be used. Small weighted spinners are also good, especially with a treble hook covered with feathers or hair. Tiny jigs weighing from ⅟₆₄ to ⅛ ounce are highly effective, especially those with white or yellow heads and hair or feathers. Tiny jigs with white or yellow plastic grub or worm bodies are popular, as are spinners with a strip of pork rind, a wet fly, or a sponge spider behind them. Tiny plugs not much longer than 2 inches also draw strikes.

Most bluegills, however, are caught on natural baits, the most popular of which is the earthworm. Big nightcrawlers aren't as good as the smaller varieties of worms. Bluegills will also take tiny minnows up to 1½ inches long. Insects such as grasshoppers, crickets, roaches, catalpa worms, mealworms, corn borers, goldenrod grubs, mousies, waxworms, nymphs, and hellgrammites can all be used for bait. Fresh-water shrimp are excellent baits, especially in our southern states. If you run out of bait try a tiny strip of pork rind, a piece of bread or dough, or a tiny strip cut from a bluegill or other fish.

The fastest bluegill fishing takes place in the late spring or early summer, when they are spawning or have just finished guarding their nests. Then they are pugnacious, hungry, and easy to locate. But they also bite most of the summer and into the late fall. You can catch them all day long with bait or sunken lures. For fly fishing, the early-morning, late-afternoon, and evening hours are best. Bluegills will bite at night in some waters, but for the most part they are daytime fish. Big bluegills also tend to bite best when the skies are cloudy and the water murky.

When bluegills are spawning they tend to stay close to shore over their nests, which are circular and light in color and stand out against the rest of the bottom. These nests are usually formed over clay, sand, or gravel bottoms. If you can locate several of these nests or nesting areas you can move from one to the other, catching fish along the way. Most of the nests will be in water from two to six feet deep.

When bluegills are feeding in shallow water

(particularly in the morning, evening, and at night), you'll find them around weedbeds, submerged logs, sunken trees, stumps, brushpiles, rocks, boulders, lily pads, pilings, docks, and under overhanging branches of trees. In rivers look for bluegills in the deeper and quieter pools and coves, backwaters, eddies, below dams and falls, and along bushy banks. They tend to stay close to vegetation such as lily pads, hyacinths, reeds, mossbeds, and similar growth.

During the hot summer days, bluegills go into deeper water. The big ones, especially, will spend most of their time in deep water, as far down as twenty to thirty feet in the middle of the day. Most of them, however, prefer water anywhere from ten to twenty feet along structure. So look for them over bars or sloping points near the deeper water and along dropoffs, over sunken islands, submerged weedbeds, sunken trees, roots, stumps, and rock piles.

Most bluegills are caught by still fishing from shore, bridges, piers, docks, and boats. Here you can fish with or without a float or bobber and drop your live bait into likely spots. A float is

Most youngsters start their fishing careers by catching bluegills or other sunfish. (Pennsylvania Fish Commission Photo)

usually more fun because you can watch it bob up and down, and when it is pulled under, you can set the hook. Use the smallest and lightest float you can get for bluegills. To hold the bait down deeper in the water, add a single, small split-shot sinker between the float and hook on the leader.

One of the best baits you can use for bluegills is a live cricket on a small, light No. 8 or No. 10 wire hook, with a split-shot sinker on the leader above the hook. The cricket can also be fished on a light $\frac{1}{64}$-ounce jig hook. You can make one of these jigs yourself by pinching a split-shot sinker at the eye of a hook. Then impale your cricket on this hook and lower it among lily pads or alongside brush or weeds, sunken trees, or stumps where bluegills hang out.

Some of the larger bluegills are smart and wary and take off when you get too close. For taking these larger fish, a light spinning rod is ideal because you can usually cast your bobber or float and bait, from shore or boat, a good distance. The first splash may chase the bluegills away, but they'll soon return and investigate the bait. It is also a good idea to jerk the bait or move it every so often to keep it from hiding in the weeds and also to attract the fish to the scene.

In deeper water, fish the live baits without a float or bobber, add a split-shot sinker on the leader, cast out the rig, and let the bait sink toward the bottom. When it reaches bottom let it lie there a few minutes, then reel it back slowly along the bottom. Another way to fish baits in deep water is to make up a bottom rig with a light dipsey sinker on the end of the line and a

hook on a short ten-inch dropper tied about a foot above the sinker. This can be used with most natural baits and can be cast out and allowed to lie in one spot for a while. Then reel the rig in slowly a few feet and allow it to rest again. Or you can drift in a boat with the wind and let the rig and bait drag along the bottom slowly.

When bluegills are inclined to take flies or panfish bugs off the surface, a lot of fun can be had by wading in the water along the shoreline or moving in a boat some distance from land. Then you cast small dry flies or tiny panfish bugs into likely spots. Drop the fly or bug close to logs, rocks, stumps, lily pads, or near the shoreline and let it lie there a minute or so. Then twitch it gently so that it moves a few inches. Let it lie a few seconds more, then twitch it once again. Keep doing this until the lure is too far away from where the fish are likely to be. Then lift the fly or bug off the water and cast it to a new spot. Dry flies or small bugs are most effective in the evening and when the water is calm.

During the middle of the day and when the water is ruffled or whenever the fish are feeding below the surface you can use a wet fly, nymph, tiny streamer, or a sponge-bodied spider (see page 118). One of these lures can be tried first without any weight a few inches to a couple of feet below the surface. It should be retrieved very slowly in short jerks. If no results are forthcoming try sinking the lure still deeper. To save time you can add a split-shot sinker to the leader above the lure or right in front of it. A sinking fly line can also be used to get these lures down.

Flies and panfish bugs can also be used for

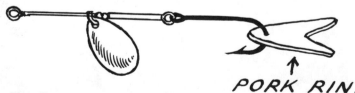

Two spinner rigs for bluegill.

PORK RIND

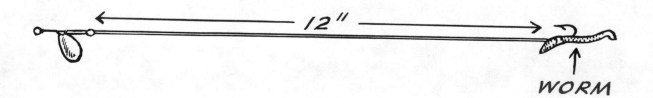

12"

WORM

Kids aren't the only ones who like to fish for bluegills for fun, sport, and food. (South Carolina Wildlife & Marine Resources Department Photo)

bluegills with light spinning or spin-casting tackle or even bait-casting tackle. Here you add a clear plastic float on the end of the line and then tie a dry fly or panfish bug behind the float on a short leader. This six- or eight-pound-test leader can be about twelve or fourteen inches long. Instead of a plastic float you can use any small float or even a small surface plug or weighted bass bug in front of the fly or panfish bug. You can't cast the fly or panfish bug alone with spinning tackle, but with a float or lure up ahead you can cast it a good distance.

When using this combination rig, cast to a spot, let the rig lie there for a minute or so, then give it a short jerk. The float or plug makes a small splash while the fly or panfish bug behind makes a ripple. Then let it lie still again after you jerk or twitch it once more. Keep doing this until a bluegill comes up and grabs the small bug or fly. Sometimes a bass will come up and grab the plug ahead of the smaller lure.

When fishing with lures or combinations such as small spoons, spinners, tiny plugs, jigs, and spinner with flies or baits, cast them out and let them sink to different depths. Work the lures very slowly with regular pauses and short twitches to give the 'gills time to catch and grab the lure.

Bluegills can also be caught during the winter months through the ice. They will take such baits as mealworms, wax worms, maggots, corn borers, goldenrod grubs, and nymphs. Small ice flies or teardrop spoons baited with any of the baits above are also good. These are lowered through the ice and kept moving up and down with gentle jigging motions. Since bluegills move around under the ice, you have to try different spots and depths until you locate them.

They are usually caught in depths from five to thirty feet, and submerged weedbeds attract them. The best fishing usually takes place early in the morning, in the evening, and on dark, overcast days rather than on bright, sunny ones.

A bluegill hooked on light tackle puts up a very satisfactory fight. It is usually of short duration, however, because the bluegill and other sunfish lack the staying power of the larger game fish. But it is spirited and lively while it lasts, and a good-sized bluegill will make circle after circle using its broad body to the utmost.

In most waters where bluegills are found, a half-pound fish is a good one, and a fish around a pound is considered a big one. In some lakes bluegills and other sunfish may become stunted and never reach a good size. In other lakes they grow larger than average if conditions are suitable. An example of the latter is Ketona Lake in Alabama, where bluegills weighing over four pounds have been caught. The largest on record weighed four pounds, twelve ounces, and was taken by T. S. Hudson on April 9, 1950.

Large or small, bluegills and other sunfish make excellent eating. Their meat is firm, sweet, and delicious. But since it takes some time and trouble to clean the smaller bluegills or sunfish, many anglers save only the larger ones and throw back the smaller ones. Or they fish only in lakes or rivers where big ones are commonly found. Fishery biologists frown on this practice, however, and would much rather have anglers take as many bluegills of all sizes as they can. There are so many bluegills, and other sunfish, of all sizes in many lakes and ponds that thinning is a necessity. Those that remain will grow larger, as will the game fish, which need plenty of living space and food.

Chapter 18

CRAPPIES

The crappie, a denizen of large lakes and reservoirs, is one of the more popular panfish for a number of reasons. Traveling in large schools, they are fairly easy to catch. In addition, the season for crappie fishing is long, starting in March and continuing into November in many areas. They are even caught through the ice during the winter months. When crappies are running it is not unusual to see a hundred or more boats congregated over the crappie beds in large lakes such as Lake Okeechobee in Florida. In addition to the boat fishermen, hundreds of other anglers line the piers, bridges, banks, and shorelines to catch crappies.

There are two kinds of crappies—the black crappie and the white crappie. The deeper-bodied black crappie has a black back, is darkly mottled, and has seven or eight dorsal spines.

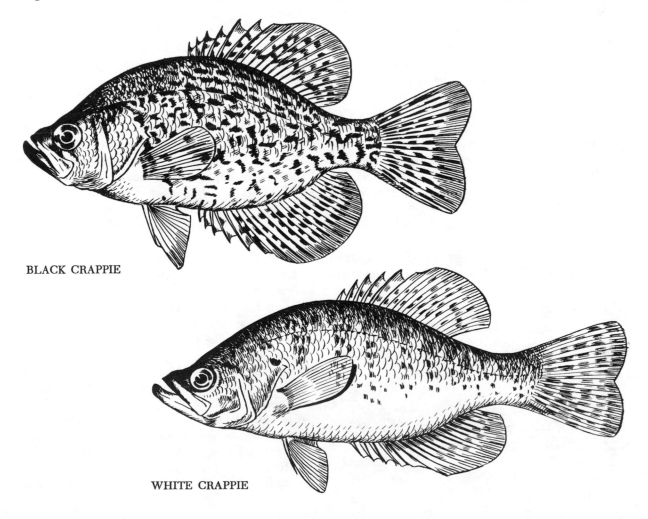

BLACK CRAPPIE

WHITE CRAPPIE

The white crappie is not so deep-bodied or so dark as the black crappie. The white crappie also has only five or six dorsal spines.

Crappies are called by almost sixty different names in various parts of the country, but the more popular ones are calico bass, speckled perch, strawberry bass, silver crappie, and bachelor. In Florida and other southern states they are often called "specks."

The black crappie is more numerous in northern waters than the white crappie; the black crappie's range extends from southern Canada through the Great Lakes and Mississippi River system to Nebraska and south to Texas, Florida, and North Carolina. The white crappie, which is most plentiful in southern waters, is found from Nebraska to Lake Ontario and south to the Mississippi River, Texas, and Alabama. Both crappies, however, have been introduced widely in other states as far west as California, Oregon, and Washington.

Fishing tackle used for crappies is similar to that used for bluegills and other panfish. Cane poles and glass poles are popular with many fishermen from boats and shore. They are particularly useful for fishing around brush, sunken trees, logs, lily pads, hyacinths, and other weeds where the bait can be lowered in the openings and holes between such snags. Bait-casting rods and reels are good for casting and trolling. And, of course, spinning and spin-casting rods and reels can be used for casting small, light lures as well as for still fishing and trolling. Fly rods are great for fishing for crappies when they are in fairly shallow water.

Crappies will strike such artificial lures as tiny underwater plugs, spoons, weighted spinners, spinners and flies, and jigs. Fly fishermen can catch them with small streamers and bucktails,

wet flies, nymphs, dry flies, and bass bugs or panfish bugs. In recent years tiny jigs with weighted heads and bodies of chenille and marabou tails have become popular for jigging and casting for crappies. Other jigs with hair, feathers, or nylon dressings, and especially those with plastic-tail or grub bodies, are also good. Spinner baits with a small spinner blade on one arm and a plastic-body jig on the other are excellent. Jigs and spinner baits should be small and weigh from $\frac{1}{64}$ to $\frac{1}{8}$ ounce; white and yellow are favorite colors for these lures.

Natural baits that will catch crappies include minnows, worms, fresh-water shrimp, grasshoppers, crickets, mealworms, nymphs, and other land and water insects. But the most dependable bait is a small minnow from $1\frac{1}{2}$ to $2\frac{1}{2}$ inches long. After you catch the first crappie you can cut a strip from its silvery belly or sides and use it for bait. Strips about $\frac{1}{4}$ inch wide and $1\frac{1}{2}$ inches long can be cut from other fish such as suckers, chubs, and gizzard shad and used for bait.

Crappies may start running and biting as early as January and February in Florida and other southern states. March and April are good months in most of our eastern and midwestern states, while in our northern and western states, May and June are top months. These are the months when crappies come close to shore to spawn and are easiest to locate and catch. But they can be caught most of the year if you locate them in the depths where they are present.

Crappies will bite most of the day, but since they do not like the bright sun, during the middle of the day they will seek shady spots and deeper water. Cloudy, overcast days will usually provide better fishing than bright, sunny days. Many crappie fishermen also go after them at night; the best period for this is usually a few days before and during the full moon.

In the spring, crappies make their nests in shallow water near shore from three to six feet deep, and fishing is best for them in water from three to twelve feet deep at this time. On warmer days they'll stay in the shallow water, but will drop back into deeper water during a cold spell. As a general rule, black crappies prefer clearer, cooler waters, while white crappies are often found in warmer, sluggish, muddier waters.

Both species like cover and shade. They hang

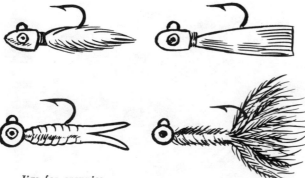

Jigs for crappies.

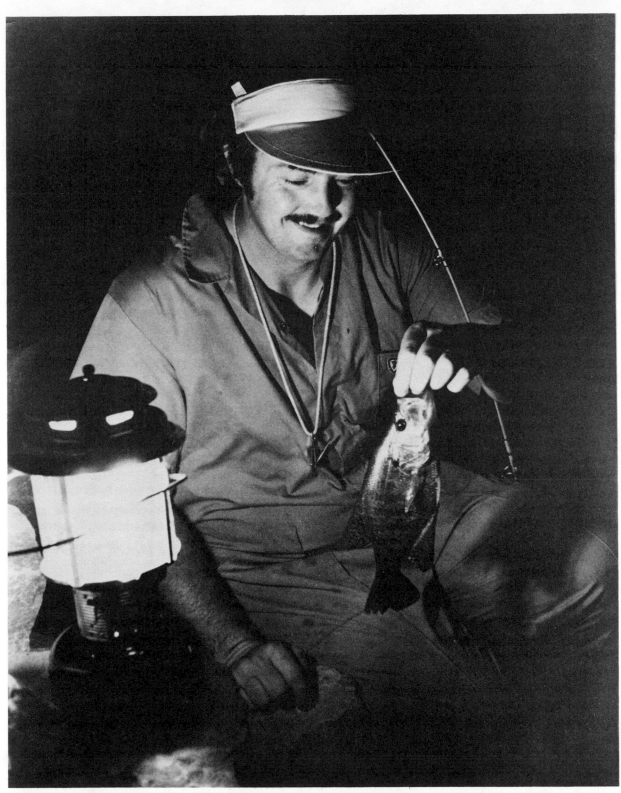

Crappie fishing is often good at night. A bright light (from a lantern, lamp, or other source) shining on the water attracts minnows and bugs, which in turn draw the crappies. (Coleman Company Photo)

out in coves, bays, around old stumps, logs, brush, sunken trees, lily pads, hyacinths, bullrushes, and other weeds and vegetation. Rivers, streams, and inlets entering a lake are usually hot spots. So are the waters below spillways and dams. Any trees, stumps, or brush showing above water or submerged below the surface are great attractions to crappies. They also lurk in shady spots under overhanging tree branches, bridges, piers, docks, rafts, and anchored boats. During floods look for them in flooded pasture lands, coves, bays, and inlets. When the water is muddy they'll be in the clearer areas near shore. Usually on the more popular lakes and reservoirs locating crappies is easy during the big runs of fish in the spring. At this time you'll see many other anglers lined up along shore or fishing from bridges or from boats, and you can take your cue from their location.

It is during the hot summer months, when crappies go deep to seek cooler water, that fishing for them can get difficult. They may be on the bottom or suspended at various depths. They may be in schools or scattered. Your best bet will be to fish in water from ten to thirty feet in depth. Here again, the crappies will hang out over a structure of some kind, usually in deeper water not too far from the shallow spots where they spawned earlier. Look for submerged islands, shoals, rockbars, rock piles, sloping points, bars, sharp dropoffs, channels, and old creek- and riverbeds. A depth finder or a fish finder is a big help in locating such bottoms and even the fish themselves.

For still fishing, which is the most popular way to catch crappies, the long cane or glass pole is generally used. In fairly shallow water you can add a float or bobber high enough on the line so that the bait just clears the bottom or weeds. In deeper water, a small dipsey sinker tied on the end of your line, and two hooks tied on short droppers or snells about a foot apart make a good rig. Special crappie rigs with two hooks on wire spreader arms can be made, or bought in tackle shops. (See accompanying illustration for such a rig.)

Minnows or any other crappie bait can be used on Nos. 4 or 6 hooks for small crappies and on Nos. 1 or 2 hooks for the bigger fish. A minnow can be hooked through the lips or eye sockets and lowered to the depth at which the specks are lying or feeding. This usually means right in or alongside any vegetation, such as lily pads, hyacinths, sawgrass, stumps, logs, sunken trees, and weedbeds.

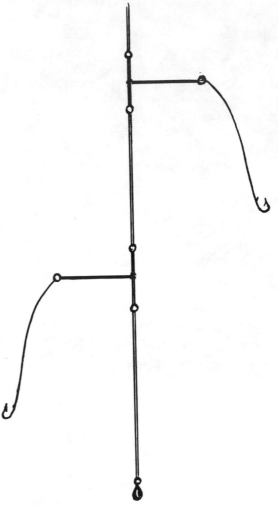

A wire spreader crappie rig.

When fishing from shore with a casting rod and a bottom rig with sinker, cast your rig and minnow out a good distance, and when it reaches bottom, reel it in very slowly, letting it lie a few seconds in different spots. The same thing can be done from a boat when the specks are in the deeper holes and channels. Here you can try casting all around the boat and reeling in the rig along the bottom.

Another good way to locate and catch crappies is to let the bottom rig with a minnow or other bait down to the bottom and drift with the wind or current slowly as the sinker drags along the bottom. When you get a bite or hook a fish, drop anchor and fish in that spot. In this instance, it pays to give the baits some movement by raising and lowering the rod tip or moving the rod back and forth in an arc.

Usually crappies stay at a certain level when feeding, and it is important to find out what this is if you want to get action. Try different depths until you find the right one. Crappies are school fish, so if you find one, you'll usually catch more. If you don't get action in one spot or if the crappies stop biting, move to other spots.

Crappies tend to bite gently, mouthing the bait, then moving into the depths with it. Don't strike too soon, especially when using big baits such as minnows, or you'll pull them out of their mouths. Let the bobber or float disappear or wait until you feel a strong pull on the line before you set the hook. Do not strike too hard, since crappies have soft, paper-thin mouths, and a hook tears out easily.

Crappies bite well at night, at which time you can suspend or hang a lamp or light with a reflector from a dock, bridge, pier, or boat to shine into the water. The light will draw bugs and insects, which will draw minnows, which will in turn attract crappies. Most night fishing is done with baits such as minnows.

When using lures such as small spoons, weighted spinners, small plugs, and jigs, you also have to explore different depths and try different spots. When the fish are in shallow water near shore you can retrieve the lures near the surface or a foot or two below. But in deeper water you have to let the lure sink and work it several feet below the surface and even along the bottom.

When crappies are in heavy cover, ease the boat up to lily pads, hyacinths, sunken trees, or brush, and lower a jig down deep to the bottom or just above any cover. Hold it there, giving the lure an occasional short, gentle jerk upward, then let it drop back. You can also do this vertical jigging in deeper water among suspended crappies or those lying near the bottom.

At other times you can cast out a small jig and let it sink to the bottom, then retrieve it very slowly along the cover or structure. Straight reeling will bring strikes, or else you can work the jig with short up-and-down twitches of the rod tip. This can be done from shore or from a boat. From a boat, cast all around it to varying distances until you locate the fish.

Another way to fish a jig is to rig it below a small ¾-inch-round plastic bobber or float high enough so that the lure just clears the weeds, sunken trees, brush, or bottom. When the jig reaches this cover or the bottom, retrieve it very slowly, barely turning the reel handle. Or you can give the bobber or float a short twitch or jerk at intervals to move the jig. You have to watch the bobber or float closely to see a bite. At the slightest sign of a hit, set the hook.

In more open waters, trolling is often a good way to locate and catch crappies. A slow-moving boat is used to follow the shoreline around points of land, along bars, edges of lily pads, and other weeds and over sunken rocks, trees, brush, or other cover. You can let out anywhere from 75 to 150 feet of line, depending on the depth you are trying to reach. You can also add a split shot or two or a small clincher sinker above the lure. Trolling is most effective in depths from 8 to 30 feet with tiny spoons, spinners, spinner baits, and jigs. You can troll with 3 or 4 lines and with different lures working at various depths. Once you catch a fish, adjust all the other lines to the same depth and use the same lure on all of them. Trolling should be done at very slow speeds, for which an electric motor is best. Or you can back-troll with a low-power, regular outboard motor.

A fly rod can also be used to catch crappies when they are in fairly shallow water. Here a sinking fly line is best with wet flies and tiny streamers or bucktails. And when crappies come into the shallows in the evening to feed on surface insects you can sometimes catch them on dry flies, small bass bugs, or panfish bugs. Work these slowly with plenty of pauses and twitches to bring the crappies to the top and make them hit.

Crappies can also be caught through the ice during the winter months. Here, too, minnows make the best bait and should be lowered to the bottom. If you get no action, raise the minnow a couple of feet and try at that depth. If still no takers, raise it a bit higher and let it swim there. Keep doing this until you find the depth at which the fish are lying. Crappies will also hit tiny spoons, jigs, and ice flies fished through the ice if these lures are jigged gently up and down. Adding a grub or tiny strip of fish to the lure will usually bring more bites and hook more fish.

It would be dishonest to say that the crappie

Lakes with standing timber and weedy shores, like Virginia's Chickahominy Lake, shown here, are ideal for crappie fishing. (Virginia State Travel Service Photo)

is a great fighter on the end of a line. They usually wage a slow, uninteresting, short fight and give up too easily. In addition, they have soft, paper-tissue mouths, and a hook will often pull out or drop out readily. So light tackle is best in getting the most out of them and for saving those that are hooked.

Crappies in most waters will average about a pound or a bit less, though in some lakes and reservoirs they are often caught up to two or three pounds in weight. Both species of crappies have been known to reach about five pounds or slightly more in weight and a length of about twenty inches.

The crappie is one of the tastiest panfish. They are especially good in the early spring and late fall and during the winter months when the flesh is firm. Those taken from muddy waters during the hot summer months may be softer and not so well flavored.

Some of the better crappie lakes, reservoirs, and rivers are found in Wisconsin, Minnesota, Iowa, Idaho, Kansas, North Dakota, South Dakota, Oklahoma, Missouri, Colorado, Illinois, Nebraska, Ohio, and most of the states bordering the Mississippi River. In New York, Chautauqua Lake, Lake Ontario, Croton Reservoir, and other reservoirs near New York City contain crappies. In Pennsylvania, Pymatuning Lake, Glendale Lake, Pinchot Lake, Lake Wallenpaupack, Kinzau Lake, and Lake Erie have crappie fishing. In Mississippi, the Enid Reservoir, Sardis Reservoir, Grenada Reservoir, Moon Lake, Eagle Lake, Lake Rodney, and Lake Mary can be fished. In Louisiana, Toledo Bend Reservoir, Lake Bistineau, Bussey Lake,

Black Lake, Turkey Creek Lake, and D'Argonne Lake are noted for crappies. In Tennessee, you can try Kentucky Lake, Reelfoot Lake, Percy Priest Reservoir, Woods Reservoir, and Douglas Reservoir. In Kentucky, you can fish Kentucky Lake, Lake Barkley, and Lake Cumberland. In Texas, such reservoirs as Spence, Sam Rayburn, Dam B, Navarro Hills, Toledo Bend, Amistad, and Belton have crappies. So do such lakes as Texarkana, Buchanan, Travis, Belton, and Texoma, also in Texas. In Virginia, try Philpott Reservoir, Smith Mountain Lake, Kerr Reservoir, Gaston Reservoir, Buggs Island Lake, and Claytor Lake. Florida has many lakes, rivers,

and canals that contain crappies. Some of the more popular ones are Lake Okeechobee, Lake Harris, Lake Griffin, Lake Eustis, Lake Dora, Lake Jessup, and the St. John's River. On the Pacific Coast, crappies are found in California's West Valley Reservoir, Back Butte Reservoir, Comanche Reservoir, Clear Lake, and Success Reservoir. In Oregon you can fish Owyhee Lake, Siltcoos Lake, Brownless Reservoir, Cold Springs Lake, Fern Ridge Lake, Coffenbury Lake, Smith Lake, and the Columbia River and Willamette River sloughs. In Washington, crappies are found in Coffee Pot Lake, McNary Reservoir, Palmer Lake, Vancouver Lake, Loomis Lake, and Silver Lake.

Crappies, which on the average are larger in size than most panfish, can provide a lot of fun and sport when caught on light spinning tackle or fly rods. (Virginia Commission of Game & Inland Fisheries Photo)

Chapter 19

WHITE BASS

How would you like to catch a fresh-water fish that is bigger than the average panfish, fights harder, strikes many kinds of artificial lures, and makes delicious eating? And when these fish are really running it's a cinch to catch the limit. Many of you are probably already familiar with the fish in question, but those who are not should become acquainted with this silvery little scrapper. He's the white bass, also called sand bass, sandy, silver bass, barfish, gray bass, silversides, striper, and striped bass. But the last two names are better reserved for his relative—the true fresh- and salt-water striped bass, which grows much larger and is a longer, more streamlined fish. The white bass is shorter, deeper, much smaller, and strictly a fresh-water fish. His back is greenish and the sides are silvery, with six or seven stripes running along them.

At one time the white bass had a limited range from the Great Lakes region to the St. Lawrence and Manitoba, from southern Ontario to New York, and south through the Mississippi Valley to Texas. But in the past thirty years or so they have been introduced in many waters in the central, eastern, and southern sections of the United States. They prefer large rivers, lakes, and reservoirs, and are very plentiful in the man-made impoundments in Texas and in the TVA system in Tennessee. As its range increases, the white bass is becoming very popular with many anglers; today it occupies a position somewhere between the panfishes and the black bass.

For casting light lures to white bass, the ideal outfit is a light fresh-water spinning rod and reel. The line should be about 4- or 6-pound-test, and the rod should be able to cast lures ranging from 1/8 to 1/2 ounce. The spin-casting rods with push-button-type reels are also good for casting. These are usually used with 8- or 10-pound-test lines.

If you prefer a bait-casting outfit, get one

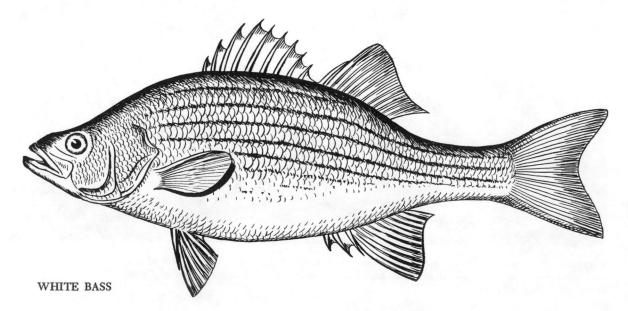

WHITE BASS

Popping plug (top) and dowel (bottom) with trailing lures.

about 5½ to 6 feet long and light enough to be able to cast the light lures used for white bass. Lines testing about 10 or 12 pounds can be used with such a rod. If you use a heavier bait-casting rod and line you'll have trouble casting the small lures required in white-bass fishing, especially if you have to reach schools of fish at a distance. However, the heavier bait-casting or spinning outfits would be good for trolling or bottom fishing with sinkers and bait.

When white bass are actively feeding on top they'll usually strike almost anything that moves through the water and even remotely resembles a shad or other minnow. They'll take small surface and underwater plugs, spoons, spinners, streamers, bucktails, and weighted jigs of all types. The important fact to remember when choosing lures is that they should be small. The big plugs used for black bass and other large fish are not effective in this case. The white bass has a small mouth and you'll miss too many fish if you use large lures.

If you have no outfit capable of casting very light and small lures you can get around this by making up a "popping" or "chugging" block to add weight (see above). This can be a small section of broomstick or dowel from two to three inches long, with two small screw eyes fastened to both ends. Your fishing line is tied to one screw eye, and an eighteen-inch mono leader is tied to the other eye. At the end of this leader, attach a tiny spoon, bucktail, or streamer fly, or a small jig. When this rig is cast and reeled in with short jerks, the wooden block creates a commotion and acts as a fish attractor in addition to providing weight for casting the small lure. This rig may be a bit clumsy to cast at first, but it gets a light lure out much farther and attracts fish. Instead of a wooden block you can also use a small surface popping plug with the hooks removed.

The peak season for white-bass fishing is usually in the spring, when they run up creeks or rivers to spawn. This may start as early as March and April in our southern states or later, in May and June, in our northern states. But white bass can also provide good fishing from spring through fall, and even in the winter months in the South.

Locating white bass during the spring spawning season is easy in waters where they are plentiful and popular. You'll usually see hundreds of anglers lining the shores and banks or in boats over areas where white bass are gathered. If you join these anglers, you'll have a lot of fun and action pulling in the whites.

During this spring run look for concentrations of white bass below falls, dams, riffles, and rapids in rivers. They will bunch up in the deep runs, quiet pools, eddies, and in the slow water behind big rocks and boulders. In the smaller streams or narrow spots they can be so thick that their backs and fins will protrude above the surface. Feeder streams and brooks entering the bigger river are also hot spots.

In lakes or reservoirs that do not have tributary streams for spawning, white bass will deposit their eggs on shallow, rocky, or gravel shoals and sandbars. Though the spawning season is short, lasting only about two or three weeks, white bass will remain for some time in fairly shallow water in lakes and reservoirs around the mouths of creeks, under bridges, around islands, along dropoffs, and also along gravel points, sandbars, rockbars, and reefs.

During the summer months when the water warms, white bass will seek deeper waters toward the middle of the lake. They may be as deep as forty to fifty feet, especially during the middle of the day on bright, sunny days. But even in the summer, they usually come closer to the surface or move into shallower water to feed around daybreak, toward dusk, and during the night. Gizzard shad and other small fish and minnows are the preferred food of the white bass, and they'll follow these baitfish all over the lake.

So one of the best times to fish and catch white bass is when they are actually chasing the shad minnows on the surface of a lake or reservoir. Calm days are best for spotting and locating them. At other times, the best fishing will take place early in the morning or toward evening. When white bass are chasing small fish on the surface they often turn the water to a froth, and the commotion can be spotted a long distance away. In some of the larger reservoirs and lakes, like Lake Erie, gulls and terns congregate over such feeding white bass and pinpoint the fish for you. Since white bass tend to wander all over the lake or reservoir you either try to follow them from spot to spot, or wait in one spot and hope they will pass by a few times during the day.

Fishing for white bass when they are feeding on top calls for quick action. Their rods rigged with a lure, anglers cruise around in their boats looking for feeding schools of fish. As soon as they spot a commotion or see birds working, they speed toward the spot. When they get within casting distance they cut their motors and everybody in the boat starts casting small plugs, spoons, jigs, or popping blocks. Fast reeling usually produces the best results at this time. You have only a short time before the school sounds and goes down or is frightened by too many boats getting too close. Then you have to locate another school or drift and wait till the fish reap-

Trolling is a good way to locate and catch white bass, especially on large lakes, reservoirs, and broad rivers. (Mercury Motors Photo)

pear near you. This is an exciting sport known as "jump" fishing, but it can become hectic with too many boats trying to get in on the act.

When white bass are not showing on top you have to locate them below the surface. They will gather at the mouths of streams and rivers, over old creek channels below the surface, off rocky points, and along dropoffs, underwater islands, shoals, bars, and reefs. A depth finder or a fish finder is good for locating such bottoms and even picking up the schools of fish themselves. Then you can drift or anchor in a boat and fish the spot with such lures as jigs, spoons, weighted spinners, and deep-running or sinking underwater plugs. Cast out and work the lures first just below the surface, then try deeper water until you are working the lures along the bottom. Cast all around the boat until you cover all the water in a circle and at different depths. Once you get a strike or hook a fish, of course, you let the lure sink to the correct depth on the next cast. If you get no action, move on to a new spot and repeat.

Trolling is a good way to locate and catch submerged white bass. Some anglers even prefer to troll when the fish are surfacing. At such times fast trolling up to five or six miles per hour with the lure a short distance behind the boat will catch them. At other times a slower-moving boat with a long line is better. When the whites are very deep, you'll have to troll with weights, wire lines, or downriggers to reach them. You can use spoons, spinners, small plugs, or jigs, and troll over and along such structure as the edges of shoals, bars, reefs, the ends of sloping points, and along dropoffs. Here again, try different depths by trolling with two or three rods set at varying depths. Keep letting out line with one rod until you get a strike, then mark your line so you can let out the correct length to reach the depth where the fish are. It is also a good idea to mark the spot with a marker or buoy so you can troll in the exact spot.

When the white bass are down deep during the summer or winter months, vertical jigging is a good way to reach and catch them. Here you can let a small but heavy spoon or jig down to the bottom. Then work it up and down in short jerks close to the bottom. Or else when the lure reaches bottom, you can start reeling it back with slow jerks to activate it. This can be done from a drifting boat if you are over a wide shoal or if you are still trying to locate the fish. Once you find them, however, drop anchor and fish that spot thoroughly.

White bass that are down deep can also be caught by still fishing with small, live minnows between 2 and 2½ inches long. This is often a very productive method at night. To attract white bass at this time, hang one or two lanterns or lights on the boat so that the light shines into the water. This is also a good way to catch fresh bait for your fishing. The minnows gather below the light and you can scoop them up with a dip net. To use the minnow, impale it through the back on a bottom rig with sinker and lower it to the depth where the white bass are present. This minnow fishing can be done day or night from a boat, dock, bridge, or any other spot with deep water harboring white bass.

White bass put up a good scrap for their size and have more zip and endurance than most panfish. They do most of their fighting below the surface and don't leap out of the water. But on light tackle they are a lot of fun and sport.

White bass don't grow too big, averaging from ¾ pound to 2 pounds in weight, which is still larger than the average panfish. Fish weighing 4 and 5 pounds or a bit more have been caught from time to time in various waters.

However, the white bass is so prolific and has such a short life span that most states have liberal bag limits for them. Most of them live only three or four years, and if not caught, they die and are wasted. So biologists claim that it's a good idea to catch your limit as often as you can, which is rather easy when white bass are really running. If you can't give them away to your neighbors, try cleaning or filleting them and putting them in a deep freeze, if you have one. They make good eating, having a firm, tasty flesh.

White-bass fishing is best in the Deep South where the season is long and the fish are large and plentiful. In Texas, for instance, you'll find them in lakes Texoma, Travis, Buchanan, Marshall, Livingstone, Sulphur, Caddo, and Dallas, and in such rivers as the Rio Grande, Colorado, and Pedernales. In Tennessee most of the man-made reservoirs and lakes have white bass, with Kentucky Lake, Watts Bar Reservoir, Pickwick, Douglas, and Center Hill lakes offering good fishing. Kentucky has Kentucky Lake, Herrington Lake, Lake Cumberland, Dale Hollow Lake, Lake Barkley, Nolin, Dewey, Buckhorn lakes, and such rivers as the Dix and the Rockcastle. Lake of the Ozarks and Bull Shoals in Missouri are noted for white bass. In Arkansas, Lake Hamilton and Ouachita River are fished. Virginia's South Holston Lake, John W. Flannagan Lake, Claytor Lake, and Smith Mountain Lake all contain white bass. In South Carolina, you'll find white bass in Lake Hartwell, Clark Hill Reservoir, Lake Murray, Lake Greenwood, Savannah River, Catawba River, and the Santee-Cooper waters. In Wisconsin, Lake Mendota, Lake Winnebago, Lake Monona, Wisconsin River, and Wolf River contain white bass, as do the Illinois River, Quiver Lake, Lake Matanzas, and the Fox Chain o' Lakes in Illinois. Georgia's Lake Hartwell, Clark Hill, and Lanier are all productive. In Florida, you can fish Lake Seminole and the Apalachicola River. In New York, white bass are found in Oneida Lake and the St. Lawrence River. With the exception of Lake Superior, where they are rare or nonexistent, all the Great Lakes contain white bass.

Of course, this is only a partial list of white-bass waters. Write your state fish and game department for further information. And remember that white bass are constantly being stocked in many states and waters.

Chapter 20

WHITE PERCH

The white perch is a panfish like the sunfishes, crappies, yellow perch, rock bass, and others in this class. But among most outdoor writers and many anglers, he's a much-neglected panfish. You rarely read about white perch in books or magazines, and few anglers go fishing deliberately for them. Yet the white perch has many qualities that make some fresh-water anglers rate him over most of the other panfishes.

The white perch is not related to the yellow perch, or any perch, for that matter. He's a member of the sea-bass family, which includes the white bass and the striped bass. In fact, he resembles both of these fish in general outline but lacks the stripes. The upper surface or back varies in color depending on where a white perch is found. But it is usually olive, dark grayish-green, or silver-gray on the back and upper sides. These colors shade into a paler olive or silvery green to silvery white on the belly. When found in fresh water, these fish are usually much darker than when found in brackish or salt waters.

The white perch is also called the bluenose perch, gray perch, black perch, silver perch, silver bass, and sea perch. But "white perch" is the name most often used.

The white perch is found from Nova Scotia down to the Carolinas, mostly in rivers, creeks, salt-water ponds, and bays near the Atlantic Ocean. Though they have also been introduced into many fresh-water lakes and ponds in the eastern states, their natural habitat remains the rivers emptying into the sea, and salt-water and brackish ponds formed by sandbars that cut them off from the ocean. These ponds usually "salt out" in time and become mostly fresh water. But white perch live and thrive in them anyway.

White perch can be caught on various kinds of outfits, from cane poles to light salt-water rods and reels. For fishing in quiet ponds or creeks in shallow water near shore, an ordinary cane pole does the trick nicely, with or without a float or bobber. When white perch are in shallow water near shore or feeding on the surface, a

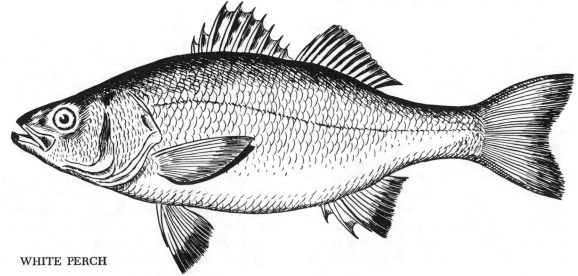

WHITE PERCH

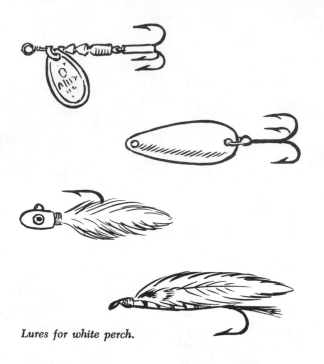

Lures for white perch.

fly rod makes an excellent outfit. A light fresh-water spinning rod or spin-casting or bait-casting outfit can be used for casting. In brackish or salt water with strong currents or tides, a heavier fresh-water or a light salt-water spinning rod, or a conventional revolving-spool rod and reel can be used with heavy sinkers to hold bottom or to fish among rocks.

The white perch will often hit artificial lures such as wet flies or streamer flies on a fly rod. Those with silver bodies are especially good. Other effective lures include small silver and gold spoons and weighted spinners. For trolling and casting, a small spinner rigged in front of a wet fly, a streamer, or a worm is a good combination. And in recent years tiny jigs with buck-tail, feather, nylon, or plastic bodies or tails have been used with good results.

White perch will also take natural baits such as earthworms, nightcrawlers, minnows, baby eels, and small, soft-shelled crayfish. Also good are various kinds of insects such as grasshoppers, crickets, and grubs. In brackish and salt water, white perch are susceptible to grass shrimp, bloodworms, clamworms, sandworms, and pieces of clam or shedder crab.

The white-perch season lasts from early spring to late fall and even through the winter months

in most waters where they are found. They spend the winter in deep water or brackish bays, then move into rivers and creeks to spawn in April, May, and June. The spawning run often takes them up big rivers into fresh water many miles from the sea.

You can catch white perch pretty well during the daytime, although they will probably be in deeper water (from eight to twenty feet) at that time. They move into shallow water (from two to eight feet) near shore toward evening, at dusk, and at night, which are the best times to fish for them in the shallows. Although their usual range is from two to twenty feet deep, in some large fresh-water lakes, or in the larger salt-water bays, like Chesapeake Bay, white perch may be anywhere from thirty to one hundred feet down.

The white perch is quite an adaptable, hardy fish, able to live in warm and cold waters, ranging from fresh to brackish to salt. However, they prefer, and are most plentiful in, the brackish waters of bays, sounds, lagoons, tidal creeks, and river mouths. They may be found over mud, clay, sand, or rocky bottoms.

White perch are school fish and may move about in groups of several fish or in big schools numbering hundreds or even thousands of fish. They also tend to travel around quite a bit, which of course makes them difficult to locate. When you fish unfamiliar waters, it is wise to consult a fishing guide or an angler who knows the lake about the usual whereabouts of the fish. Or you can look for anglers fishing from shore or boats; if they are catching white perch, go ahead and join them.

Early in the morning or toward evening when the lake is calm, you can often see schools of white perch close to the surface. At such times they may be showing their backs or even breaking water. If they are merely swimming around, you may not be able to entice them to hit a bait or a lure. But if they are feeding on insects or chasing minnows, you can usually get some action.

Still fishing with a cane or glass pole near shore, in shallow creeks, or in other shallow waters is a popular way to catch white perch. Since they start feeding early in the spring soon after the ice is out, they attract many anglers at this time. You can use a bobber or float above a

White-bass bag limits are extremely liberal in most states, and big catches like this one are commonly made. (Walker: Missouri Tourism Photo)

hook baited with worms, minnows, or any of the natural baits mentioned above. White perch like a moving bait, so when you toss out your bait let it sink as far down as it will go. Then move it gently to one side or raise it a foot or so and let it sink again. Keep doing this at regular intervals so that the bait just doesn't hang motionless. Of course, with a live bait like a minnow this isn't as important as with a dead bait.

After you catch your first white perch, cut a thin, narrow, tapered strip from its belly or side about an inch and a half in length and put this on a No. 4 or No. 6 hook through its wide end.

Then flip the baited hook out, let it sink a few feet, and then bring it in with short, gentle twitches.

In fast rivers or tidal creeks, or when you are trying to reach a spot some distance from shore, a casting outfit such as a spinning rod is a good alternative. Use a standard bottom rig with a small sinker tied on the end of the line and a hook on a short snell or leader above it. This can be baited with a worm or minnow in fresh water or a bloodworm or grass shrimp in brackish or salt water. Cast the rig out from shore, put your rod in a holder or against a log or rock on the

White perch usually bite best in shallow water near shore early in the morning or the evening. During the middle of the day fishing is better in deeper waters. (Coleman Company Photo)

bank, and wait for a bite. White perch bite with vigor, but because of their small mouths, give them time to mouth the bait before you set the hook.

You can use the same bottom rig with sinker and bait from a boat, too, but here, instead of anchoring, you drift with the tide, current, or wind. This is a good way to locate and catch white perch because you cover more water and run into more fish. Once you hook or boat a fish you can drop anchor and fish that spot as long as the perch keep biting. Some anglers also tie a small balloon with a long string around the tail of the first perch they catch and then release it in the water to follow the rest of the school. This way you can keep up with the school as it moves around.

At times white perch will take artificial lures; when this is the case, you can cast for them from shore or a boat using small spinners, spoons, jigs, or spinner-and-worm combinations. These can be worked near the surface if the fish are on top, or else you can let them sink down close to the bottom and work the lures slowly toward the surface. In a stream or river with a current, cast a spoon, jig, or spinner upstream and across and let it sink and travel close to the bottom. Do not reel or retrieve lures too fast for white perch. They like movement and action in their lures, but these shouldn't move too fast.

Trolling is also a good way to locate and catch white perch. You can troll spoons, spinners, jigs, and spinner-bait combinations with a long line out so that the lure travels close to the bottom at a slow speed. Here again, once you catch a perch you can throw out a buoy or float with a weight as a marker. Then you can either troll around that spot, anchor and fish with bait, or cast lures.

Trolling can also be done with small streamer or bucktail flies such as the Mickey Finn, Gray Ghost, or Black Ghost tied on No. 6 or No. 8 hooks. Late evening, when white perch move into shallow water, is best for this. But the ultimate in sport with white perch is to cast dry flies, wet flies, nymphs, or streamers when the fish are on top or in shallow water. When you see them rising to the surface to feed on insects, you can use dry flies such as the Light Cahill, March Brown, Wulff patterns, and the bivisibles. Toward evening you can also try the small

This big white perch shows the typical sea-bass body shape. It resembles its relatives, the white bass and the striped bass, except that it lacks their stripes. (New Hampshire Fish & Game Photo)

panfish popping bugs. Move or twitch the dry flies or bugs gently to make them ripple the surface. When casting wet flies, streamers, or bucktails, use a weighted fly or sinking fly line, or both. Then try different depths right down to the bottom to find the level at which the fish are lying or feeding.

When white perch are in very deep water, vertical jigging from a boat is one of the best ways to catch them. Here you can use a leadhead jig, a spoon, or other small metal lure about ⅛ or ¼ ounce in weight. Let it down to the bottom, reel in 1 or 2 feet, and then start working it up and down in short jerks. Many times you don't even have to jig the lure because white perch are usually in thick schools, and some of them will hit the lure as it flutters or sinks. Vertical jigging for white perch can also be done through the ice during the winter months. Or you can use tiny minnows on a hook when fishing through the ice.

White perch put up a much better fight on the end of the line than the yellow perch, crappie, or rock bass. The big ones, especially when hooked in a river with a strong current or in salt water where a strong tide is running, will often put up a long, spirited battle. However, the tackle must be light for them to show their best, since they are small fish.

The average white perch runs from 8 to 10 inches long and weighs less than 1 pound, though in some lakes and brackish waters fish going 2 or 3 pounds have been caught. One of the largest was a 19½-inch white perch weighing 4 pounds, 12 ounces caught in Messalonskee Lake in Maine in June 1949.

The white perch has a firm, flaky, sweet-tasting flesh and makes excellent eating when cleaned and fried in deep fat or even pan fried. Fillet of white perch can be used to make a delicious chowder. In the early spring or late fall when the females have eggs or roe, you can remove these, dip them in flour and egg, and fry them.

White perch abound in Canada, particularly in Nova Scotia and in New Brunswick. Maine is noted for the white perch found in most of its coastal rivers, lakes, and ponds. They have also been introduced to many inland lakes here. Other New England states such as New Hampshire, Massachusetts, Rhode Island, and Connecticut all have good white-perch fishing. In New York you'll find white perch in many waters on Long Island and in the reservoirs and larger lakes upstate. They are very plentiful in the Hudson River, Delaware River, Toms River, Mullica River, and many lakes and ponds in New Jersey. In Virginia and Maryland the Chesapeake Bay and its many tributaries contain white perch. So do Lake Waccamaw and the Albemarle Sound and its tributaries in North Carolina.

Chapter 21

STRIPED BASS

The salt-water striped bass has long been a popular food and sport fish in this country. Way back in 1634, the early settlers in New England were catching striped bass on a cod line baited with a piece of lobster tail. They would toss this line and bait into the sea from shore and when a bass took the bait, the line would be hauled in quickly and the fish clubbed on the head.

Striped bass have also been caught for a long time in many coastal fresh-water rivers from Maine to Mississippi during their spawning run in the spring. Many of these stripers were caught accidentally by anglers fishing for salmon, trout, bass, shad, and other game fish. But a few anglers were deliberately catching stripers on flies in these fresh-water rivers as far back as the Civil War.

When the Santee and Cooper rivers in South Carolina were blocked by dams in 1941, some stripers were trapped in the two lakes that were formed by the blockage—Lake Marion and Lake Moultrie. The striped bass thrived and spawned, and sport fishing for them became popular with local and visiting anglers.

After World War II attempts were made to stock striped bass in other fresh-water lakes and reservoirs. At first these weren't very successful, but gradually as biologists learned more about striped-bass culture, the stripers began to thrive in many fresh waters.

Striped bass were introduced into many fresh-water lakes, reservoirs, and impoundments not only to provide sport fishing but also to control the big populations of small fish and minnows that were threatening the existence of black bass and other game fish. It was found that introduced striped bass ate gizzard shad, threadfin shad, glut herring, and alewives in sufficient quantities to keep their numbers down, thereby improving the game fishing. In addition, the stripers feeding on these forage fish grew even faster than they did in salt water. So at this writing we find striped bass present in the fresh waters of at least thirty-three states. No doubt other states will soon begin stocking striped bass in their fresh waters.

Striped-bass fishing in fresh water is now booming as more and more anglers discover

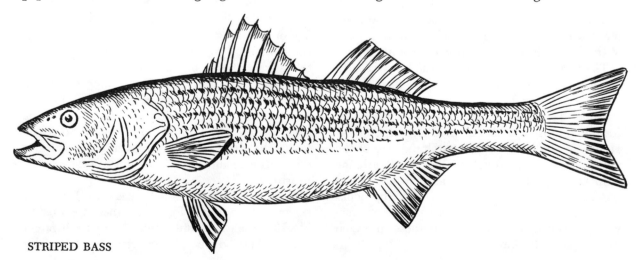

STRIPED BASS

these fish and learn how to catch them. Many of these anglers already are spending less time fishing for black bass, walleyes, and panfish, concentrating instead on catching striped bass. Like many anglers fishing for salt-water stripers, some of these fresh-water anglers will also become striped-bass "specialists," spending most of their time seeking this highly prized newcomer. So great is its popularity that the fresh-water striped bass has been called by many "The Super Fish" and "The Fish of the Future."

In the past the striped bass was also known as the squidhound, linesides, greenhead, rockfish, and rock. But most anglers today refer to it simply as the striper—an apt name given the seven or eight longitudinal stripes on its sides. The back of the striped bass will vary from a light tan to a dark olive or bluish green, depending on where it is found and the color and depth of the water. This upper color changes to silver along the sides and to white along the belly. The striped bass resembles the white bass, except that the body of the striped bass is longer and it grows much bigger. Striped bass crossed with white bass produce a hybrid bass that grows bigger than the white bass but not so big as the striped bass. The hybrid also has a deeper body and is less streamlined than the striper.

The fishing tackle used to catch fresh-water striped bass can be the same as the outfits used to catch big black bass, walleyes, pike, muskellunge, coho, chinook, lake trout, and other big fish in fresh water. Your regular fresh-water spinning, spin-casting, bait-casting, and trolling outfits will all catch stripers. Some anglers also use the heavier fly rods for this fishing. In some areas where you have to make long casts or fish fast tailwaters below dams you can use two-handed salt-water spinning rods, including some of the longer surf rods up to ten or twelve feet.

The same is true of many of the lures used to catch striped bass. Most of the same surface and underwater plugs, spoons, spinners, jigs, streamer flies, and plastic lures used for other fresh-water fish can also be used for striped bass. However, the lures should match the size of the minnows, shad, herring, or other small fish the stripers are feeding on. So you should have some bigger sizes in your tackle box. Also, the hooks on lures used for striped bass should be somewhat larger and stronger than those used on most fresh-water lures.

When it comes to natural baits, the striped bass can be caught on live and dead gizzard shad, threadfin shad, herring, alewives, needlefish, waterdogs, small eels, minnows, panfish, and other small fish. Some anglers have even used dead salt-water anchovies, sardines, and herring for fresh-water stripers with great success.

The season for catching fresh-water striped bass is a long one, especially in our southern states, where they can often be caught the year round. In most states, however, the best fishing starts in the spring, when the stripers move up the rivers to spawn. This can be as early as February and March in the South and as late as May or June in the North. During the summer months fishing can be good in the deeper rivers, lakes, and reservoirs. Then in the fall, there is usually another surge of fast fishing in most waters during September, October, and November.

The time of day you fish for stripers depends on the season, the weather, water temperature, and the presence of baitfish. As a general rule you'll find that most striper activity peaks in shallow water or close to shore (or when they are chasing baitfish) during the early morning and evening hours. This is especially true during the summer months. During the fall and early winter there can often be surface action during any part of the day. Stripers are also more apt to show on top and feed closer to the surface and in shallow water on cloudy, rainy, or overcast days than on bright, sunny ones. And some of the best striper fishing takes place at night from dusk to midnight and then just before daybreak.

Striped bass are easy to locate when they are chasing shad minnows, alewives, or herring on top of the water. Then you can see them breaking or churning the water and creating a big commotion on top. In some lakes and reservoirs this attracts flocks of gulls, which you can spot at a distance, especially if you have a pair of binoculars. Of course, stripers, which also chase and feed on baitfish below the surface, do not show on top too often or too regularly. So try to locate the shad minnows or baitfish even below the surface and you'll usually find stripers nearby.

Striped bass are usually easy to locate in rivers with a dam, falls, or other obstruction blocking their spawning run. The fast tailwaters below these dams attract stripers, especially

Striped-bass fishing in fresh water is often good in the turbulent waters below dams. Stopped by these barriers on their journey upstream, striped bass feed on the shad minnows and other small fish found in these waters. (Oklahoma Department of Wildlife Conservation Photo)

when the turbines are turned on and the water boils out, often bringing stunned, injured, or chewed-up shad minnows or small fish that stripers feed on.

Finding stripers in a large lake or reservoir is more difficult, since they tend to move around quite a bit following the schools of baitfish and feeding at different spots, depths, and periods. In such waters, look for structure and cover such as fallen trees, driftwood, submerged brush, or trees especially along sloping points, on humps, bars, and along dropoffs bordering deep water. Stripers also hang around pilings, rocks, bridge supports, breaklines, and channels. The mouths of rivers and creeks entering a lake or reservoir are other productive areas. Stripers like fast currents and rips and will gather at such spots to wait and feed.

Early in the morning, at dusk and during the night, when stripers move into shallow water near shore to feed, they will be found at the entrances to coves and bays and along bars and points. During the middle of the day and during the summer months they will often be suspended in deeper water, from fifteen to forty feet in most lakes. In some deep lakes and during the hot summer months and cold winter months stripers may be down in depths up to sixty or seventy feet. For fishing in deep water, a depth finder or a fish finder is a big help in reading the depth and bottom and in locating baitfish and even the stripers themselves.

The most exciting fishing for stripers occurs when they are showing on top, chasing shad minnows or other small fish. For this type of fishing, called "jump" fishing, you rush over to the spot, preferably in a boat with a fast motor, when you see birds working or fish breaking. You should also have two or three rods rigged with different lures all ready to cast.

It is important here not to speed up too close to the fish and frighten them or put them down. Instead, approach the outside edge of the school on the upwind side, shut off your motor about a hundred feet away, and drift toward the fish. Then you make long casts into the feeding fish, using surface plugs such as the poppers, chuggers, swimmers, torpedo shapes, and crippled minnows with propellers. Work these fairly fast, with plenty of commotion or splash on top.

But whether the stripers are showing on top or go down, you can still catch them by using underwater plugs, spoons, and jigs at this time. In fact, it is usually the smaller stripers that break on top—the bigger ones will be down below anywhere from a few feet to twenty or thirty feet down. Here you should try reeling in a lure fast with no added rod action. If this fails, try a spoon or jig and make long upward sweeps of the rod, then drop the tip so that the lure rises and sinks in an attractive manner. You have to keep an eye on the line at all times and also try to feel a hit because the stripers will usually grab the spoon or jig while it is dropping. For this reason you should also try to keep the slack out of your line while the lure is sinking.

On many rivers and lakes you can also drift in a boat or move it slowly along shore and in shallow water and cast lures for stripers. Here you will have best results early in the morning, toward dusk, and during the night. The best fishing is usually off points, bars, along dropoffs, mouths of coves and creeks, rocks, steep shorelines, and overhanging trees. At night fish near marinas and docks where lights shine into the water. You can often hear the stripers or see splashes when they chase shad minnows and small baitfish. The best lures at such times are usually underwater plugs such as the Rapala, Rebel, Pikie Minnow, Redfin, Hellcat, Hellbender, and similar types. Another good lure for this inshore fishing is a white or yellow bucktail or feather jig, weighing about ¼ to ½ ounce, with a long strip of pork rind. Both plastic-tail jigs and spinner baits also work well in shallow water near shore.

Casting lures for stripers from shore is usually most effective when you are fishing in rivers, especially below dams and in the tailwaters. Here you can also use surface plugs early in the morning and evening or when you see fish breaking or chasing baitfish. You can try underwater plugs, spoons, spinners, and jigs from shore. Jigs are especially deadly because they get down deep and reach stripers lying near the bottom. In fast currents cast well upstream and across and let the jig swing, sink, and bounce along the bottom or rocks. For such shore fishing in many spots you need the longer two-handed spinning rods similar to salt-water surf rods to reach the best spots or breaking fish.

When striped bass are down deep, vertical jigging is the best way to reach and catch them. For this, use a fairly stiff bait-casting rod or popping-type rod with fifteen- or twenty-pound-test line. The deadliest lures for such jigging are the heavy spoons such as the Hopkins 75, the Kastmaster, the Nebco Tor-P-Do No. 2, the Slab, the Topo, the Little Cleo, and the thicker Dardevles. In somewhat shallower water the bucktail, feather, nylon, and plastic-tail jigs can also be used.

Vertical jigging is most effective during the summer, fall, and winter months when stripers are in water from twenty to seventy feet deep. They may be suspended at middepths or down over some kind of structure or cover such as sunken trees, brush, and rocks. A depth finder or fish finder is almost a must for such vertical jigging. If you locate the fish or are directly over the right structure or cover, anchoring is best. But you can also try drifting over a broad underwater island, hump, bar, or along a dropoff or break.

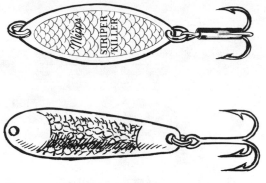

Two spoons used for striped bass.

For vertical jigging, let your spoon or jig flutter down freely until it reaches the level where the fish are suspended or until it hits the cover or bottom. Many strikes will come while the spoon or jig is sinking, so watch the line closely. It is best to let your lure drop while you are measuring the depth with one- or two-foot strips of the line. When the spoon reaches the correct depth, start working it up and down in three- or four-foot sweeps of the rod, lifting it high sharply and then lowering the rod as the spoon flutters and sinks. If you are over sunken trees, brush, or if the fish are right on the bottom, it's a good idea to try to touch and feel this cover or bottom with your spoon.

When using a jig with a bucktail or plastic tail for vertical jigging, let it hit the cover or the bottom and take up the slack line. Then give the jig three or four short, quick jerks, let it settle back toward the bottom, and be prepared for a hit while it is sinking.

In any vertical jigging, you have to experiment with the rod action you use to see what the stripers want. In cold water or very warm water less energetic or short lifts will usually be best. On other days the stripers may want a faster, more active sweep of the rod and more movement in the lure before they hit.

Fresh-water striped bass can also be caught by trolling in most of the rivers, lakes, and reservoirs where they are found. Trolling is especially effective when stripers are scattered or when concentrations are difficult to locate. But it can also be done effectively even when stripers are feeding on top or when you are over known structure or along dropoffs.

For trolling, somewhat heavier tackle than that used for casting is best; spinning tackle with a stiff action rod and ten-to-fifteen-pound-test lines will do the trick. But if you plan to do a lot of trolling for stripers, conventional, heavy fresh-water rod of the bait-casting type but with a longer handle or light salt-water rods are better. These can be fitted with heavy-duty bait-casting-type reels or light salt-water reels with revolving spools. The reels can be filled with lines testing from fifteen to twenty-five pounds.

Most of the lures used for casting such as underwater plugs, spoons, spinners, jigs, and plastic lures can also be used for trolling for striped bass. In shallow water or when trolling the lures a few feet below the surface for stripers feeding on top, you can use plain monofilament line and let it out anywhere from 50 to 150 feet behind the boat. But when stripers are deeper you have to add trolling weights ahead of the lure or else use wire lines. Downriggers, of course, are best for holding your lure at the correct depth for deep trolling and for fighting a striper without any heavy weight on the line.

There are days when stripers want the real thing, and then live baits can be deadly. Live shad minnows, herring, alewives, shiners, small eels, or even small sunfish can be hooked through the back for still fishing or through the lips for drifting or reeling in the bait. Nos. 1/0 to 4/0 hooks are usually used, depending on the size of the stripers expected.

You can lower a live baitfish into the depths by adding a light clincher or Rubbercore sinker so that it swims at various levels depending on how much line you let out. When fishing in strong currents such as the tailwaters below dams, you can add a heavier egg sinker about two feet above the bait. A barrel swivel on the line at this point will act as a stop to keep the weight at the proper distance above the bait.

One highly effective way to use this rig is to cast it out from a boat or shore and let it sink, then reel it in slowly like a lure. If the bait is lively no added rod action is needed, but if it is sluggish or dead you can try moving the rod tip in short jerks. You may also have to change weights to get the baitfish down to the level where stripers are present.

You also use a bottom rig with a three-way swivel when fishing with live or dead baits. Tie a two-to-three-foot leader with the hook to one eye of the swivel. Then add a shorter dropper line to another eye of the swivel to hold

These anglers fishing Kerr Lake in North Carolina have just netted a husky striper. These fish attain an even bigger size in many fresh waters. (Photo by Joe Arrington)

the sinker. This line holding the sinker should be weaker than the fishing line or the leader holding the bait so that it breaks off when caught on the bottom. The fishing line, of course, is tied to the remaining eye of the swivel.

Live baits can be used on both rigs described above. But you can also use a small whole dead baitfish or cut a big one into sections and use these on the same rigs. Cast this bait out from an anchored boat or from shore and let it go down to the bottom and "soak" there until a striper finds it.

When using any kind of live bait for stripers give the fish plenty of time to swallow it before trying to set the hook. The bigger the bait you use the more time you should give the fish to swallow it.

A hooked striper puts up a long and determined fight, but rarely on the surface. When first hooked the striper will make a long, fast run and head for deeper water. Do not try to stop or even slow down this first run; rather let the fish take line freely. Several other runs will be made, but these will be shorter. In a river you may

Striped bass grow fast in fresh water. The fingerlings on the left were placed in Lake Talquin in Florida, and within two years had reached the size of the specimen on the right. (Florida Game & Fresh Water Fish Commission Photo)

have to follow a striper if it's a big one, because they usually head downstream. When a striper tires, a big, wide-mouthed net or a gaff should be used to bring it up to the boat or shore.

Most of the fresh-water stripers you catch will run from about a pound or two up to fifteen or twenty pounds in weight. But fish in the thirty-, forty-, and even fifty-pound class have been caught through the years. One of the largest was the fifty-nine-pound, twelve-ounce striper caught by Frank W. Smith in 1977 in the Colorado River, near Bullhead City, Arizona. But no matter what their size, fresh-water stripers make good eating and can be prepared in many ways.

Today you'll find fresh-water stripers in Alabama, Mississippi, Louisiana, New Mexico, Kansas, Utah, Nevada, Arizona, Colorado, West Virginia, Virginia, Texas, Tennessee, Arkansas, North Carolina, South Carolina, Oklahoma, Kentucky, Georgia, Florida, Indiana, Missouri, Nebraska, New York, New Jersey, Pennsylvania, Connecticut, Rhode Island, Massachusetts, New Hampshire, Maine, California, and Oregon.

The future of the fresh-water striped bass looks bright. Stripers are reproducing naturally in some of the waters where they are now found. In other waters they are being stocked annually or at intervals to maintain a fishery. Biologists welcome the stripers because they keep the forage-fish populations down and because in lakes where they cannot reproduce naturally, they can be kept under strict control. Many states are building their own striper hatcheries so that they do not have to depend on other states for a supply of eggs or young stripers. So it looks like fresh-water striped-bass fishing is not only here to stay, but also will increase in the future to provide sport for more and more fresh-water anglers.

Chapter 22

ROCK BASS

The rock bass is another neglected fresh-water fish, often overlooked in the outdoor columns of newspapers or in magazines or books. In fact, most anglers seem to ignore this fish and rarely brag about catching rock bass, probably because very few of them deliberately fish for rock bass. This worthy little panfish is usually caught by anglers seeking black bass, walleyes, or some other fish.

Yet the rock bass can provide some excellent sport and fine eating afterward. He is a very willing biter and is usually easy to catch once you locate him. Rock bass are found in almost two thirds of the United States, from the Great Lakes to the St. Lawrence River west to Wyoming, Colorado, and Arizona, and south to the Gulf of Mexico and Florida. They have been introduced widely, especially in the East, where formerly there were none.

A member of the sunfish family, the rock bass resembles the sunfishes in general outline and shape. The major difference is that the rock bass has a much larger mouth than any sunfish and a red eye. The back is olive-green to black, blending into a yellow or bronze on the sides. There are dark patches of scales on each side, which give the fish a mottled effect. The belly is a yellowish white.

The rock bass is also called the goggle-eye, redeye, sun perch, lake bass, sunfish bass, frogmouth perch, redeye sunfish, redeye bream, redeye perch, rock sunfish, and just plain "rock."

Many rock bass are caught by youngsters with cane or glass poles about ten or twelve feet long, with or without a bobber above the hook. A light or ultralight spinning outfit or spin-casting outfit is good for bait fishing or for casting small lures. And a fly rod as always will provide the maximum in fun and sport with rock bass.

Rock bass will hit spinner-and-fly or spinner-

ROCK BASS

and-bait combinations when cast and reeled in slowly. Wingless or hackle flies should be used behind a spinner. Rock bass will also strike small underwater and surface plugs, as well as small weighted spinners and small spoons. In recent years the small jigs with bucktail or hair, feathers, nylon, or plastic tails have proven very effective. Since rock bass have large mouths, they will hit somewhat larger lures than those used for most panfish. In fact, many anglers fishing for bass with lures usually used for these fish, often find that rock bass will grab them too.

Fly-rod anglers have caught rock bass on dry flies such as the Royal Coachman, the Wulffs, bivisibles, Irresistible, Goofus Bug, and Muddler Minnow. These can be somewhat bigger in size than those used for trout and most panfish. Wet flies such as the Black Gnat, Western Bee, Red Ibis, Coachman, Colonel Fuller, Wooly Worm, and any nymph patterns can also be used. Small streamers and bucktails also work well since rock bass often feed on small minnows. Bass bugs and panfish bugs can also be used. The more colorful, gaudier patterns of flies work as well if not better than the darker, somber patterns.

However, most rock bass are caught on natural baits such as worms, hellgrammites, grasshoppers, crickets, catalpa worms, mealworms, crayfish, and minnows. Small crayfish about 1½ or 2 inches long make an excellent bait. With big crayfish, peel the hard shell off the tail and just use the meat. One big tail will make two or three baits. Minnows should be about 2 or 2½ inches long.

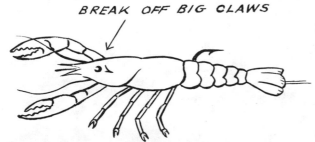

BREAK OFF BIG CLAWS

How to hook small crayfish for rock bass.

The season for rock bass is long because this fish starts to bite early in the spring and continues into the late fall. In the colder creeks, rivers, and lakes, they will often bite during the entire summer—a time when bass and trout refuse to co-operate. However, during warm weather the best fishing will usually take place in the evening just before dark. Since the rock bass continues to feed after dark, some good fishing can also be had at night.

As the name implies, the rock bass loves to hang out around rocks. In fact, he prefers the same rocky areas as the smallmouth in most waters, except that he likes the slower, quieter spots rather than the fast, turbulent currents. In lakes, rock bass are found over rocky shoals, reefs, and bars in shallow water, and will be close to shore especially in the spring and fall. During the hot summer weather, they may move off into somewhat deeper water along dropoffs, around big boulders and rocks, and along cut banks. They like shade and will hide under ledges, lily pads, overhanging branches of trees, stumps, logs, brush, docks, piers, and rocky cliffs.

In rivers and streams rock bass also frequent rocky stretches and gravel bottoms. Look for them under overhanging banks, rock ledges, under trees and branches, bushes, logs, tree branches, and anywhere else they can find shade and cover. Rock bass in rivers usually stay out of the main currents and fastest water, preferring instead the quieter pools, eddies, and backwaters. The big rock bass in rivers will often be found in the tails of pools, below dams, and around bridge supports and sunken trees. Look for them on the upstream side of obstructions waiting for the lazy current to bring them food. They are usually in shallow water in the morning, evening, and at night. In the daytime they stay hidden in shady spots or in deeper water.

When using natural baits for rock bass in creeks, streams, and rivers it's a good idea to keep the bait moving and drifting slowly with the current into spots where rock bass may be lying. In shallow streams one good way to do this is to wade in the water a good distance from shore. Then drop your bait upstream above the spot where you see a rock bass or think one may be lying. Let the current sweep the bait as close to this hideout as you can so that it passes in front of the fish. Although rock bass will take most baits readily without hesitation, they will not move too far from their shady cover to get them. When fishing shallow streams and creeks no float is needed, and unless the current is strong you don't need any weight. But if you have to get the bait deeper in a fast current, add

Rock bass are most plentiful in slow rivers and streams. In faster waters, they tend to stay in the quiet pools and deadwaters. (West Virginia Economic & Community Development Photo)

Most rock bass are caught accidentally by anglers fishing for smallmouth bass in rivers or for largemouth bass or other panfishes in lakes and ponds. However, in waters where they are plentiful, rock bass are sometimes sought deliberately. (Pennsylvania Fish Commission Photo by Johnny Nicklas)

a split shot or two on the leader above the hook.

When fishing in the deeper pools or lakes near shore you can use a float or bobber on the line high enough so that the bait will sink almost to the bottom. In still deeper water in a lake you'll find the biggest rock bass along dropoffs, breaklines, rocky shores, and bottoms. Here in the hot summer months when they are down in water from ten to twenty-five feet deep you can let the bait sink to that level without a float, or fish right on the bottom with a sinker and bottom rig.

When using such lures as small plugs, spinners, spoons, or spinner-and-fly combinations in streams and creeks, you can cast downstream and across, let the lure swing with the current, and then bring it back close to the bottom. Here again, it is important to have the lure pass right in front of and close to the rock bass. And work the lures slowly for rock bass, since they are not very fast fish. In lakes you can use the same lures, casting them into likely spots and reeling them in slowly along the bottom.

Jigs can also be used for rock bass in streams, creeks, and lakes. Here small crappie jigs with marabou tails or small jigs with plastic worm or grub tails are highly effective. These are cast out, allowed to swing toward the rock bass in a stream, and then reeled in close to the bottom. In a lake cast out to a rock bass hangout, let the jig sink to the bottom, then retrieve it slowly, bouncing it along the bottom.

The fly-rod angler can catch rock bass with wet flies or small streamers or bucktails. In a stream or creek cast upstream and across, above the spot to be fished, and then let the current swing the fly toward the fish. In shallow water a floating fly line will work well. But in deeper water and fast currents, use a weighted fly or a sinking fly line or both. Rock bass will also take dry flies, bass bugs, or panfish bugs on top, especially toward dusk and at night. Work them up close to the shore in short twitches or pops.

Small rock bass will often swarm all over in small schools and are usually easy to catch. The bigger rock bass are more wary, more solitary, and more likely to be found in deeper water. To catch them you have to approach their hiding spots carefully and make fairly long casts, especially when the water is clear.

Unfortunately, rock bass are feeble fighters on the end of a line: They give up rather quickly and do not pull too hard. They show the most spunk when you catch them on a fly rod or ultralight spinning tackle. A good-sized fish in a fast current or in snag-infested waters may give some trouble and fight a bit harder.

But most rock bass that are caught are lightweights, ranging from about 4 to 8 inches in length and weighing about ½ pound or a bit less. Some waters may contain good-sized fish up to 1 pound or somewhat more in weight; and several weighing more than 2 pounds have been caught in the South. The biggest rock bass ever caught on rod and reel was a 3-pounder taken in the York River in Ontario by Peter Culgin in August 1974.

Rock bass make good eating if taken early or late in the year from cold, clean waters. Those taken from lakes and ponds or slow-moving muddy waters, especially during the summer months, may be soft and have a muddy flavor. This can be avoided to some extent if the big ones are skinned or filleted.

We won't list any waters containing rock bass because most anglers will continue to fish for other species and take the rock bass if they happen to come along.

Chapter 23

CATFISH

Fishing for catfish is very popular in waters where these dark, smooth, bewhiskered fish are numerous. Down South, for example, you'll often see the banks of the larger rivers, lakes, and reservoirs lined with hundreds of eager catfish anglers. Additional hundreds will be out in small boats dangling their lines near the bottom hoping a big catfish will come along and engulf the bait. Even in northern lakes and rivers where channel catfish have been stocked, they have proven more popular than black bass.

The reasons for this popularity are simple: Catfish often come big and make delicious eating. Also, they are found in warmer, muddier waters, often near cities, where trout, bass, and other more delicate game fish have tough going. In addition, catfish bite well at night: Many working anglers do a bit of catfishing after dinner without missing a day's work.

When we talk about catfish we must mention the fact that there are at least twenty-four species found in North America. But of these we are mainly concerned here with the four usually caught by anglers. They are the blue catfish, channel catfish, white catfish, and flathead catfish, of which the biggest is the blue catfish, also called the chucklehead, great blue catfish, great forktail catfish, and Mississippi blue catfish. This species is gray or dusky blue on the back with a silvery white belly and a deeply forked tail. The blue catfish can weigh up to 150 pounds or more.

The channel catfish resembles the blue catfish but is smaller and more streamlined. Also known as the squealer, willow catfish, fiddler, forktail catfish, speckled catfish, and silver catfish, this species is usually gray or grayish blue on the top, with a silvery tinge and black spots along the sides. Its tail is also deeply forked. Channel catfish may reach fifty pounds or more in weight.

The white catfish is pale olive or blue-gray on top and white on the belly. The tail is forked but not so deeply as in the channel catfish. The

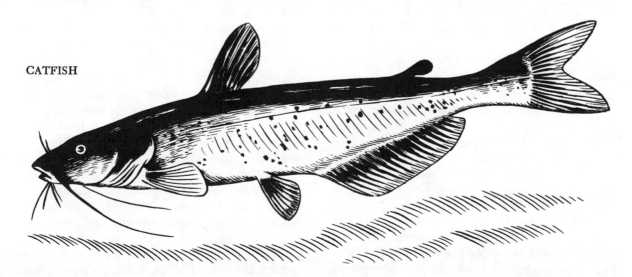

CATFISH

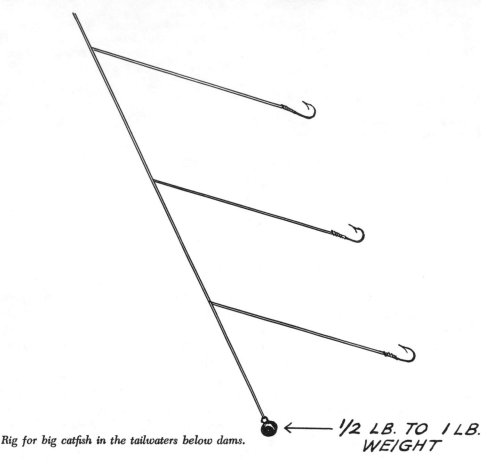

Rig for big catfish in the tailwaters below dams.

← 1/2 LB. TO 1 LB. WEIGHT

white catfish may reach sixty pounds in weight in certain waters but rarely goes over fifteen pounds in most areas. It has also been called the Potomac catfish.

The flathead catfish is yellow or olive-brown on the back with brown blotches along the sides. It is also called the yellow cat, mud cat, and shovelhead cat. It sometimes reaches over one hundred pounds in weight in the larger rivers.

Catfish have been caught on all kinds of tackle, from simple drop or throw lines to deep-sea rods and reels. The ordinary cane pole is often used when the catfish are close to shore or in narrow creeks. For the smaller catfish, weighing from two to fifteen pounds, you can use spinning rods, spin-casting tackle, and bait-casting tackle. But for the big catfish in large rivers and where strong currents prevail, you need heavier outfits. For boat fishing, a salt-water boat rod and reel will serve the purpose. Here if the bottom is rocky or filled with obstructions and the catfish are big, you often need lines testing up to eighty or one hundred pounds. For fishing from

shore where long casts may be required, the shorter surf-spinning or even revolving-spool conventional outfits are effective. You can use twenty-to-twenty-five-pound-test line with the heavy surf-spinning rods and thirty- or forty-pound-test lines with the conventional surf rods and the revolving-spool reels.

Various types of rigs are employed in catfishing. For fishing in quiet pools or lakes, the baited hook is merely tied to the end of the line, cast out, and allowed to sink to the bottom. But when distance is needed or when you are fishing in a strong current, a bottom rig, consisting of a sinker on the end of the line and a hook on an eighteen-inch leader tied a few inches above the weight, is often used. Some anglers like to use two or three hooks on such a rig with up to a pound of weight in strong tailrace currents.

Another popular catfishing rig is the sliding-sinker rig. This is similar to the one often used for carp fishing and merely employs an egg-shaped sinker with a hole in it. The line runs through the hole, and the sinker is stopped by a barrel swivel tied about two feet above the hook. For fishing from shore or boats in deep water with strong currents, heavy sinkers up to eight or ten ounces may be required to hold bottom. In most catfish waters, however, you can use much lighter weights.

Hooks in size Nos. 1/0, 2/0, 3/0, and 4/0 are usually used for the smaller catfish. For the big catfish hooks in size Nos. 7/0, 8/0, and 9/0 are preferable. These should be strong, salt-water types that do not straighten too easily under a strain. The Eagle Claw and the O'Shaughnessy patterns are usually favored. Treble hooks are also used to hold the softer baits such as dough-balls, cheese baits, and stinkbaits. Some of these treble hooks even have a coil spring around the shank of the hook to hold the soft baits better.

The list of suitable catfish baits is long and varied. Earthworms such as the garden worms and nightcrawlers are tops; up to a dozen or more of the smaller worms may be needed on a single hook. Another good bait is a fresh-water clam or mussel, opened and allowed to stand for a day or two to ripen. Various chunks and strips of meat such as beef, lamb, pork, and poultry can be used. The heart, liver, and lungs of such animals are also worth a try, as are the entrails of smaller animals such as rabbits and poultry, and fish such as carp and buffalo. Big catfish have been taken with small dead birds, mice, chicks, and frogs. For smaller catfish, insects such as grasshoppers, catalpa worms, locusts, and grubs (usually two or three on a single hook) can be drifted in the currents during the summer months. Another excellent bait is a soft-shelled crayfish tied to a hook. (With hard-shell crayfish, just use the meat from the tail.)

Various kinds of small fishes and minnows make effective catfish bait. In Tennessee, Kentucky, and other southern states, gizzard shad and river herring are commonly used. The smaller ones are hooked whole, while the larger ones can be cut into strips or chunks. Don't overlook the entrails or guts from such fish when baiting your hook. Other fish such as small perch, sunfish, suckers, carp, small catfish, and bullheads can also be used as bait for big catfish. The really big baitfish can be sliced into strips an inch wide and seven or eight inches long and used for bait.

Catfish have also been caught on fruits, berries, laundry soap, congealed chicken and animal blood, and various stink and doughball baits made from strongly scented combinations of cheese, meat, fish, and flour. Most catfish anglers like to make their own stink and doughball baits, but they can also be bought in tackle stores already prepared and packaged.

When you go catfishing, it's a good idea to take along several different kinds of baits and try them all until you find the ones the fish want. Although catfish will eat almost anything, they have their preferences and fussy feeding periods when they want a certain kind of food and ignore all others.

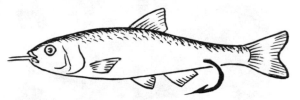

Minnow on hook for catfish.

Catfish have also been caught on slow-moving artificial lures such as underwater plugs, spoons, jigs, spinners, and plastic lures, but this is usually accidental. Though in a few spots they are deliberately fished for with jigs or other artificials, in most waters catfish are caught on lures being used for other, livelier game fish. The speedier channel catfish is more likely to be caught on artificial lures than the other species. But day in and day out, the natural baits are more dependable for all kinds of catfish.

The season for catfishing may begin as early as March or April in southern waters and continue through October or November. Farther north it may start later and end earlier, but usually the months from May to October are best. They are more likely to be congregated in rivers below dams during May, June, and July when they are spawning. In the northern states catfishing is often good during the summer months, and June is usually a good month in most areas. In Florida, of course, catfish can be caught the year round.

The best time to go catfishing is when a river is rising from a recent rain and is becoming discolored. At this time, catfish go on a feeding binge, eating around the clock on foods washed by the rains into the river. After the water has been muddy for a few days the fishing may fall off since the catfish have filled their bellies.

The best catfishing usually takes place at night. With two or three lines out, all you have to do is sit back and wait for a bite. (Oklahoma Department of Wildlife Conservation Photo)

Although most catfish are caught from shore, you can also make some big catches from a boat, as these two anglers have done. (Walker: Missouri Tourism Photo)

When the water is clear the best fishing takes place early in the morning, in late afternoon, in the evening and dusk, and during the night. In fact, you can't choose a better time to go catfishing than at night. That's when they leave their hideouts and roam the shallows and shorelines looking for food. During the daytime they bite better on cloudy, overcast days than on bright, sunny ones. And as was mentioned above, daytime fishing can be good when the water is muddy.

If you do fish during the daytime when the water is clear you have to locate the deep-water spots and holes where catfish lurk. Big catfish will often stay in water from thirty to sixty feet deep, in the larger, deeper rivers. Look for catfish along underhanging banks, beneath rocks and ledges, along brick walls, cement blocks, caves, stumps, logs, sunken trees, brush-piles, tree roots, and similar cover. The mouths of creeks or rivers entering a lake or reservoir are prime hot spots, while deep pools, channels, and eddies are best during the daytime. At night you can try the rapids, riffles, and shallows near shore.

Big catfish are often found in the deeper pools, channels, and holes below big dams. In many southern states with such dams and tail-waters the best spots are the "boils"—that is, the turbulent water flowing through the turbines and coming out of the openings. Here the catfish feed on fish that are stunned, crippled, or chopped up by the turbines.

Such turbulent waters usually call for boat fishing: anglers in a small boat head close to the boils, lower their sinker and bait, and then drift slowly downstream. The outboard motor is left running, with the boat heading into the current as it slowly backs downriver. This can be a dangerous method, since you never know when water will be released from the turbines and perhaps capsize your boat.

Some anglers like to head through the boils to fish the quieter water next to the dam. And still others run their boats up to the boils, then cut the motor and drift downstream, bouncing bottom with their sinker and bait. Another method is to anchor your boat above a hot spot and then drift the bait into it. The same thing can be done from a bridge or small dam, in which case you should let the current move the baited rig along the bottom as you let out line.

From shore, fishermen cast sinker and bait with long surf rods out into the river and let them go down to the bottom. Then they put their rod in a rod holder or prop it against a log or rock and wait for a bite. A catfish is usually slow about taking a bait and must be given plenty of time. Don't try to set the hook on the first nibbles but wait until the fish really swallows the bait and starts moving off with it.

Anglers seeking channel catfish in the smaller, shallower rivers and creeks like to wade for the fish and drift the bait into likely-looking spots. In the faster waters you can drift the bait without a float or bobber to let it sink deep enough. But in the slower-moving stretches a bobber or float can be used to keep the bait moving with the current. The bait should be close to the bottom at all times. Take a position in a rapid or riffle above a pool or hole and let the bait wash down into the deeper water. Do this slowly with the bait held stationary for a few minutes in one spot, then lift the rod tip and let it move off downstream to a new spot. You can also let the bait drift under overhanging trees or bushes, undercut banks, and tree roots. It will also be worth your while to cast the bait on the upstream side of logs, stumps, and rocks and let the current sweep the bait past the obstruction into any hole or depression alongside or below it. Usually a long fly rod or extra-long spinning rod is best for such fishing.

When channel catfish are in the mood you can have a lot of fun trying to hook them on artificial lures. Here a weighted spinner or a jig is good, especially when the hook is tipped with a strip of pork rind or a worm. Plastic worms that are not too long and minnow-type plugs such as the Rapala or Rebel will also work at times. When using any of these lures in a river or a lake, reel them in very slowly as close to the bottom as you can. The same lures can also be trolled on a long line very slowly so that they travel deep along the bottom.

In states where this is allowed, catfish are caught on drop lines, hand lines, or set lines with hooks and baits on the end. The baited hooks are thrown out, the lines tied to stakes, trees, or branches and left for hours in the water. Or trotlines may be stretched across a stream or river and tied to trees on both banks. Short lines with baited hooks are tied to the main line at regular intervals. The trotlines are usually set in the evening and allowed to remain in the water until morning, when they are checked.

An effective and popular way to catch catfish from a boat is by jugging. Years ago people in search of catfish actually used regular stone or glass jugs, then later metal gallon cans. Now plastic containers and styrofoam plastic floats are more popular. A strong line with a hook is attached to the handle of the container or around the float. This line will vary in length according to the depth of the river being fished. Baits such as beef liver, beef heart, minnows, small fish, or chunks of meat or fish are put on the hooks tied to the floats. When the fishing area is reached, the "anglers" toss the whole contraption overboard to form a group of big, floating bobbers. If the current is strong a strip of lead or clincher sinker is added to the line above the hook, to keep the bait close to the bottom. The floats are followed downriver in the boat, and when a float starts to dance up and down or submerges and bobs up, the anglers in the boat head for it and pull in the catfish. Jugging is usually most effective during the hot summer months when the river is low and not too fast.

Still another method used legally or illegally, depending on which state you fish in, is grabbling, also called groping, tickling, and noodling. This involves catching catfish with the bare hands and is done mostly in the late spring or during the summer months when big catfish are holed up spawning and guarding their eggs. The grabbler probes with his arms in the holes under banks or logs, enticing a catfish to attack his hand. Then the braver individuals may shove

This husky catfish was caught in South Carolina waters; even bigger ones are taken from time to time in various states. (South Carolina Wildlife & Marine Resources Department Photo)

their arms through the catfish's mouth and out through the gill opening. Thus caught, the catfish can be hauled out. Other grabblers prefer to tickle the catfish along its belly, slowly working their hands toward the gills. Then they quickly thrust their fingers under the gill cover and grab the catfish to pull it out. But before you attempt this, check your state laws to see if grabbling is legal in your area.

A catfish, however, is at its best when caught on rod and reel: If you use the lightest tackle that is practical for the waters you are fishing and for the size of the fish running, you can have a lot of fun and sport. Channel catfish, especially, will put up a great scrap making fast runs and sometimes splashing around on the surface. But most catfish fight deep, boring toward the bottom for a submerged rock, log, tree root, or other spot where they can foul or cut your line. Big catfish will give you the most trouble, and in some waters heavy tackle is essential for holding them and pulling them off the bottom.

Smaller ones can be lifted directly into a boat or on shore if the line is strong enough. Larger ones can be netted with a wide-mouthed net or gaffed with a big hook.

Catfish, of course, must be skinned before you eat them. This is done by cutting the skin around the head and down the back and belly. Using pliers, grab the skin and pull it off toward the tail. Small catfish can be cooked whole, but the larger ones should be filleted or steaked. Frying and stewing are the usual methods of cooking the fish, with the former particularly popular in the Midwest and South.

In the Midwest and South, the Mississippi, the Missouri, the Ohio, the Tennessee, the Illinois, the White, and the Green rivers are noted for catfishing. Also good is the Tennessee River, especially in the tailwaters below dams such as Watts Bar, Chickamauga, Guntersville, Wheeler, Wilson, Pickwick, and Kentucky. White catfish and channel catfish have been planted in many waters throughout the country, and have joined bass and bluegills in many farm ponds. The white catfish has been introduced to the Great Lakes and in California, where they are plentiful in the lower Sacramento and San Joaquin rivers. White catfish are also found in the Connecticut River and in many lakes and ponds throughout the state. In Virginia they are found in the Potomac River, while in North Carolina they are common in the Cape Fear and Roanoke rivers. White catfish and channel catfish reach a big size in South Carolina, especially in the Santee-Cooper reservoirs. Many rivers and reservoirs in Texas have catfish, with the Rio Grande one of the best. In Florida, the St. John's River and its bulge, Lake George, as well as Lake Okeechobee, are great catfish waters. This is only a partial listing, since many other waters in the states listed above and in other parts of the country contain catfish. A little exploring and fishing with the right baits at the right time of the year will determine whether catfish are present in waters in your area.

Chapter 24

BULLHEADS

The bullheads are the smaller members of the catfish family, but what they lack in size they make up in numbers and popularity. This is the fish which, together with the sunfish, is usually sought by small boys and girls. But don't get the idea that bullheads are only for youngsters and have nothing to offer older anglers. They are just as popular with many older anglers all over the country. In fact, it's a common sight to see many men, women, and kids fishing for bullheads on levees, shores, banks, bridges, and docks where these fish are numerous. Many other anglers fish for them from boats.

Bullheads are usually plentiful in most waters where they are found. Their ability to live in polluted or warm waters that other fish find uninhabitable makes them available to all anglers, even those from large cities and towns. Actually, the bullhead is the most prevalent species in many park ponds and lakes in big cities.

Three kinds of bullheads are found in the United States. One is the brown bullhead, also called the speckled bullhead, pond catfish, red catfish, marble catfish, brown catfish, and polly-wog. Its back ranges from olive to brown in color, while its sides are mottled with light and dark patches. The second species, the yellow bullhead, also called the pond bullhead, has a white chin and whiskers, slightly round tail, and yellow belly. The third is the black bullhead (or the creek bullhead, black catfish, and stinger). The body color of this bullhead varies from greenish brown to black shading into a greenish bronze. It has a light vertical bar at the base of the tail.

Bullheads, also known as "horned pouts" in some areas, are now found in many parts of the United States outside of their original range. They are very popular as a pond fish on farms throughout the country and are beginning to rival the usual inhabitants of these ponds, the black bass and the bluegill.

There is one drawback, however, to stocking bullheads in farm ponds. Though they grow slowly, they breed rapidly and may overpopulate a pond or lake to the detriment of game fish such as trout or bass. If there are too many bullheads in a small body of water, they fail to reach a good size. Because of this they should be caught as rapidly as possible or seined at regular intervals to reduce their numbers in farm ponds. In many states there are no closed-

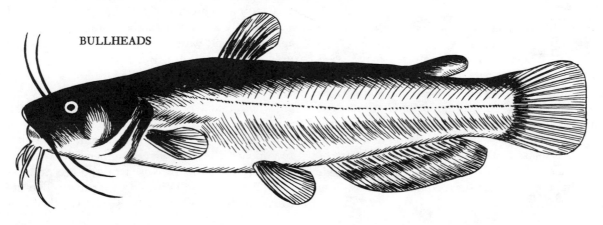

BULLHEADS

season or bag limits on bullheads. You can fish for them the year round and take as many as you like.

It would be foolish to recommend any specific fishing tackle for bullheads because they can be caught on almost any outfit available. Cane poles are popular with kids and many older anglers. But you can also catch them on spinning rods and reels, spin-casting rods and reels, and bait-casting tackle as well as on fly rods. Of course, if you want to have the most sport and fun you should use the lightest tackle possible. There's a big difference between catching a bullhead on a big, heavy cane pole and hooking one on an ultralight spinning rod or a fly rod.

Although bullheads have been known occasionally to follow and strike an artificial lure such as a plug, spinner, spoon, jig, or fly, they are usually caught on natural baits. The list of such baits is long, but day in and day out the lowly earthworm takes the most bullheads. If you are using big nightcrawlers, one or two worms on a hook are sufficient. But when using the smaller garden worms or angleworms you can use a half dozen or more on a single hook.

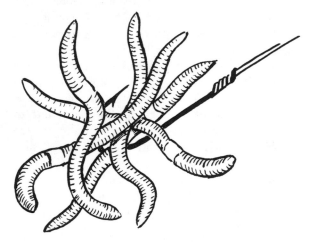

A bunch of worms on a hook for bullheads.

Strips of beef liver or meat often make good baits. In fact, you can use small pieces of meat from almost any animal (including poultry) to catch bullheads. Small minnows are excellent bait, as are small pieces of almost any fish. Bullheads have also been caught on doughballs, bread, insects, stink baits, shrimp, and most of the other baits used for catfish. (See the previous chapter on catfish for a complete list of these baits.)

Bullheads bite from spring to fall, but the best fishing usually starts around April in the South and continues from May to September throughout most of their range. When the water warms up past fifty degrees Fahrenheit they start to become active but bite best when the temperature goes over sixty degrees.

Although bullheads will bite during the daytime, they are not very active in waters that are too clear at this time. The best fishing in rivers and creeks usually takes place when the water is rising and brown from a recent rain or shower. Under such circumstances, the bullheads will bite well all day long. In clear lakes and rivers you'll find your best fishing early in the morning, toward dusk, and during the night. Cloudy or rainy days are better than clear, bright, sunny days for daytime fishing. As soon as it gets dark, however, bullheads become active and prowl the shallows and shorelines in search of food.

Consequently, many bullhead fishermen do most of their fishing at night. To get in on the fun and the large catches that can be taken at this time, take along a lantern or build a fire on shore, cast out your lines, and wait for a bite. If bullheads are present in the waters being fished it won't be long before they find your baits and give you some action.

Bullheads are gregarious by nature, and where you find one there will usually be others. They like the slower pools, eddies, and deeper parts of a stream or river, and though they prefer mud bottoms of rivers or lakes, bullheads are also found over gravel, sand, and rocky bottoms in many waters. Look for them under bridges, below dams and riffles, and along under cut banks and tree roots.

In quieter river waters and in most lakes, you can fish for bullheads with a cane pole or rod and reel without using a sinker, since the bait will usually go down to the bottom of its own accord in such waters. A float or bobber can be used to indicate bites. But make sure the baited hook reaches and rests on the bottom.

In the faster waters of rivers and streams or anywhere that you have to cast some distance, a sinker can be used. Attach this to the end of your line and tie a short leader with the hook a few inches above it. Since bullheads have large mouths, hooks in size Nos. 1 or 1/0 are preferable. (Big hooks will also be easier to remove because a bullhead usually swallows the bait

Bullheads, present in most ponds, lakes, streams, and rivers throughout the country, are a favorite with the cane pole set. (Arkansas Department of Parks & Tourism Photo)

deeply.) Cast this rig out and allow it to sink to the bottom. Next, place your rod in a forked stick or rod holder, or prop it against something solid like a rock or log, and then sit and wait for a bite. The click should be set on your reel, especially if you are fishing at night. Small dock bells can also be used to indicate bites at night when you are fishing with two or three lines or rods.

When you get the first nibbles, wait a few seconds more until the bullhead swallows the bait before you set the hook. A good-sized bullhead in a fast river will put up a good fight on light tackle. But most fishermen using cane poles just yank them out of the water without much ceremony, remove them from the hook, and then cast out for another one.

When you do catch a bullhead hold it carefully so that you don't get stuck with the sharp, and poisonous, spines. They aren't dangerous, although the wound they leave may be painful and cause the fingers or hand to swell. The best way to remove a bullhead or small catfish is to grab the fish so that the spines emerge between your fingers and the fish can be held firmly. Still safer is to pin the fish to the ground with your foot and then remove the hook. Since bullheads often clamp their jaws on a hook or swallow it deeply, a stick with a notch on one end or a hook disgorger is a big help in removing it. So is a pair of long-nosed pliers sold to fishermen for holding fish and removing hooks.

Bullheads rarely grow big, averaging between ½ and 1 pound in weight. A few may reach as much as 3 or 4 pounds, but such big specimens are rare. However, bullheads weighing over 5 pounds have been taken; the largest on record, in fact, came in at 8 pounds.

Like most catfish, the bullhead makes good eating but must be skinned beforehand. Most anglers cut the skin around the head, grab the edge with gripping pliers, and pull it off the body. A quick way to do this without pliers is to cut a slight depression just ahead of the dorsal fin on the fish's neck and deep enough to cut through the backbone. Grasp the head of the fish, and cutting away from the head, remove the dorsal fin and spine. Then slit the skin on top of the bullhead's back all the way down to the tail. Finally, grab the fish's body near the tail with one hand, hold onto the head with the other hand, and bend the two sections sharply until the backbone emerges. Grip the end of the backbone between your thumb and a knife blade and pull on the fish's head. This skins the fish and at the same time removes the entrails, which stay attached to the head. This technique sounds difficult, but once you get the knack, it is easy and quick.

Bullheads are found in many parts of the United States, with the brown bullhead ranging from Canada, throughout the Great Lakes, St. Lawrence region, south to Virginia. A subspecies is found from southern Illinois to Arkansas, the Carolinas, and Florida. The black bullhead is found from Canada to North Dakota, and from the Great Lakes region south to Colorado, Wyoming, Tennessee, and Kansas. A subspecies is found in Alabama, Texas, and Louisiana. The yellow bullhead ranges from North Dakota through the Great Lakes to New York and south to Texas and the Tennessee River system. Another subspecies is found from New Jersey southward. Of course, as stated earlier, bullheads have also been stocked in many other areas throughout the country.

These anglers fishing a New Jersey lake have just caught a good-sized bullhead. Although they are not noted as fighters on the end of a line, bullheads make up for this deficiency on the table, where they provide excellent meals. (Photo by Harry Grosch)

Chapter 25

EELS

The first eel I ever caught as a young boy was taken in a small country brook where the current had pulled the worm and hook under the roots of a large tree. The bait rested there a few seconds, then I felt a sharp tug. I yanked on the pole and an eel about two feet long came flying out.

That was the end of fishing for the day. I grabbed my string of sunfish, and holding the squirming eel as far away from myself as possible, I ran almost all the way back to the farm a mile away, thinking that I had hauled in a snake!

The snakelike appearance of the eels has no doubt repelled many anglers, who do their best to avoid catching them. But thousands of anglers, having discovered that this unique fish can provide fun and is a table delicacy second to none, fish for eels often.

The eel, of course, is a true fish, despite its appearance. It breathes in the water by means of gills like any other fish, whereas a snake breathes out of the water by means of lungs. An eel has two small fins near the head and a long, continuous fin along the back and around the tail. A snake has no fins.

Eels vary from gray to greenish-brown to black on the back; these colors gradually blend with the whitish belly.

For a long time the eel was a creature of mystery, and little was known about its spawning habits or migrations. Ancient Europeans thought that eels originated spontaneously from slime, dew, grass, horsehair, and mud.

It was not until the middle 1880s that the larva of an eel was first examined, by a German naturalist named Dr. Karp, who unfortunately thought it was a new species and failed to identify it as the larva of an eel. In 1896, two Italian ichthyologists identified the larva in question as that of the European common eel. And in 1906, a Danish scientist named Johannes Schmidt began a series of investigations, lasting more than fifteen years, that proved that both the American and European eels travel to the Sargasso Sea region near Bermuda to spawn.

EEL

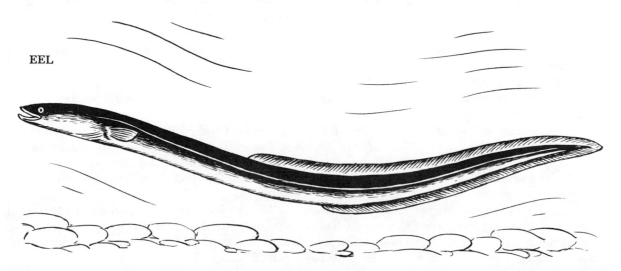

(The two species, which look very much alike, are distinguished by the number of their vertebrae: The American eel has from 103 to 111 vertebral segments, while the European eel has from 110 to 119. This differentiation has been challenged, however, by some scientists who claim that there is only one eel—the American eel.)

The migrations of the common eel are even more remarkable than those of the salmon. The females of both species spend most of their lives (six to eight years before maturation) in fresh-water lakes, rivers, and streams. These "silver eels" descend the rivers in the autumn to meet the males, which have been living in brackish and salt-water bays. Together they slowly move toward their spawning area in the Sargasso Sea. Here, in the deep water, the females lay their eggs and die.

When the eggs hatch, the larvae of the eels are tiny (less than ¼ inch long), shaped like a willow leaf, and transparent. For a time the tiny eels remain several hundred feet below the surface of the ocean. Then they slowly rise to the warmer waters above.

Now the most amazing episode of all takes place. The American larvae start to drift and swim toward the west, while the European larvae move toward the east. Since the American larvae are closer, they reach the coast in about a year. The European larvae, being much farther away from the Continent, require three years to complete the journey.

When the larvae reach the coastlines of their respective continents they change from the leaf-like shape into the cylindrical form of the adult eel. They are still transparent, only about two or three inches long, and are known as "glass eels" or "elvers." Soon they lose their transparency and take on the dark colors of their parents. Then the females ascend the fresh-water rivers, while the males remain in the brackish and salt-water bays and estuaries.

The American eel is found along the East Coast from Labrador to the Gulf of Mexico. They migrate up the Mississippi River and its tributaries and are found in many states east of the Rocky Mountains.

To catch eels you can use ordinary hand lines, cane poles, spinning rods, spin-casting rods, bait-casting rods, and fly rods. Most eels run pretty small (rarely more than a pound or two in weight), so light tackle will provide the most fun.

Eels feed mostly on or near the bottom, poking their pointed snouts into every crevice or hole in search of food. Although an eel at times will strike a wet fly fished slow and deep, they are rarely interested in artificial lures, preferring instead natural baits. They are more or less like catfish in that they feed on a wide variety of animal matter, including crayfish, frogs, worms, insects, and small fish. Worms and small minnows usually make the best eel bait.

It is best to use a rather thick, heavy line and a long-shanked hook such as the Carlisle in size Nos. 1 or 1/0. Eels will wrap themselves around a line and often swallow a hook deep. A long-shanked hook is easier to remove and is less likely to be swallowed all the way down. A thick line is easier to untangle when an eel makes a mess out of it.

Eels can be caught from April to November in most waters, but the spring and fall are the best times. If you can find a river where the eels are migrating to the sea in the autumn, you'll have some great fishing at that time, particularly in September and October. But the summer months also produce plenty of eels.

The best eel fishing takes place at dusk and throughout the night. They seem to bite actively for two or three hours after sundown, then there is a lull. Usually the darker the night, the better the fishing. Eels can also be taken during the daytime, especially in rivers or creeks that are muddy from recent rains.

Eels will come into very shallow water at night to feed, and are often found close to shore then. During the daytime they hide under ledges, banks, rocks, weeds, and roots. In small creeks and streams, the deeper pools are the best places to fish.

Most eels are caught by still fishing from shore, with the angler casting out his line and bait and letting it lie on the bottom. In lakes or quiet pools and eddies no sinker is required, but in fast currents a small sinker is needed to take the bait down and hold it close to the bottom. A weight is also good if you want to cast to a distant spot.

You can have more fun and catch more eels if you use more than one rod or line. Usually two, three, or more rods and lines are cast out and placed along the shore. Set the click on your

A nice spot to keep cool. Also an ideal spot to catch eels, especially toward dusk and at night.
(Virginia Commission of Game & Inland Fisheries Photo by L. G. Kesteloo)

reels or attach the lines to small dock bells, so that you will be alerted if you have a bite. This is especially valuable at night, when the line can't be seen. A lantern or light also comes in handy at night for baiting the hooks and removing the eels.

When you catch an eel, haul it in quickly to prevent it from doubling up and tangling your line. A big eel caught in a rocky area can give you plenty of trouble by crawling into a hole; unless your line is strong you'll probably break off and lose him. If caught over a muddy bottom or other areas free from obstructions, you can fight a big eel on a light outfit for a few minutes. However, the long, slim body of an eel isn't built for fighting, and the best it can do is shake its body and head from side to side in an attempt to get free.

A potato sack to keep the eels in as well as a dry rag or a bucket of sand are necessary on any eel-fishing trip. When you bring an eel in, grab it with the rag or drop it into the sand and you'll be able to hold the eel firmly in order to remove the hook.

Another way to catch eels is by the old-time method of bobbing. To make an eel bob bait, take a long needle and attach several feet of fine linen thread to the eye. Now thread as many earthworms as are needed to fill the string and roll the whole mess into a ball. Wrap some more thread around the worms and then attach the works to a fishing line and a cane pole.

Lower this to the bottom of the lake or river at night and let it lie there. When you feel any bites and are sure that several eels are chewing on the worms, start lifting the bait slowly toward the surface. Then when the eels are near the top of the water, lift them out quickly and swing them over a bushel basket or open potato sack. The eel's fine teeth get tangled in the thread and they hang on for a short while, but soon start dropping off.

Eels can also be speared at night during the spring, summer, and fall months. This can be done from a boat with a light suspended at the bow or by wading in shallow water with a headlight or searchlight. A wide spear or gig with several tines is best for this. Eels are also speared through the ice in rivers, especially brackish ones, as well as in salt-water bays when they hibernate in the mud.

Eels can also be taken in eel pots baited with dead fish, meat, or similar foods. Great numbers are caught commercially in traps, racks, weirs, and seines in the autumn, when eels are migrating down rivers to the sea.

Female eels caught in fresh water usually run from about 1½ to 3 feet in length. Occasionally one over 3 feet and weighing several pounds is caught. A few female eels that do not mature sexually may reach a length of 4 or 5 feet and weights up to 15 or 16 pounds. The much smaller males run from 1 to 2 feet in length in the salt-water and brackish bays where they live.

To skin an eel, first stun it by whacking its head against something hard and solid. Then cut through the skin completely around the neck but not into the meat. Now either hold the head with a dry rag or nail it down to a board or tree. Grasp the loose flap of skin below the head with a pair of pliers, and with a sharp pull toward the tail remove the skin.

Eels have a firm, sweet flesh and can be fried, pickled, or boiled. Smoked eels are considered a delicacy and bring a fancy price in the larger cities.

Anglers who pursue the wily trout or the fighting bass may turn up their noses when eels are mentioned, but the fact remains that many fishermen get a kick out of catching eels. In some sections of the country it is the only fishing that can be had because of heavy water pollution. The pollution has killed off or driven away the more delicate game fishes, but the eel doesn't mind or at least manages to survive. He's tough, rugged, and takes a long time to die, which is the only thing he's got in common with snakes, aside from the elongated shape. Year after year eels complete their fascinating life cycle and at the same time furnish food and sport for thousands of anglers.

Chapter 26

SHAD

There are records of shad being taken on rod and reel in the Connecticut River as early as 1869. But anglers who enjoyed sport fishing for shad remained a handful until after World War II, when spinning tackle came into use and more and more outdoor writers began popularizing shad fishing in their newspaper columns and magazine articles. Now thousands of anglers fish for shad not only along the Atlantic Coast but also along the Pacific Coast, where shad were introduced from the East back in 1871.

Shad were so plentiful in the early days of this nation that they choked the rivers and were caught by the colonists in great quantities for use as fertilizer. Since Atlantic salmon were also plentiful in those good old days, the colonists saw little reason to eat the bony shad. Later on, when salmon started to disappear because of pollution, dams, and overfishing, shad became more popular. But they too became less plentiful as time went on; by 1900 the runs of shad were small or nonexistent in many rivers. Then steps were taken to eliminate pollution, some of the

dams were removed, and permanent fishways were established on the remaining dams. As a result, shad have gradually been making a comeback, and good runs have been re-established in many rivers.

The American shad is also called the common shad, white shad, Atlantic shad, jack, and silver herring. Anglers have also dubbed it the "white lightning" and "poor man's salmon" because of its fast, flashy, fighting qualities on the end of a line. There is also the Alabama shad, which is smaller than the American or white shad. Both are members of the herring family and are sometimes mistaken for the hickory shad—a close relative often found in the same waters.

The American shad has a deep, compressed body. Its back is greenish with a metallic luster, and the sides and belly are silvery. There are dark spots on the shoulder often followed by smaller spots.

Shad are found along the Atlantic Coast from the St. John's River in Florida to the St. Lawrence River in Canada. The Alabama shad

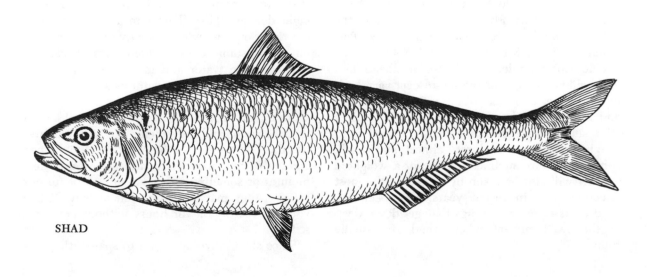

SHAD

is found in the Gulf of Mexico and ascends some of the rivers there. On the Pacific Coast they range from Southern California north to Alaska. Shad spend most of their lives in salt water but return to fresh-water rivers and streams to spawn. Although they eat little or no food during the fresh-water run, they will hit lures. Almost all shad are caught on rod and reel in fresh water during the spawning journey.

You can use different kinds of fresh-water outfits to catch shad: Bait-casting, spin-casting, spinning, and fly rods have all been used. Since shad lures are small and light, you should have a rod that can cast lures from $\frac{1}{16}$ to $\frac{1}{2}$ ounce. The most popular outfit is a light, limber, fresh-water spinning rod and small spinning reel filled with 4- or 6-pound-test line. This is best for casting from shore or a boat. For trolling, a similar outfit or a slightly heavier spinning rod can be used. Fly rods suitable for trout or bass can also be used to cast flies for the silvery scrappers. These are best for casting from shore, in shallow water, or from boats. Light, limber bait-casting or spin-casting rods can also be used to cast lures from shore or boats and for trolling.

Shad flies are usually simple lures, often effective with a fly rod or when let out in a strong current from a boat with any tackle. These flies are usually tied on Nos. 3, 4, 6, or 8 hooks and consist of a body of silver tinsel and sparse white, red, or yellow feathers for wings. They are often used together with red beads ahead of the hook. In fact, a hook wrapped with silver tinsel and two or three beads ahead of it will often catch shad. Flies with Mylar ribbing or tubing are also good. Two popular old-time shad flies are the Enfield Shad Fly and the Chesapeake Bay Shad Fly. You can also use the gaudier, standard trout flies such as the Parmachene Belle, Scarlet Ibis, and Yellow Sally. Pacific Coast anglers often use steelhead flies with yellow, orange, or red fluorescent yarn bodies and silver or Mylar ribbing. Small streamers and bucktails such as the Black Ghost, Mickey Finn, and White Marabou can also be used.

When it comes to lures, almost any small, shiny metal lure such as a spoon or a weighted spinner will also be taken by shad. But the most effective lures in recent years have been the shad darts or other tiny jigs that get down deep in the swift current where shad are usually found.

On the St. John's River in Florida, anglers often troll with a double or tandem rig consisting of a small spoon attached by swivels to the line and another lure, usually a small yellow jig, attached to a three-foot leader, which in turn is tied to the swivel on the line. This is trolled, sometimes with split-shot or clincher sinkers added on the line to get the shad rig down into deeper water.

Shad are occasionally caught on natural baits such as worms, tiny minnows, and grass shrimp. But few anglers fish for them with such baits; most prefer to use the flashy and effective artificials.

The shad-fishing season varies according to the location, weather, and water temperature. It may start as early as December, with good fishing during January, February, and March on the St. John's River in Florida. Farther north it usually begins in April or May, with May and June usually the top months. In California, the season may start in March and continue through May. In Oregon and Washington, May and June are good months, with the fishing often continuing into July. It must be remembered that on some of the longer rivers the shad takes more time to reach the upper stretches of a river, so fishing here will be later than on the lower sections.

The time of day to go shad fishing will also depend on where you fish. On the St. John's River some of the best fishing has taken place during the middle of the day. Farther north good fishing is often had early in the morning and late in the afternoon and evening. In the Connecticut River it was found that shad like water temperatures around sixty-seven or sixty-eight degrees. They don't bite as well in northern rivers on raw, windy, cloudy days as they do on bright, sunny ones. Sudden rains or showers that raise the water and muddy the river may ruin the fishing until the water clears.

An important fact to keep in mind is that shad travel in schools at various depths, and their behavior and movements are highly unpredictable. There may be hours of inactivity—then suddenly they may start hitting. After a few minutes or sometimes an hour or two of furious activity, they may suddenly quit or leave. Then you can cast again for hours without getting a strike.

Since shad move upstream to spawn, they fol-

This big shad was caught in the Delaware River. Most of the larger rivers along the Atlantic Coast have runs of these fish in the spring. (Pennsylvania Fish Commission Photo)

low the main channels and the strongest flow of water. You will therefore find them moving or darting in and along the edges of such currents. They often flash and turn in the current or may even roll, break, or "wash" on top. In shallow, clear water you can also see them swimming or milling around or lying in the current. But more often than not, shad will be near the bottom in the deeper holes, pools, and eddies. The best fishing is usually found in spots where there are obstructions such as falls, dams, or shallow rapids that concentrate the shad in a small area. The curve or bend in a river where the water is deep and the current strong is also a hot spot.

On some rivers it's easy to locate the best shad-fishing spots, since you'll find anglers lining the banks shoulder to shoulder and casting to the fish. Or you will see small fleets of boats anchored in a spot or trolling where shad are present in numbers.

When you are using lures, the usual procedure is to cast a spoon or jig slightly upstream and across the current and allow it to swing and sink toward the bottom. Most strikes will occur at the end of the arc when the lure starts to rise. Although most of the time you can reel in steadily to take up the slack and obtain strikes, you can also retrieve the lure in short jerks or twitches. You should feel the lure touch bottom every so often. If you are not getting down deep enough, add some weight to the line or change to a heavier lure.

Fly-rod anglers either use weighted flies or add weight to the leader or use sinking fly lines to get their flies down deep enough. Here again, the best results are obtained by casting up and across stream and letting the fly swing downstream close to the bottom. If the current is fast you usually don't have to give the fly any added action. But in the slower currents or quieter waters you can give the fly short pulls or twitches during the drift or swing.

Shad have also been known to hit a dry fly in size Nos. 12 or 14 when they are in very shallow water not more than a foot or so in depth. Here best results are obtained by pulling the fly on the surface so that it creates a slight ripple or streak on top. This fishing is most productive late in the season when the shad are in the clear, shallow upper reaches of the river, and especially when caddis flies are hatching.

Casting for shad can also be done from an anchored or drifting boat, but most anglers prefer to troll. Blind trolling can be done in a general area to locate the shad. Then you can troll through the spot repeatedly. Anywhere from 50 to 150 feet of line is let out, and the spoon, spinner, or jig is trolled slowly, close to the bottom. A combination rig with the small spoon on the end of the line and a tiny jig about two feet above it on a dropper is effective for such trolling. You can work the rod up and down in short jerks while trolling. Or you can let the motion of the boat, rod tip, waves, and current do the work of activating the lures.

On the West Coast, anglers often fish from an anchored boat (sometimes two or three lines of boats will be tied up alongside one another) by simply dropping the lures back in the current. In a strong current, however, a rig with a three-way swivel is often used: A three-foot leader holding the lure is attached to one eye of the swivel; a dropper with a sinker is attached to another eye, usually two or three feet below the swivel; and, of course, the fishing line is tied to the remaining eye on the swivel. The lure is generally a small spinner or spoon.

Shad will often hit a lure hard, but at other times you'll feel only a series of light taps. Keep casting or letting out the lure or keep on trolling, since these light hits show that the fish are present and are interested in the lure.

When you hook a shad you'll know why it has been called "white lightning." It will make a fast, long run, then leap out of the water so quickly your eyes can barely follow it. It is a game fish that will fight right up to the end; many are lost during the battle or near the end.

Combo spoon-and-jig rig for shad.

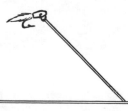

Shad are very fast and put up a great fight on light tackle, often leaping like this out of the water. However, since they have thin mouths, many are lost during the fight. (Florida News Bureau Photo)

Shad have soft mouths, and a sudden pull or shock will rip the hook out of their jaws. They must be played with extreme care, and even then you'll probably lose more fish than you will land. A long-handled, wide-mouthed landing net is needed to scoop a shad up near the boat or in shallow water when you are wading.

Shad can reach fifteen pounds in weight, but most will range from about three to five or six pounds. Nowadays, a seven- or eight-pound shad is considered a big one. The record on rod and reel is a nine-pound, two-ounce shad caught near the Enfield Dam in the Connecticut River on April 28, 1973, by Edward P. Nelson. The Alabama shad runs from one to one and a half pounds, but has been known to reach three or four pounds in weight.

The females or "roe shad" grow larger than the males or "bucks." Shad roe is considered a delicacy, and the females command a higher price in the fish market than the males. Shad are very bony and unless properly prepared are difficult to eat. Boning a shad to remove the fine bones is an art that few anglers know.

Starting in Florida, we find shad in the St. John's River in the northeastern part of the state. On the Gulf of Mexico side of Florida the smaller Alabama shad run in the Chipola, Apalachicola, and Suwannee rivers and up Alabama rivers. In Georgia, the Ogeechee, Woodbine, Satilla, Altamaha, and Savannah rivers have shad. In South Carolina, the Edisto, Cooper, Santee, Black, and Pee Dee rivers can be fished. North Carolina's shad rivers include the Tar, Cape Fear, Neuse, and Roanoke. In Virginia you can try the James, York, Mattaponi, Chickahominy, Appomattox, Rappahannock, and Potomac rivers. Maryland's Potomac, Susquehanna, Patuxent, and other rivers and streams entering Chesapeake Bay all contain shad. In New York, Pennsylvania, and New Jersey they are found in the Delaware River. There are also runs up the Hudson River, with some fishing below the Troy Dam in upper New York State. One of the best fishing spots for shad is the Connecticut River in Connecticut. Here such spots as the Enfield Dam, Windsor Locks Bridge, and Holyoke are well known for their shad fishing. The Farmington River and its tributaries in Connecticut also have some shad fishing. In Massachusetts you can find shad in the Connecticut River, the Merrimack River, Palmer River, and North River.

On the Pacific Coast shad are found in California in the American, Russian, Sacramento, Feather, Yuba, and Trinity rivers. In Oregon, the Columbia River, Coos Bay, Coos River, Sandy River, Willamette River, and Umpqua River have shad runs. And in Washington, you can catch shad in the Columbia River, the Washougal River, the Chehalis River, and the Willapa River.

On the Pacific Coast many anglers who formerly were strictly salmon and steelhead fishermen have tried shad fishing and become enthusiasts. Some of them claim that pound for pound the shad will outfight a steelhead or salmon.

Chapter 27

CARP

No fresh-water fishing guide would be complete without mention of the carp. Although many anglers, especially the purists, may disagree, the carp is highly popular with many thousands of fresh-water anglers in this country.

However, the carp still hasn't attained the same popularity in this country that it has in Europe. There, carp fishing is a time-honored sport, and carp fishermen are a highly skilled group who take their sport seriously. They prepare their tackle and baits with utmost care, check the weather, the wind, select their spots, walk carefully and quietly, and fish for many hours. If they catch a really good-sized carp they consider it a trophy worth mounting. In England, especially, carp are rated very highly as a sport fish, as is evident in the number of carp-fishing clubs, contests, and tournaments that have been established there.

At one time there were no carp in the United States, or in Europe, for that matter. Carp are natives of Asia and are especially plentiful in China, where they have been raised in ponds for over twenty-five hundred years. From China they were introduced to Europe around the thirteenth century. Carp were present in England during the time of Izaak Walton, who wrote about them in his classic *The Compleat Angler*.

In many European countries carp were raised in ponds for food and were considered a delicacy. Even to this day tons of carp are cultivated selectively in ponds for sale to fish markets.

The very first introduction of carp into the United States is hard to pin down, but there are records of carp being brought over from Holland as early as 1832 by a Captain Henry M. Robinson. He kept them in a pond near Newburgh, New York, and it is said that some of the carp escaped into the Hudson River. A Californian, J. A. Poppe, introduced carp into that state in 1872. These fish were brought over from Holstein, Germany, and placed in a private pond in Sonoma County. Of the eighty-three carp only

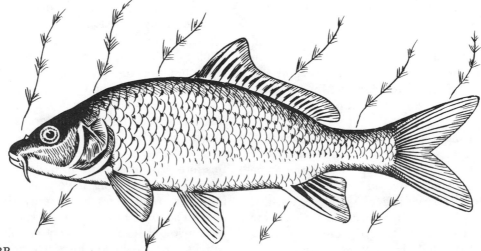

CARP

five survived the trip, but these spawned and soon were numerous enough to be sold and stocked in many waters in the West.

But the real march of the carp began in 1877, when the United States Fish Commission imported 345 carp from Germany and placed them in ponds in Druid Hill Park in Baltimore, Maryland. From there they were transferred to Babcock Lake in Washington, D.C. By 1879 the lake had produced 12,265 carp. Soon there were shipments of young carp going out to twenty-five states and territories.

By 1900, carp had become so plentiful that many fresh-water anglers turned against them. Unfortunately for the carp, other game fish began their decline at around this time and many anglers blamed the carp for this development. They were accused of eating fish and spawn, of muddying the waters, and of not being much of a game or food fish.

We now know that carp can make waters unsuitable for many game fish because of their rooting, feeding, and spawning habits. They compete for living space and food with the game fish, they roil the waters, and they make them unsuitable for spawning for such fish as black bass and sunfish.

But it has also been found that carp do not eat the spawn of other fish. In addition, the carp has been blamed unfairly for conditions that are really the result of siltation, pollution, fluctuating water levels, and warm-water temperatures. There are many waters in which game fish cannot live or reproduce, but in which the hardy carp often thrives and multiplies. Thus the carp provides fishing in many ponds, rivers, and lakes that would otherwise be barren, at least as far as the angler is concerned.

So while many anglers and some fish and game departments consider it a pest in certain waters, the carp is a highly regarded sport fish among many fresh-water anglers. In any case, the carp is here to stay and can provide a lot of fun and sport.

Although there is only one species of carp in the United States, this species have been divided into three types: "Scaled carp" are, as the name implies, completely covered with scales; those with patches or large irregular scales are called "mirror carp"; and those with no scales are called "leather carp." Of the three, the completely scaled variety is the most common. Carp

are also called German carp, golden carp, silver carp, mud carp, mudhog, waterhog, riverhog, bugle-mouthed bass, and old puckerpuss.

The carp resembles its close relatives, the goldfish and the buffalo fish, which is native to this country. (See Chapter 29 for information on the buffalo fish.) The carp is usually olive-green on the back with bronze sides and a white or yellow belly. It has a long dorsal fin with a serrated spine in front. The carp's sucker-type mouth is toothless but it does have teeth in its throat. It has two barbels or "whiskers" on each side of the mouth.

Carp fishermen use all kinds of tackle, from an ordinary hand line or drop line to salt-water rods and even fly rods. In waters where the fish aren't too big, a light spinning rod can be used. But for all-around carp fishing in waters containing big fish, a heavier spinning rod and reel is preferred. This can be a 1- or 2-handed heavy fresh-water spinning rod or a light salt-water model, with appropriate reels. The latter should hold at least 150 to 200 yards of 8-, 10-, or 12-pound-test line. Another good outfit for all-around carp fishing is a bait-casting rod and reel filled with 14-to-20-pound-test line.

Carp have been caught on artificial lures such as bass bugs, wet flies, nymphs, small streamers, and bucktails. This is especially true during the summer months, when carp may be feeding on insects such as Japanese beetles. (Bass bugs and dry flies are particularly effective at this time.) But most of the time wet flies, nymphs, and small streamers are best. When using these lures, wait until you see a fish lying in the water or slowly cruising below the surface. Then cast the fly about 3 or 4 feet in front of the carp and let it settle slowly with no added action.

Carp have also been known to hit lures such as plugs, spoons, spinners, and jigs at times. One of the top lures for them is the "Ugly Bug," a jig-type lure made by the Gapen Tackle Company. This lure has long rubber legs and resembles a small crayfish. The best colors are black or brown, and the $\frac{1}{16}$- and $\frac{1}{8}$-ounce weights are most effective. Dan Gapen, the manufacturer of this lure, has taken carp up to 24 pounds on the Ugly Bug by working it very slowly along the bottom in river pools where crayfish are abundant. The lure also works in lakes, especially those without weeds or vegetation. Dan has also caught carp on sinking lures. He finds that add-

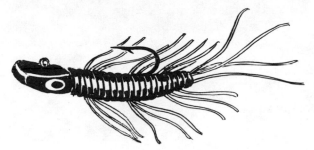

Ugly Bug lure for carp.

ing a bit of natural bait such as a worm, or corn kernels to the lure produces more strikes. You might also try dipping your lure or fly in some kind of scent or flavoring that appeals to fish.

Most fishing for carp, however, is done with natural or prepared baits, and at the top of the list is the time-honored doughball bait. These are usually prepared from flour or corn meal mixed with various sweetening or flavoring agents. You can make such a bait quickly and easily by combining a cup and a half of boiling water and a cup and a half of corn meal. Stir this mixture over a low flame for about five or six minutes, adding about two or three tablespoons of sugar, molasses, or honey as you do so. When the corn meal becomes thick and sticks to the sides of the pot, it is ready. Let the mixture cool and then knead it until it becomes thicker and smooth. You can keep this bait wrapped in aluminum foil or wax paper in a refrigerator until it is ready to be used.

Some anglers also add vanilla flavoring or strawberry gelatin to the corn meal or flour. The package of gelatin should be added to the boiling water at the same time as the flour or corn meal and stirred constantly. The gelatin makes the dough softer and more gummy and also gives off a scent that carp evidently like.

Doughball bait is used either on a single hook (such as the Eagle Claw, in size Nos. 1 or 2 for small fish, and Nos. 2/0 to 5/0 for big fish) or on a small treble hook. Single hooks can be covered entirely, right up to the eye, with the doughball formed into a large, pear-shaped bait. This will also provide weight for casting, thereby eliminating the need for sinkers in quiet lakes or pools. Carp sometimes prefer smaller baits, in which you should make a small doughball that will cover just the bend of the hook, or an even smaller one covering only the point and barb. Such small doughballs are also best for small carp.

When using a treble hook, you can cover the entire hook right up to the eye. Though the bait adheres better and longer to a treble hook, this type of hook gets fouled more quickly on rocky or weedy bottoms.

Another good bait for carp is fresh white bread. Just break off a chunk from the inside of a loaf, knead it to form a ball, and put it on the hook. Carp will also take bread crust floating on top of the water or suspended just off the bottom. Some anglers use floats or bobbers with the bait on or near the bottom. This helps to indicate a bite. But most anglers fish with the bait lying on the bottom either by itself or on a bottom rig with a sinker, especially where long casts are needed or where there is a strong current. Here an ordinary bottom rig with the sinker on the end of the line and a long snelled hook tied a few inches above the weight can be used. Since carp are suspicious and cautious and will often refuse a bait if they feel the weight or sinker, many anglers prefer to use a sliding egg sinker slipped on the line above a barrel swivel. An eighteen- or twenty-inch leader and the hook complete the rig. This enables the carp to pull

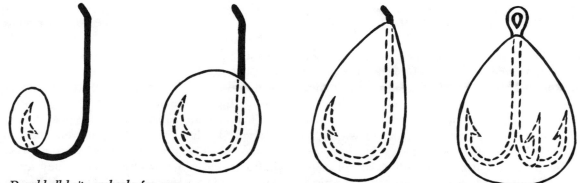

Doughball baits on hooks for carp.

Fishing for carp demands a lot of time and patience. You have to sit quietly and wait, often for hours, before you get some action. (Virginia State Travel Service Photo)

the line through the sinker without feeling the weight.

Carp have also been caught on many other baits such as fresh and cooked corn kernels, peas, lima beans, parboiled potatoes and parsnips, mulberries, marshmallows, hominy, pieces of meat, minnows, fresh-water clams and mussels, soft-shelled crayfish, and worms.

No expert carp fisherman in Europe would go carp fishing without first "baiting" the waters to attract carp to the area. This is similar to chumming in salt water where you scatter some kind of fish food to attract fish to the boat or shore. For carp fishing, scatter boiled potatoes, oatmeal, bread, crackers, canned corn, and similar foods all around the area to be fished for two or three days before you start to fish. This should bring the carp around so that you won't have to wait so long for a bite. However, baiting or chumming is illegal in many states or waters, so check your local laws before doing this.

The best carp fishing usually takes place in May and June, when carp start to feed after a long winter fast. At this time they also come into shallow water right up to the shoreline to spawn. Carp like warm water and move about a lake in search of it. They feed in the shallows if the temperature is between sixty and seventy degrees Fahrenheit. When the shallows cool, they head for deep water, and do not feed much in water below fifty degrees.

In the spring and fall, carp fishing can be good throughout the day. But in the middle of the day during the summer months carp will be in the shallows either lying just below the surface or slowly cruising back and forth on top, but usually not biting. At such times the best fishing takes place early in the morning, in the evening, and at night. On cloudy, rainy, or windy days, however, carp will often feed even during the middle of the day.

Though carp can adapt themselves to many different kinds of water, they prefer, and thrive in, lakes, ponds, rivers, and streams with mud bottoms and a lot of vegetation. They are less abundant in rocky rivers or lakes with hard bot-

Carp are not protected in most states and can be speared, snagged, or shot with a bow and arrow, as this one was. (Michigan Travel Commission Photo)

toms. Carp also like the warmer, quieter, and slow-moving rivers or streams rather than the colder, faster-moving waters. The areas below dams, quiet pools and coves, shallow bays, lagoons, and swampy or marshy waters are often productive spots.

Carp swim near shore or lie near the surface in groups of varying numbers. Other times you will see or hear them leaping out of the water. In the spring, when they come very close to shore to spawn, you can see and hear them splashing loudly in the water next to dry land. One large female will be surrounded by several smaller males crowding against her.

But after spawning, the carp becomes a smart, wary, and cautious fish, and the only way to take it is with a quiet approach. Keep out of sight or crouch low so that the carp won't see you or your shadow. Walk softly and don't make any unnecessary noises or vibrations, like stamping or running on shore. You need a lot of patience to be a good carp fisherman and often have to sit quietly for hours waiting for a bite.

Carp do not rush a bait, as do bass, trout, or even sunfish, but rather feed very slowly and deliberately, grubbing in the mud and vegetation along the bottom for their food. They may pick up a bait and drop it several times before they finally take it for good. Most carp fishermen use two or three rods, which they place in forked stakes or rod holders along the bank. They cast out, let the bait sink to the bottom, and then set the clicks on their reels.

The first indication of a bite will be a slight movement of the line where it enters the water. Don't try to set the hook when you see these first nibbles. Keep waiting; if the carp decides to take the bait, the line will suddenly straighten out fast and rise from the water. That's the time to grab the rod and set the hook.

If you are using light tackle you'll probably be surprised at the speed and strength of a carp. The small ones are fast and are often mistaken for bass or other game fish when they make their runs back and forth. A big carp will be slower but will often take off on a long, powerful run.

You can bet this angler had his hands full fighting and landing such a big carp on a fly rod. A big carp will put up a long and stubborn fight on almost any tackle. (Pennsylvania Fish Commission Photo)

They also have plenty of endurance, which means that you can't rush or horse them when using light tackle. The best procedure is to play the carp until, exhausted, it can be beached, netted, or gaffed.

The carp is not protected in most waters, and fishing for them by various methods is permitted in many states most of the year. They are shot with bow and arrow when they come into shallow water near shore to spawn or feed. They are also speared with a long-handled spear, mostly at night from a boat equipped with a powerful light. Carp are also snatched or snagged with single or treble hooks on the end of a strong line and pole as they run up narrow brooks, streams, or canals, or whenever they gather in any numbers before some obstruction such as a dam or falls. In the winter they are snagged through the ice in areas where they are found hibernating on the bottom. And skin divers have taken many carp with spear guns in waters where such underwater hunting is allowed.

Though most of the carp you catch on rod and reel will weigh from about two to ten pounds, carp weighing from ten to thirty pounds are not rare. Carp in the forty-to-sixty-pound class are sometimes taken in nets by commercial fishermen and from lakes being cleared by fish and game departments. The record on rod and reel is a fifty-five-pound, five-ounce giant caught in Clearwater Lake, Minnesota, on July 10, 1952. There is also a report of a carp weighing seventy-four pounds caught by an angler in Mississippi. But it wasn't recognized as a record because the rod was handed to another angler when the reel froze, and the first angler waded in to grab the fish. It is believed that carp can reach eighty or ninety pounds in weight.

What do you do with carp after you catch them? Eat them, of course; properly prepared, they make a fine meal. In Europe and some of the larger cities in the United States carp, sold alive or dead, are relished by gourmets. They can be fried, broiled, steamed, baked, pickled, and made into fish cakes or balls or smoked. Any good fish cookbook will have recipes for preparing and cooking carp.

Chapter 28

SUCKERS

Suckers, like sunfish, are very popular with younger anglers throughout the country. But a surprising number of older anglers also fish for suckers early in the spring. When word gets around that suckers are running in a nearby stream, there's usually a rush of men, women, and children to those waters. In a short time, it's standing room only as the eager anglers line up to catch these fish. Suckers are usually the first fish to run in any numbers early in the spring soon after the ice is out. Many anglers who can't wait to start fishing welcome these rubber-lipped fish after the long winter months. Sucker fishing is relaxing fishing—you bring a chair, build a fire or light a stove, make coffee, and then sit back and wait for a bite.

Since North America has nearly one hundred different kinds of suckers, there is in almost every state some brook, river, or lake containing these fish. However, only a few species are big enough to be considered sport fish, and only a few bite readily on a hook. Among these are the white sucker (also called the common sucker, black sucker, and rainbow sucker); the redhorse sucker (also known as the redfin or redfin sucker): and the long-nosed sucker (or northern sucker). These are the three main species of suckers caught by anglers, though many others are taken at times in various areas. The white sucker has a wide range from Canada southward to New Mexico, Arkansas, Oklahoma, and Georgia. The northern redhorse suckers are found from eastern Canada to the Great Lakes, and from the St. Lawrence watershed south to New York and west to Montana, Arkansas, and Kansas. The long-nosed sucker's range extends from the St. Lawrence River and the Great Lakes westward to the upper Missouri basin and to the upper Columbia and north to Alaska. Still other species of suckers are found in our southern and western waters.

Suckers vary in color depending on the species, but they are all similar in their general outline and mouth structure. They have suckerlike, fleshy lips, underslung mouths, large scales, and large, soft-ray fins.

Suckers are caught on all kinds of fishing tackle, from ordinary hand lines or drop lines to fancy casting outfits. Probably the cane or glass poles catch more suckers in the smaller brooks and streams than any other outfits. A fly rod provides a lot of sport on these narrow, confined

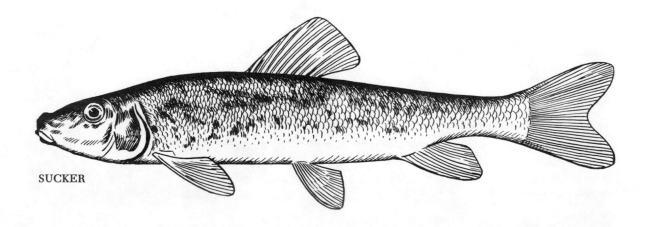

SUCKER

waters. On larger, wider rivers and lakes a light bait-casting, spin-casting, or light spinning outfit is suitable.

Every once in a while you'll hear of a sucker grabbing a wet fly, nymph, or streamer being fished for trout. Suckers have also been known to grab a lure fished for bass or panfish. But this doesn't happen enough to make it worthwhile to fish for suckers with such lures.

Most suckers are taken on natural baits such as worms, which are the top bait early in the spring. (The smaller earthworms are much better than the larger nightcrawlers.) Usually one worm will catch a sucker, but there are times when two or three small worms on a hook are better. Another good bait, especially during the summer months, is the tail of a crayfish peeled down to the white meat and wrapped around a hook. Also effective bait is the soft muscle of fresh-water clams or mussels. Cut this meat into small squares and use it on a small hook. Still other baits for suckers include grubs, insects, small pieces of meat, and doughballs. All of these should be used on small hooks in size Nos. 2 to 8, depending on the size of the suckers present.

The best time of the year to catch suckers is early in the spring, as soon as possible after ice-out, when the warm rains swell the streams and the suckers move up narrow creeks, streams, and brooks to spawn. This may occur as early as February and March along their southern range and as late as May or June farther north. April is usually a good month in many areas.

Later on during the summer months suckers are harder to catch because they scatter more widely and do less feeding during the hot weather. You'll often see them at this time gathered in small groups or schools suspended midway between the surface and the bottom. When this is the case, they won't be interested in baits and are hard to hook. However, if you see them feeding along the bottom you can sometimes make them take a bait by casting well in front of them and letting it lie quietly until they approach it.

That's one way to locate suckers when the water is clear—by watching until you spot them lying, swimming, or feeding below the surface. In the early spring, let the concentrations of fishermen along the banks be your guide. At this time, suckers may be in the riffles, or just below them, spawning or getting ready to spawn. Pools just below riffles and dams are also worth investigating. Suckers will bite all day long in the spring, even when the water is high and muddy from recent rains. Of course, if the water is too high or too muddy, fishing may have to come to a halt. But as soon as the water drops and starts to clear, you can try fishing again.

Still fishing is done by casting out your baited hook with a cane pole, casting rod, or spinning rod, and letting the bait lie quietly on the bottom. If you are fishing in a strong current or want to cast out a good distance in a lake or big river, add a small sliding sinker above the hook, or else tie the sinker on the end of the line and then tie a leader and a hook a few inches above it. Some anglers use multiple hook rigs with anywhere from two to four hooks on short leaders tied one above the other. The main thing to remember is that the baited hook should lie on the bottom without moving. And it's a good idea to cover the point and barb of the hook with the bait.

Suckers, somewhat like carp, feed slowly but deliberately, moving along the bottom and sampling a variety of tiny animal and vegetable matter. They'll come across your bait sooner or later while feeding, but they rarely take it in a hurry. Give them plenty of time to mouth the bait and don't strike at the first nibbles—wait until the line starts to move away fast before you set the hook.

Most suckers put up a disappointing fight and rarely show any speed or endurance. But every so often a big specimen hooked on light tackle in fast water will take off and protest being hauled in. Such battlers have often been mistaken for trout, bass, or other game fish.

Another, not exactly sporting, way to catch suckers is by snagging or snatching. This is done

Snagging rig for suckers.

Though suckers provide sport and fun for anglers at any age, they are especially popular with youngsters. (Pennsylvania Fish Commission Photo)

mostly in the spring, when suckers are concentrated in thick schools, and entails dragging a line with a series of treble hooks and a sinker on the end for weight through the school. The goal here is to foul-hook a fish in the body.

Still another technique is gigging, or spearing with a long-handled spear. This too is done in shallow water when the suckers are moving up to spawn. Though suckers can be speared in the daytime, you will usually be most successful at night. Gigging is usually done on the larger rivers and lakes along shore from a boat equipped with a light in the bow. Or you can wade in the shallow water near shore or in the rapids of streams, using a headlight or searchlight to spot the fish.

However, before you do any snagging or gigging, check your local fish and game laws to make sure the method is legal in your state or in the waters being fished.

Suckers usually average anywhere from ten to sixteen inches in length and weigh up to a pound or so. White suckers have been known to reach thirty inches in length and a weight of eight pounds. The redhorse sucker also reaches a large size—up to two feet in length and a weight of eight or ten pounds.

Suckers are good food fishes but they have never become popular with anglers because of their small bones. Even so, large numbers are caught commercially and sold in the larger cities. They have a sweet, tasty flesh, which is at its firmest and best early in the spring. They aren't as good during the summer months, when they turn soft and may also have a muddy flavor from certain waters. The bones can be removed from the larger fish; in the smaller ones cut the bones crosswise and fry the pieces in deep fat or oil (this will usually soften the bones). Suckers can also be baked and broiled.

Chapter 29

OTHER FISHES

Several other fishes taken on rod and reel in fresh water deserve attention, even though they are frequently overlooked. Some are not numerous enough or have too limited a range to be truly popular. Others are not readily available or are difficult to catch. And still others may require special techniques and methods not known to most anglers.

One group of fishes neglected by many anglers are the whitefishes. These silvery fish with large, smooth scales and forked tails are fairly numerous and are being discovered as a sport fish by more and more anglers. Although there are many species of whitefish found in North America, only three are highly valued as sport fish at the present time.

One of the largest and most numerous is the lake whitefish, whose range extends from New York to New England, Canada, Newfoundland, Labrador, and Alaska. It is very common in the Great Lakes region, where millions have been caught commercially.

The second popular whitefish species is cisco or lake herring. It resembles in habits and ap-pearance the lake whitefish and is found in many lakes and some rivers in the Great Lakes region, in Canada, and in Alaska.

The other member of this group is the mountain whitefish, also called the Rocky Mountain whitefish. Found mostly in lakes and streams from the Rocky Mountains west to the Pacific and British Columbia, it is most plentiful in Montana, Wyoming, Utah, Idaho, Oregon, and Washington.

Most of the tackle used for other game fish can be utilized for whitefish. For deep fishing, the spinning rod and bait-casting rod are best. For shallow water and surface fishing, the fly rod has proven effective. The lighter, limber rods are preferable because whitefish don't run too big and have tender mouths.

Whitefish will often hit wet flies, dry flies, nymphs, tiny streamers or bucktails, spoons, spinners, and jigs. They'll also take natural baits such as worms, small minnows, cubes of fish meat, salmon eggs, nymphs, and other insects.

It's a common practice when fishing for whitefish to "chum" the area ahead of time for

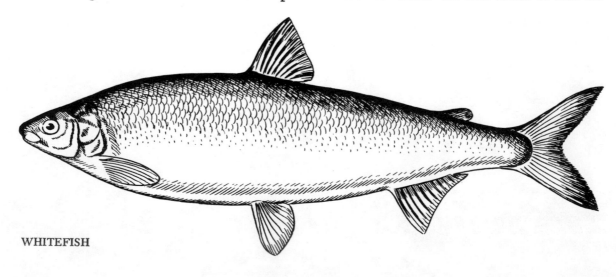

WHITEFISH

This angler is catching whitefish through the ice on one of Maine's northern ponds. They can also be caught at other times of the year in many waters. (Maine Fish & Game Department Photo)

several days, since the whitefish tend to gather in spots where they get a free handout. (Canned sweet corn, boiled rice, and tiny pieces of fish or meat can all be used as chum.)

You'll find lake whitefish at various depths depending on the season. In spring and fall they may be in depths from 10 to 60 feet, while in the summer they may go down as far as 150 feet or even more. Lake whitefish tend to gather around shoals or rivermouths. During the summer they may come up to feed on hatching insects, especially mayflies, at which time you'll see them dimpling the surface. During the winter they can be caught through the ice in water from 20 to 50 feet deep.

When lake whitefish or ciscoes are rising for insects on the surface, this is the time to bring out your dry or wet flies. Rocky Mountain whitefish will also hit wet flies or nymphs in the streams where they are most often found. When you see whitefish dimpling the surface to feed on insects, cast your fly right to the spot. Since whitefish hit fast, you have to be alert to set the hook. The best time for this sort of fishing (that is, the best feeding period) is usually from the late afternoon until dark.

Casting or trolling with tiny spinners and spoons very slowly will often take lake whitefish and ciscoes. Tiny jigs are also effective, but you have to retrieve these lures at various depths until you locate the whitefish.

Bait fishing can be done near the bottom in spring, summer, fall, and winter for lake whitefish and ciscoes. Small, Nos. 6, 8, or 10 hooks, baited with tiny live or dead minnows or cubes cut from larger fish, can be used with or without a sinker, depending on the depth.

A hooked whitefish often puts up a surprising fight, somewhat like a trout's struggle. The whitefish may thrash on the surface, roll, twist, then bore deep. Stream-dwelling whitefish, like the Rocky Mountain species, are exceptionally lively and strong. Whitefish must be handled carefully on the end of the line because they have tender mouths, from which hooks pull out easily.

Most lake whitefish will range from one to five pounds in weight, though specimens weighing from fifteen to twenty pounds have been caught commercially in the past. Ciscoes average from ½ to one pound in weight, but have been known to reach eight pounds. Rocky Mountain whitefish average about a pound and sometimes reach three or four pounds.

Highly prized as food, whitefish have a sweet, delicious flesh that can be fried or baked. Smoked whitefish is a delicacy sold in many stores.

Though not often caught by anglers on rod and reel, the sturgeon offers the nearest thing to big-game fishing in inland fresh waters. There are several species of sturgeon found in North American waters, but the one usually caught by anglers is the white sturgeon. This is the largest of the sturgeons in our waters, sometimes reaching 12 feet in length over 1,000 pounds in weight. The white sturgeon is found in rivers from California to Alaska, and penetrates far inland during its spawning run. Anglers fishing for striped bass, salmon, and steelhead in Pacific Coast rivers often hook sturgeon by accident, but only the smaller ones are landed on the light tackle used.

Sturgeon were once plentiful in most river systems along the Pacific Coast. The Snake River in Idaho formerly produced many each year, but now the fishing has fallen off drastically and big sturgeon are scarce. A few still run up the Columbia and Willamette rivers in Oregon, but since dams have blocked their runs, they are also becoming scarce here. Your best bet is to fish the Fraser River in British Columbia, where sturgeon over 700 pounds have been caught on rod and reel in recent years. Some sturgeon are

STURGEON

They're measuring and tagging a sturgeon before releasing it. These fish are becoming scarce in many waters and need protection. (Idaho Fish & Game Department Photo)

caught in California bays and rivers, and there is also good sturgeon fishing in Florida's Apalachicola River below the Woodruff Dam.

If you want to catch big sturgeon you have to equip yourself with heavy tackle. Although many fish up to 360 pounds have been taken on heavy salt-water surf-spinning tackle, a conventional rod and reel is much better. For this type of fishing, big salt-water reels are loaded with lines testing anywhere from 50 to 100 pounds. Large hooks from Nos. 6/0 to 9/0 are attached to short leaders and tied above a sinker weighing from 3 to 16 ounces or even more to anchor the bait on the bottom in a strong river current.

Various baits are used for sturgeon depending on the area being fished. Anglers fishing in Washington and Oregon often use several lamprey eels on a big hook. Others like to use smelt, sardines, herring, or other small fish. Pieces of meat can also be tried as well as several big nightcrawlers on a hook. Anglers fishing in the Apalachicola River in Florida find that a large clump of river moss or green algae gathered from rocks in the water and rolled into a big ball makes a good bait.

Sturgeon are usually found in the deeper pools and fairly fast-flowing water along the edges of the main current in rivers. The deep water below dams or high falls blocking their spawning runs upriver are also hot spots. Most of the fishing for big sturgeon is done from boats, though they have also been caught from shore. You have to give a sturgeon plenty of time to find and take the bait. A sturgeon swims along the bottom slowly, sucking up the food found there or in the mud or sand. It will usually take the bait gently at first and play with it for quite a while. But when it does swallow the bait, the line will move off steadily, at which point you can set the hook.

A hooked sturgeon is not a spectacular fighter, but it is powerful and has plenty of endurance. The fight may last an hour or two or even longer, depending on the size of the fish and the strength of the current. In a boat you can follow the big fish downriver and thereby stand a better chance of boating it than when fishing from shore, where many of the biggest ones are lost.

Sturgeon along the Pacific Coast are caught all year round, but the spring, early summer, and winter months are usually most productive. In the Apalachicola River in Florida the best months are from April to September.

The lake or rock sturgeon is a species of sturgeon sometimes caught on rod and reel in the Great Lakes region. They are also speared through the ice in Wisconsin.

The sturgeon, as almost everyone knows, is an expensive fish and the source of genuine caviar. But the meat can also be eaten fresh, either fried, broiled, or baked. Smoked sturgeon is sold in many delis in the larger cities.

Another relatively unknown but, at times, worthwhile fish is the fresh-water drum. Also known as the drum, sheepshead, gray bass, silver bass, white perch, grunt, grunter, croaker, grinder, gou, and gaspergou, it is a member of the drum family, which includes many species of drums and croakers in salt water. Most of these fish, including the fresh-water drum, are capable of making a "croaking" or "drumming" sound, hence the name "drum."

The fresh-water drum is found from the Hudson Bay drainage south to Lake Champlain and in the Great Lakes drainage through the Mississippi River region south to the Gulf of Mexico.

It lives in lakes, rivers, and streams in clear or muddy waters and usually prefers shallow waters near shore. It can be caught on almost any fresh-water tackle, such as that used for bass. Most of the fresh-water drum hooked on artificial lures are caught by anglers casting for other fish.

To catch them deliberately, a natural bait such as a soft-shelled crayfish, shrimp, worm, or piece of fish is best. This should be fished on the bottom, since the drum feeds on clams, mussels, snails, and crayfish.

Fresh-water drum average from two to five pounds. An occasional fifteen- to twenty-pounder is taken from time to time, and there are records of this fish reaching fifty or sixty pounds. It is not considered a particularly good food fish, though it is eaten quite a bit in the South.

A more popular fish is the American smelt, also known as the salt-water smelt, fresh-water smelt, frostfish, and icefish. This slender, silvery fish with a translucent green back is found from Labrador south to New York, in Newfoundland, New Brunswick, Nova Scotia, Ontario, Quebec, the Great Lakes region, and in many New England rivers and lakes.

Smelt run up into fresh water from brackish or salt-water bays and estuaries to spawn in the spring soon after the ice is out. In the larger lakes they also enter rivers or streams emptying into the lake. This may take place in March, April, or May, depending on the area and water temperatures.

During these spawning runs, millions of smelt are caught with dip nets or scoop nets at night. The congregation of men, women, and kids all engaged in smelt dipping on some of the rivers emptying into the Great Lakes is a sight to see. Equipped with hip boots or waders, a flashlight

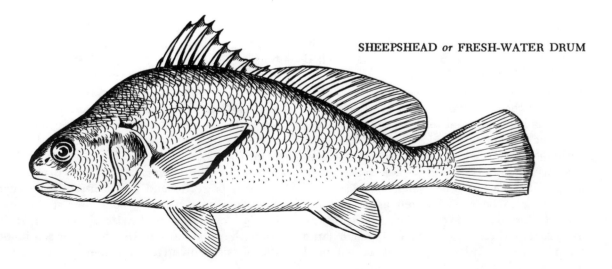

SHEEPSHEAD *or* FRESH-WATER DRUM

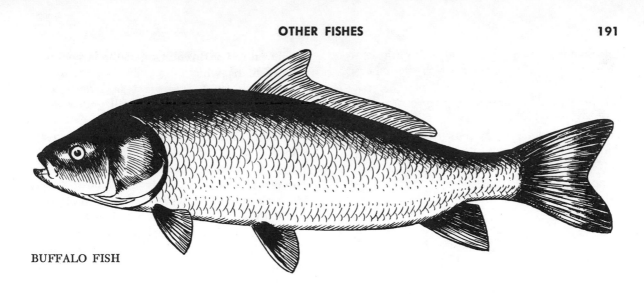

BUFFALO FISH

or headlight, and a long-handled dip net, they wade in shallow water and draw the wide-mouthed net to scoop up the silvery fish.

Smelt are also caught on tiny hooks baited with small minnows, pieces of fish, small shrimp, or bits of worm. The best fishing is usually during the fall, winter, and spring months in brackish and salt waters. Occasionally smelt will also hit a fly or a tiny, bright lure. And on the larger lakes, like New York's Lake Champlain, they can be caught through the ice during the winter months, usually on a tiny minnow or a slice of fish fished near the bottom. The bait should be raised and lowered at regular intervals to attract the smelt.

Most of the smelt caught will range from six to eight inches in length, with some reaching twelve inches. Fried smelt make delicious eating, and during the season tons are caught commercially, to be served in restaurants or sold in fish markets.

Another of the lesser fresh-water fish sometimes caught by anglers is the buffalo fish, of which there are three species: the bigmouth buffalo fish, the black buffalo fish, and the small-mouth buffalo fish. They belong to the sucker family and resemble the carp. They also have many of the same habits as the carp, preferring sluggish waters and feeding on many of the same foods. Buffalo fish which are not too common in our northern states, are found mostly in the Mississippi River region. However, some turn up as far north as the lakes and rivers of Minnesota.

Most of the buffalo fish that are caught on rod and reel are taken in southern waters on doughball baits. They come big at times; some specimens four feet in length and sixty pounds in weight have been reported. Those taken from clean waters are well flavored and make good eating. But buffalo fish caught in muddy, weedy waters may have a muddy flavor.

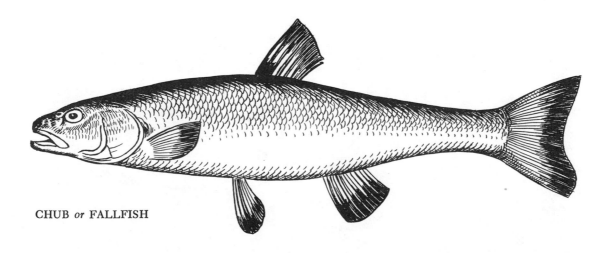

CHUB *or* FALLFISH

A fallfish caught on a spinner. (Pennsylvania Fish Commission Photo)

Not many anglers realize that the minnow family can provide great sport on rod and reel. Of course, the carp, which belongs to this family, is well known and popular with many anglers. (See Chapter 27.) But there are other members of the minnow family that can also be caught on rod and reel. One of the largest is the squawfish, of which there are several species. They reach up to two feet in length and a weight of several pounds. They'll grab a lure or bait and put up a spirited fight in fast water. The squawfishes are found mostly in our western states.

Another member of the minnow family that can provide good sport is the fallfish (or the Mohawk chub, Delaware chub, white chub, silver chub, or just plain chub). It is found from Canada south to Virginia along the East Coast.

Many fallfish are taken by trout or bass fishermen using flies, lures, or natural baits. They will hit dry and wet flies, nymphs, streamers, spoons, spinners, and tiny plugs. Of the natural baits, they'll take worms, minnows, crayfish, hellgrammites, and various insects.

Fallfish are often found in the larger rivers and streams in many of the same spots inhabited by trout or bass. They are caught either by casting or while trolling. When first hooked they put up a fast, lively fight, which has often led anglers to mistake them for a trout or a small bass. But fallfish lack the endurance of these fish, and after the first few short runs and some thrashing around they soon give up.

Fallfish or chubs run from six to ten inches, with a few reaching eighteen or twenty inches. When caught they should be cleaned as soon as possible and kept on ice, or else they'll turn soft and become unfit for the table. Those taken from cold, clean waters make the best eating. Their flesh is sweet and delicious, despite the presence of some fine bones that must be removed.